A Journey
through the
CONSTRUCTION INDUSTRY

A Journey
through the
CONSTRUCTION INDUSTRY

Hema Kanta Barua

First published in India in 2025 by Exceller Books,
An imprint of GE Group

Address: G1, Dream Apartment, Degree College Road, Belgharia, Kolkata, 700056, India
www.excellerbooks.com

EXCELLER BOOKS®
A GLOBAL PRESS

Dedication

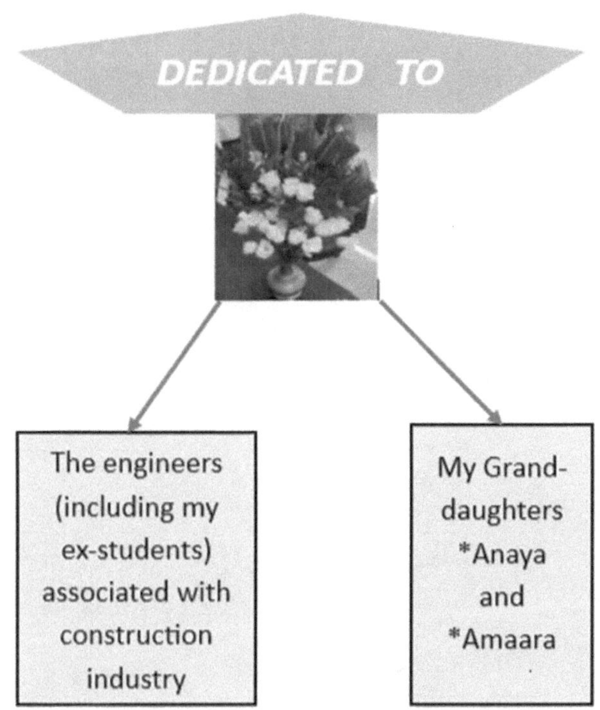

DEDICATED   TO
The engineers (including my ex-students) associated with construction industry
My Grand-daughters *Anaya and *Amaara

Acknowledgments

The energy to write this book at this stage of my life has truly been derived from two generations of my ex-students: the first generation spanning from 1966 to 1978 and the second from 2010 to 2023. The love, respect, and inspiration they extended throughout these years have been the primary motivation behind my decision to write this book. I am deeply grateful to this vibrant community of engineers.

I express my sincere gratitude to Mr. Pranav Jyoti Sharma, IRSE, the Chairman of the Railway Recruitment Board, Guwahati, Assam, for his kindness in sparing his valuable time to review the manuscript and write the **FOREWORD** for this book.

In crafting this book, I have referred to the contributions of numerous institutions, organizations, and individuals, as listed in the **References** section. I extend my heartfelt thanks and gratitude to all of them.

I am grateful to all my colleagues, friends, teachers, and well-wishers who contributed and encouraged me at various points in my long professional journey spanning more than five decades—with many important aspects of this journey going into this book.

A special acknowledgment goes to my wife, Runima Dutta, a retired teacher from the Government of Assam, for her unwavering moral and financial support throughout this journey. Her silent encouragement has been a cornerstone of my efforts in writing this book.

I am also grateful to other members of my immediate family: my son, Geetartha; my daughter-in-law, Sukanya; my son-in-law, Jnanjit; and my daughter, Tejaswinee. Their continued support and encouragement in all aspects of this endeavor have been invaluable.

Lastly, I would like to express my gratitude to the team at M/S Exceller Books for their diligent efforts in editing, printing, and marketing this book.

Hema Kanta Barua

Table of Contents

List of Abbreviations   *i*

Foreword   *iv*

Preface   *vi*

1| Construction Industry of India and Its Challenges   1
  1.1 Introduction
  1.2 Present Status of the Construction Industry in India
  1.3 Generation of Employment in the Construction Sector
  1.4 Apparent Challenges Confronting the Construction Industry
  1.5 An Approach to Meet the Challenges
  1.6 Concluding Remarks

2| Seismic Vulnerability of Structures: A Strong Warning to India   26
  2.1 Introduction
  2.2 Structural Damages Caused by Earthquakes
  2.3 Role of Civic Bodies in Mitigation of Earthquake Damages in
      Vulnerable Structures of Urban Areas
  2.4 A Modern Concept (Eews) For Reducing Loss of Life and
      Property in Earthquakes
  2.5 An Approach to Retrofitting of Structures Vulnerable To
      Earthquake Damages
  2.6 Concluding Remarks

3| Urbanization in India and Its Challenges with Specific
Reference to the North East Region   83
  3.1 Introduction
  3.2 Growth of Urban Population and Related Challenges in India
  3.3 The Flagship Missions of Government of India
  3.4 Ease of Living Index in Cities of India
  3.5 Concluding Remarks

4| United Nations' Sustainable Development Goals and
Role of Engineers   114
  4.1 Introduction
  4.2 Position of India In Respect Of Progress Made So Far
  4.3 SDG 6: Clean Water and Sanitation (Ensure Availability And
      Sustainable Management and Water for All)

4.4 SDG 7: Affordable and Clean Energy (Ensure Access to Affordable,
    Reliable, Sustainable and Modern Energy for All)
4.5 SDG 9: Industry, Innovation and Infrastructures (Build Resilient
    Infrastructures, Promote Inclusive and Sustainable Industrialization
    And Foster Innovation)
4.6 SDG 11: Sustainable Cities and Communities
    (Make Cities and Human Settlements Inclusive, Resilient and Sustainable)
4.7 Concluding Remarks

5| Sustainability and Construction Project Management   163
5.1 Introduction
5.2 Factors responsible for adverse impact on sustainability
5.3 Different stages of sustainable construction project management
5.4 Concluding Remarks

6| Maintenance of Buildings: Different Aspects of Its Management   220
6.1 Introduction
6.2 Phases of maintenance management of buildings
6.3 Maintenance of building fabric—repairs and rehabilitation
6.4 Concluding Remarks

7| Articles on Miscellaneous Topics   273
7.1 Introduction
7.2 Lessons Learnt from the Demolition of the Twin Towers of Noida (India)
7.3 Flood problem of Assam with specific reference to River Embankment
7.4 The Draft Professional Engineers' Bill, 2019 yet to become an Act
7.5 A few incidents of 'Conflict of Interest' in author's professional life
7.6 Lack of clear understanding of code provisions
7.7 Concluding Remarks

Appendices   *301*
References   *308*

List of Abbreviations

GDP — Gross Domestic Product
NIP — National Infrastructure Pipeline
PMAY-U — Pradhan Mantri Awas Yojana-Urban
SBM-U — Swachh Bharat Mission-Urban
BMTPC — Building Materials & Technology Promotion Council
BIS — Bureau of Indian Standards
EEWS — Earthquake Early Warning System
NDMA — National Disaster Management Authority
SDMA — State Disaster Management Authority
EDRI — Earthquake Disaster Risk Index
NER — North Eastern Region
DESA — Department of Economic and Social Affairs of United Nations
MoHUA — Ministry of Housing and Urban Affairs
CR — Completion Rate
SCP — Smart City Projects
ULB — Urban Local Bodies
HRIDAY — Heritage City Development and Augmentation Yojana
AMRUT — Atal Mission for Rejuvenation and Urban Transformation
SAAP — State Action Annual Plan
IHHL — Individual Household Latrine
CT/PT — Community/Public Toilet
SDG — Sustainable Development Goal
SDSN — Sustainable Development Solutions Network
SDR — Sustainable Development Report
NITI Aayog — National Institution for Transforming India Aayog
STEM — Science, Technology, Engineering and Math
DMAF — Data Maturity Assessment Framework
CPM — Construction Project Management
SCPM — Sustainable Construction Project Management
MoEFCC — Ministry of Environment, Forest and Climate Change
NBC — National Building Code of India
EIA — Environmental Impact Assessment
SIA — Social Impact Assessment
PID — Project Implementation Document

EMP — Environment Management Plan
PD — Project Director
TL — Team Leader
HVAC — Heating, Ventilation and Air Conditioning
SoR — Schedule of Rates
CEMP — Construction Environment Management Plan
EAT — Environment Assessment Team
DPR — Detailed Project Report
WB — World Bank
ADB — Asian Development Bank
TD — Tender Document
NIT — Notice Inviting Tender
GCC — General Conditions of Contract
SCC — Special Conditions of Contract
PIU — Project Implementation Unit
TAC — Technical Advisory Committee
PM — Project Manager
BEC — Bid Evaluation Criteria
CAG — Comptroller and Auditor General (Govt. of India)
OSU — Organization Set UP
CPM* — Critical Path Method
PERT — Program Evaluation and Review Technique
RMP — Resource Management Plan
RAP — Resource Allocation Problem
RLP — Resource Levelling Problem
TQM — Total Quality Management
MIS — Management Information System
GFL — Ground Floor Level
RWA — Residents' Welfare Association
NBR — NOIDA Building Regulations
CFO — Chief Fire Officer (In the context of Fire Department)
WRD — Water Resources Department
BB — Brahmaputra Board
NWP — National Water Policy
PIL — Public Interest Litigation
MHRD — Ministry of Human Resource Development

Foreword

It is indeed a matter of great pride for me to have been given the opportunity to introduce this one-of-a-kind book by Dr. Hema Kanta Barua. As the title aptly declares, the book chronicles the author's remarkable journey through the construction industry. A veteran of the field, Dr. Barua possesses the rare distinction of excelling as an academician, a researcher, and a hands-on practitioner—all at once.

An alumnus of the prestigious IIT Kharagpur and a brilliant structural engineer, Dr. Barua has witnessed and contributed to the evolution of the construction ecosystem over more than five decades. His illustrious career spans associations with renowned institutions such as Jorhat Engineering College, Tocklai Tea Research Institute, and the Regional Institute of Science and Technology. Simultaneously, his leadership roles in construction companies have seen him deliver engineering solutions to a diverse range of real-world challenges.

This extensive experience is reflected abundantly in the pages of this book. Covering a vast spectrum—from basic civil engineering principles to advanced construction project management, sustainable planning, and policy formulation—it serves as an invaluable resource for all stakeholders in the construction industry.

As a Railway Civil Engineer with over two decades of experience in asset construction and maintenance, I can personally relate to many of the issues addressed in this book. Dr. Barua delves into critical topics such as the employability of civil engineering graduates, sustainable practices in construction management, and the challenges tied to the growth of urban infrastructure. His analyses are thorough, his insights thought-provoking, and his solutions pragmatic.

Particularly noteworthy is Dr. Barua's focus on the northeastern perspective. Whether discussing smart cities, seismic vulnerabilities, or building maintenance practices, he weaves the region's unique challenges into the broader national and global context. Furthermore, his commentary on construction policies—such as the Noida Twin Tower implosion and the long-pending Draft Bill for Civil Engineers—underscores the pressing need for regulatory advancements in the sector.

As India aims to achieve its ambitious target of a $5 trillion economy by 2024-25, the construction industry plays a pivotal role in delivering the requisite infrastructure: cities, express highways, ports, and high-speed railways. In this transformative era, the insights and knowledge encapsulated in Dr. Barua's work hold immense value.

This book is not just a testament to Dr. Barua's expertise but also a beacon for the future of the construction industry. I am confident that readers from all walks of life—students, professionals, policy-makers, and industry veterans—will find immense inspiration and guidance within its pages.

I extend my heartfelt congratulations to Dr. Barua on this commendable achievement and wish the readers an enriching experience with this book.

Pranav Jyoti Sharma, IRSE
Chairman, Railway Recruitment Board
Guwahati, Assam

Preface

Objective

India is laying the major thrust on the development of infrastructure, particularly in the sectors of buildings of all types and transportation systems, including roads and bridges. During the last few decades, construction technologies, techniques, and materials have developed substantially in terms of the planning, design, construction, and maintenance of different infrastructures. The available technologies and techniques are covered in the relevant codes of practice, as summarily covered in National Building Code of India, 2016. Against this scenario of technology and techniques, it has been strongly felt by the author during his long professional life in teaching, research and construction over a period of more than half a century that there does exist a tremendous gap between the available knowledge and its application on the ground of construction industry. The different challenges confronting the construction industry in India today have been primarily caused by this factor (i.e. the gap between available knowledge and its utilization on the ground). The realization of the extent of this gap has been the basic force behind the efforts put in for writing this book. The major factors responsible for this gap include the lack of awareness among many of the stakeholders about the available technical knowledge and skill, lack of adequate training facilities, lack of legislation of the engineering profession (through an Act), degradation of ethical values, etc. The book makes an attempt to deal with some of these factors through a set of seven chapters.

Targeted Readers

All the stakeholders of the construction industry, including the technicians, budding engineers, practising engineers in different roles, contractors, owners and users of different infrastructure, teachers of technical institutes, etc., are expected to derive benefits from the different contents of the book, as briefly reflected in the *Organizations and Brief Contents of Chapters* (given below).

Organizations and Brief Contents of Chapters
Each chapter starts with an Introduction and ends with a Concluding Remark. The different topics dealt with in the book have been organized in the following order:

Chapter I deals with the topic of 'Construction Industry of India and Its Challenges'. The brief scenario of India and the challenges confronting the construction industry of the country today have been briefly discussed. The broad aspects warranting attention to meet the challenges have also been dealt with.

Chapter II covers the broad topic of 'Seismic Vulnerability of Structures – a Strong Warning to India'. The different factors leading to the growth of vulnerable structures with reference to collapse and damage of structures caused by earthquakes of the past have been discussed. In addition, a brief discussion on the proactive measures necessary for reducing the seismic vulnerability of structures has also been presented.

The topic of 'Urbanization in India and its challenges with specific reference to North East Region' has been treated in Chapter III. The challenges confronting urbanization in India, along with different flagship missions initiated by the Government of India, have been briefly dealt with. In addition, the aspects of execution of the projects under different missions have been discussed with reference to the states of NER.

Chapter IV deals with the topic of 'United Nations' Sustainable Development Goals and Role of Engineers'. The different issues relating to the achievements of SDGs and the gaps existing as of now with respect to the execution of projects formulated/to be formulated to fulfil the set targets with specific reference to the role of engineers have been briefly dealt with.

The topic of 'Sustainability and Construction Project Management' has been covered in Chapter V. The principles of sustainability, along with the stages starting from the initiation of a construction project to the end stage of project closing, have been discussed in this chapter. The different factors responsible for the adverse impact of construction projects on the environment have also been briefly dealt with.

Chapter VI covers the topic of 'Maintenance of Buildings – Different Aspects of Its Management'. The different phases of maintenance of buildings (the fabric in particular), including inspection, repair, rehabilitation and retrofitting, have been discussed in light of NBC—2016.

Lastly, Chapter VII covers a number of articles on various topics, which include 'Lessons Learnt from Demolition of Twin Towers of NOIDA, India', 'Flood Problem of Assam with Specific Reference to River Embankment', 'The Draft Professional Engineers Bill, 2019 yet to Become an Act', 'A few Incidents of Conflict of Interest in Author's Professional Life' and 'Lack of Clear Understanding of Code-provisions'. Some salient aspects of these topics have been briefly discussed in these articles.

A large number of codes of practice, books, research papers, handbooks, reports and articles have been consulted in writing this book. The salient ones are listed under References of the book. An appendix has also been added to the book to help readers appreciate some specific aspects of the book's contents.

Guwahati, Assam
October, 2024
Hema Kanta Barua

Chapter 1| Construction Industry of India and Its Challenges

1.1. Introduction

The construction sector broadly includes:

- Real Estate (which includes residential, commercial and industrial ones) and
- Infrastructure (which includes transport, power/utility projects and other projects such as dams, waterways, etc.).

This sector has a tremendous bearing on the national economy of our country. For a systematic discussion on this topic, the broad subheads chosen are:

- Present status of the construction Industry in India,
- The projected growth of the construction industry in India,
- Apparent challenges confronting the industry and
- An approach to meet the challenges.

1.2. Present Status of the Construction Industry in India

1.2.1. Present Status of Indian Economy: In Terms of GDP

The Indian economy has been estimated to be 3.942 trillion USD (Currency rate considered is Rs. 82.00 for 1 USD) as of 2024 and is positioned as the fifth largest economy globally among the top 10 countries[1] as shown in table 1.1 (2nd & 3rd column). The population[2] of these countries are given in 4th column of the table. Though India has been estimated to be the fifth largest economy in the world, its GDP is the lowest at 2.73 thousand USD (last column). This is obviously due to its population being the largest in the world (4th column). According to a projection of growth of the Indian economy (based on GDP) given by Knight-Frank Report[3], the Indian economy will be 7 trillion USD by 2030.

Country	Rank*	GDP (USD trillion)*	Population (2024) in crore**	GDP per capita (USD thousand)*
United States	1st	28.783	33.712	85.37
China	2nd	18.536	141	13.14
Germany	3rd	4.590	8.457	54.29
Japan	4th	4.112	12.404	33.14
India	5th	3.942	144	2.73
United Kingdom	6th	3.502	6.843	51.07
France	7th	3.132	6.609	47.36
Brazil	8th	2.333	20.538	11.35
Italy	9th	2.332	5.882	39.58
Canada	10th	2.242	4.087	54.87

*Based on data given in World GDP Ranking[1] 2024. **Based on data given in World Population Outlook[2] (April, 2024)

Table 1.1: The Top Ten Largest Economy of the World (As of 2024)
(Prepared by the author on the basis of data given in references[1, 2])

1.2.2. Projected Growth of Construction Industry in India

The construction sector's contribution to the total economy as of 2022 has been 18.1%. The break-up of this includes[3]:

- Construction output, which covers the value of output from real estate and infrastructure activities and
- Real estate services output, which covers the value of output from professional services such as research, consulting services, business development, etc.

This overall contribution of 18.1% consists of (i) construction output of 10.5% and (ii) real estate services of 7.6%. The stress laid by the Government of India on further growth of this sector, particularly with respect to the infrastructure, has been evident from the substantial increase in the capital expenditure (Capex) provided in the budget[4] for FY 2023—24, which is clearly indicated by figure 1.1. The capital expenditure has been rising from Rs. 4.1 lakh crore in FY 2020—21 to Rs. 10.0 lakh crore in FY 2023—24 (figure 1.1). The increase in Capex to this extent might have been due to the launching of giant projects in the infrastructure sector, such as the National Infrastructure Pipeline (NIP) and Bharat-mala.

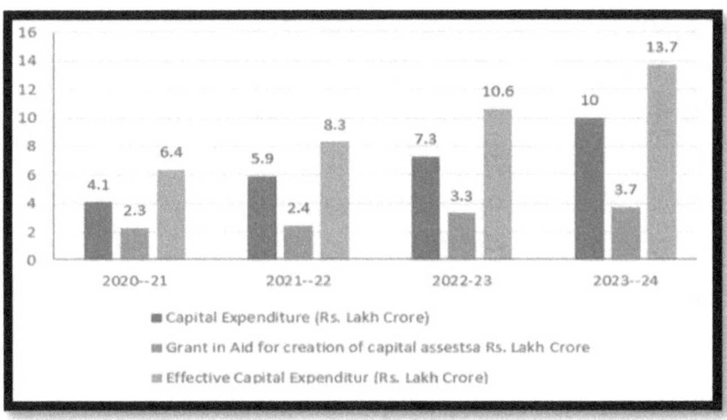

*Figure 1.1: Effective Capital Expenditure... Trend of Growth
(Prepared by Author Based on Data of References 3 & 4)*

Project (or Bharat Pari-yojana) is the second largest highway construction project after National Highway Development Project[5]. This project has two phases: Phase I and Phase II. Ministry of Road Transport and Highways[6] has given the details of Phase I. Phase 2 of this project has a total cost of Rs. 3 trillion.

The trend of growth in capital expenditure, evidenced by figure 1.1, is a clear indication of the trend of growth in the construction sector, primarily necessitated by the growth of population in India. There are many research papers dealing with the projection of the construction sector. As projected by Knight-Frank Report[3], the construction sector in India will grow from 18% in FY 2021—22 to 21% of the total economic output of the country in FY 2029—30. The major drivers of growth, as well identified in the Construction Industry in India,[7] are:

- More than 40% of the population is expected to live in urban India by 2030. This will create the additional requirement of 25 Mn of mid-end and affordable residential units.
- Under NIP, India has an investment budget of $1.4 Tn - 24% on renewable energy, 18% on roads and highways, 17% on urban infrastructure and 12 % on railways.
- Implementation of various schemes such as Smart City Mission creates many constructional activities.
- Identification of 54 global innovative construction technologies under Technology Sub-Mission of PMAY-U will

start a new era in Indian construction technology.

- Implementation of SBM-U and the development of 35 Multimodal Logistics Parks at a total capital cost of $ 6.1 Bn create a huge volume of constructional activities.

The Union Minister of Commerce and Industry, Government of India, stated[8]: *India is poised to be the 3rd largest construction market in the next 2—3 years, adding that the Real Estate Sector will provide huge business opportunities, generate employment and provide big avenues for the start-up ecosystem.* According to another research by Oxford Economics[9], the growth of the construction sector of India in terms of its contribution to the global construction growth in the decade 2020—2030 has been projected to be 14.10%, as evident from the projections given as *China – 26.1%, India – 14.1%, United States – 11.1%, Indonesia – 7%, Australia – 2.3%, United Kingdom – 2%, France – 1.8%, Canada – 1.7%, Spain – 1.5%, Italy – 1.3% and Others 31%.* According to this projection, India will be the second-largest construction market by 2030.

1.3. Generation of Employment in the Construction Sector

The growth of the construction sector, as discussed above, obviously leads to a substantial increase in the rate of employment generation in this sector. Table 1.2, prepared on the basis of data given in the Knight-Frank Report[3] indicates an encouraging scenario of employment generation in the construction sector in the period from 2023 to 2030 in India.

Positions	2023		2030	
	No. of jobs	Percentage*	No. of jobs	Percentage*
Engineers	22,00,000	3.10	33,09,000	3.30
Technicians/Foremen	22,71,000	3.20	38,11,000	3.80
Clericals	19,16,000	2.70	29,08,000	2.90
Skilled Force	68,84,000	9.70	105,30,000	10.50
Semi-skilled Force	576,95,000	81.30	797,24,000	79.50
Total	709,66,000	100.00	1002,82,000	100.00

Percentage of (jobs in each category/total jobs in each year)

Table 1.2: Estimated Employment Generation in the Period from 2023 TO 2030 (Prepared by the author on the basis of data projected by Knight-Frank[3])

The period covered in the projection of employment growth in the construction sector, as reflected by table 1.2, is from 2023 to 2030, a period of seven years. A critical analysis of this table leads to the following observations:

- **Observation 1:** The number of persons getting employed in different positions (Column 1 of the table) in the construction industry increases from approximately 7.1 crore in 2023 to 10 crore in 2030 – an average annual growth of approximately 6% concerning employment generation. Against this overall growth, the break-up of growth (or fall) category-wise (Column 1) will obviously open up a number of challenges to the construction industry.

- **Observation 2:** The growth in employment opportunities for engineers in the construction sector has been projected to be from 22,00,000 in 2023 to 33,09,000 in 2030 – an average annual growth of 5.04% - less than the annual average growth of 6% (as noted in Observation 1). The engineers involved in the construction industry are mostly civil engineers; there are a small percentage of engineers from other streams, such as mechanical/ electrical/architectural, etc. In terms of numbers, the employment potential for engineers increases annually by 158429. This number has to be critically viewed against the annual production of engineers, particularly in civil engineering (*discussed at a later stage*).

- **Observation 3:** The growth rate during this period of seven years for technicians and foremen has been projected as 9.69%, which is much higher than that for engineers (Observation 2).

- **Observation 4:** The average annual growth rate of skilled force during the period under discussion, as projected, has been 7.57%, which is higher than that of engineers (5.04%) but less than that of technicians/foremen (9.69%).

- **Observation 5:** The average annual growth rate for the semi-skilled force during this period, as projected, has been 5.45%, which is much less than that of the skilled force.

The above-noted observations will be discussed in greater detail while dealing with the next subhead (as initially chosen for this chapter).

1.4. Apparent Challenges Confronting the Construction Industry
The World Economic Forum[9] published the most recent rankings for 141 countries with respect to the quality of infrastructure. Table 1.3 shows the rankings of the top 10 construction markets (based on volume of work) in the world. India's ranking of 70 speaks of the poor quality of infrastructure. Improving this quality is the greatest challenge confronting the construction industry in India. There are, in fact, many factors responsible for this situation. It is apparent that the fundamental factors for ensuring the quality in the construction of any type of infrastructure are primarily: knowledge and skill and ethical values of the manpower involved in the implementation and maintenance of any infrastructure. Therefore, a discussion of different types of challenges facing the construction industry in India is attempted herein with reference to these two fundamental factors.

Country	Rank*	Country	Rank*
Japan	5	Canada	26
Germany	8	Australia	29
France	9	China	36
United Kingdom	11	India	70
United States	13	Indonesia	72

Rank based on quality of infrastructure (not in respect of volume of works)

Table 1.3: Quality of Infrastructure Ranking of World's Top 10 Construction Markets (Prepared by the author based on data of WEF[9])

The three civil engineering marvels, shown in image 1.1, taken from Forbes India[10] speak of the depth of 'knowledge and skill' required today with respect to both the execution and maintenance of construction projects.

Image 1.1: Three Civil Engineering Marvels of World[10]

The 70th rank of India with respect to the quality of infrastructure, as shown in table 1.3, is indicative of a number of actions absolutely necessary for the improvement of the standard and quality of construction and maintenance of different infrastructure projects in India. However, it would be absolutely wrong to attribute the reasons for this poor rank only to the gaps in 'knowledge and skills' of engineers and the workforce of the construction industry alone. The poor quality of infrastructure is apparently accountable in an unknown proportion to the degradation of ethical values in society in general, as observed (image 1.2) by the United Nations[11].

Image 1.2: Observation of United Nations[11]

The diploma holders in engineering normally start their professional career on the same ladder as graduate engineers but from a lower level, i.e., from the position of supervising sub-engineer/technician/foreman, etc. Many of the skills required at their (diploma holders') level are common to graduate engineers at the entry-level but at a lower level. They have to be skilled properly in areas such as surveying, understanding of drawings, estimations, working out of bills of quantities, labour management, basic understanding of engineering principles, communication skills, computer skills, etc. The growth of diploma holders along the same ladder as that of graduate engineers is open in a limited way with the enhancement of their knowledge and skill through higher qualifications and experiences. Ethical values are of importance, as in the case of graduate engineers. This category constitutes a growth rate of 9.69% in requirements from 2023—2030.

The average growth rate of 7.57% (Observation 4) for the skilled workforce in the construction industry of India during the period 2023—2030 has also been substantial. There are different trades requiring a skilled workforce to complete a construction project. These trades are masonry, carpentry, plumbing, welding, and other types of finishing work. A skilled workforce needs to acquire the appropriate skills in their domain of work. In addition, they have to develop the ability to coordinate with the semi-skilled workers helping them and also the ability to operate the machines and equipment used in the works of their respective trades.

The successful completion of construction projects of any type with the desired quality (as conceived in planning and design) within the specified period of completion warrants the knowledge and skills in addition to ethical values on the parts of manpower of different categories, as briefly discussed above. The issues of inferior quality of construction, delay in completion of construction leading to substantial cost over-run, the lack of some of the skills (as discussed above), and the element of pressure accountable to ethical values in society, in general, are very common. All these factors are jointly responsible for the poor ranking of 70th position of India's construction industry (table 1.3), though our country is going to be the second largest construction market as per the projection of Oxford Economics9. This is truly the situation that broadly speaks of the challenges confronting the construction industry of India. However, the discussion to follow with respect to the last sub-head, chosen for this article, is limited only to the 'knowledge and skills' and 'ethical values' of the technical manpower of the industry with specific reference to civil engineers.

1.5. An Approach to Meet the Challenges

1.5.1. General

The challenges have been basically given rise to by a number of gaps in both 'knowledge and skills' and 'ethical value'. These two aspects are, to a certain extent, interrelated. For a systematic discussion, two secondary sub-heads, (a) Engineers and (b) Skilled Workforce, have been chosen.

1.5.2. Engineers

The annual production rate of graduate and postgraduate engineers in India in civil engineering is initially a data that becomes absolutely necessary for a discussion bearing on challenges facing the construction industry. There are various types of data creating confusion with regard to a specific number of civil engineers coming out annually from a huge number of technical institutes under both private and government universities in the country. A committee of AICTE (under the chairmanship of BVR Mohan Reddy) prepared a Report[12], which covered the period from 2013-14 to 2016-17. This report shows the Approved Intake (as approved by AICTE),

Enrolment and Enrolment Percentage in each of the top 10 disciplines of engineering as of 2017-2018 for undergraduate and postgraduate courses. The average percentage of Enrolment to Intake Capacity for the 10 disciplines has been only 50%, as of 2017-18 against the total intake of 15,82,193 in all the 10 disciplines, as indicated in figure 1.4 of the report[12]. Based on the non-utilization of the full intake capacity to the extent of 50%, the report made a number of recommendations. Before discussing the major recommendations, the necessity of looking into the present position as of 2022-23 has been strongly felt. The Dashboard of AICTE[13] (visited on 11.07.24) gives the position in respect of Intake, Enrolment, Students passed, and Placement for the academic years from 2012-13 to 2022-23 for the levels Diploma, UG and PG for 12 programs – Applied Arts and Crafts, Architecture and Town Planning, Architecture and Planning, Architecture, Planning, Design, Town Planning, Engineering and Technology, Management, MCA, Pharmacy and Hotel Management and Catering for all the States/UTs of India. Table 1.4 has been prepared from this Dashboard for UG and PG courses for 8 programs exclusive of Applied Arts and Crafts, Management, Pharmacy and Hotel Management and Catering from 2017-18 to 2022-23.

The average utilization of intake capacity, as shown by the report[12] of the AICTE Committee, has been 50%. A comparison of this finding with the same reflected in table 1.4 suggests that the utilization of intake capacity improves with the reduction in intake capacity (Column 3 of table 1.4). The utilization percentage indicated in the table is only the average one for all the technical institutes of the country, indicating thereby the existence of many institutes having an intake utilization of lower than 50 %. It may be in many institutes, mostly under private and state universities (excluding IITs, IIITs, NITs, etc.). There are manifold adverse impacts of poor capacity-utilization, some of which are briefly dealt with below. As appropriately observed by the AICTE Committee[12], *"Creating any further capacity is a big drain on investments since, at the very basic level, it involves the creation of physical infrastructure like buildings and lab infrastructure. We recommend that we do not create any more capacity starting from the academic year 2020..."* The trend of capacity reduction has been evident (Column 2 of table 1.4). However, there has been an increase again in 2022-23, the reason thereof being not known. Against this situation, it is difficult to find reasons attributable to the growth of some new engineering institutes in recent years.

year	Intake	Enrolment*	Student passed	Placement**
2017---18	16,72,166	8,24,430 (49.3%)	8,16,747	3,61,534 (44.3%)
2018---19	15,99,723	7,96,144 (49.8%)	8,17,161	4,16,398 (51.9%)
2019---20	15,12,585	8,10,643 (53.6%)	6,82,514	4,18,413 (61.3%)
2020--21	14,47,342	7,87,888 (54.4%)	1,42,153	3,74,557 (***)
2021---22	14,02,365	8,80,232 (62.8%)	5,15,631	4,45,689 (86.4%)
2022---23	14,13,387	not updated	not updated	not updated

*Percentage of Enrolment to Intake shown within bracket, **Percentage of Placement to Students passed shown within bracket, ***Placement more than Students passed.

Table 1.4: *Intake, Enrolment, Students Passed and Placement For Eight Programs of UG & PG Courses (Prepared by Author based on Dashboard[13])*

As observed in Report[12], the top 10 disciplines occupy 90% of the total intake capacity of AICTE (both for UG and PG courses). In addition, it (Appendix I of the Report) suggests that the intake in civil engineering is about 15.6 percent of the total intake of top 10 disciplines. Based on these parameters, the intake in civil engineering (both UG and PG) in 2022-23 works out to approximately 1,98,440 (14,13,387x 0.90x0.156). The country, as of now, has the intake capacity to produce this number of civil engineers every year. This is in excess of what is required for the projected growth of the construction industry (as dealt with earlier). If an enrolment of about 60% (of intake) and a passed percentage of 85 are considered, the yearly production of civil engineers (UG + PG) approximately works out to 1,01,200 (excluding diploma holders). In view of the projected growth of the construction industry (as dealt with in table 1.2), the annual production at this rate does not appear to be in excess of the requirement of the industry. However, the greatest challenge facing the construction industry emerges primarily from the aspect of employability. Different views on this aspect are available today. As stated earlier, the employability of a civil engineer in today's context of the civil engineering profession is dependent on the degree of 'knowledge and skills' and 'ethical values' acquired by prospective civil engineers. The 'ethical values' may be termed as 'attitudes', as adopted internationally in the civil engineering profession. The question arises as to what extent, the fresh engineers coming out of the technical institutes in our country acquire these domains of knowledge, skills and attitudes. The Vision for Civil Engineering in 2025, published by ASCE[14] on the basis of the recommendations of an International Summit held in 2006, dealt with these areas. According to this report, a civil engineer is expected to acquire knowledge, skills and attitudes in areas as briefly stated in table 1.5.

Domain of Knowledge	Domain of Skills	Domain of Attitudes
*Mathematics, physics, chemistry, biology, mechanics and materials. *Design of structures, facilities and systems. *Risk/uncertainity such as risk-identification, data-based and knowledge-based types, probability and statistics. *Sustainability including social, economic and physical dimensions. *Public policy and administration including elements such as the political process, laws and regulations and funding mechanisms. *Business basics such as legal forms of ownership, profit, income statements etc. *Social sciences including economics, history and sociology and *Ethical behaviour including client-confidentiality, codes of ethics within and outside engineering societies, anti-corruption and the differences between legal requirements.	*To acquire skills in engineering tools such as statistical analysis, computer models, design codes and standards and project monitoring methods. *To learn, assess and master new technology for enhancing individual and organizational effectiveness and efficiency. *To learn to communicate with technical and non-technical audiences convincingly and with passion. *To learn to collaborate on intra-disciplinary, cross-disciplinary and multi-disciplinary traditional and virtual teams. *To learn to manage tasks, projects and programs for providing expected deliverables while satisfying budget, scdules and other constraints and *To lead by formulating and articulating environmental, infrastructure and other improvements and build concensus by practicing inclusiveness, empathy, compassion, persuasiveness, patience and critical thinking.	To develop---- *Creativity and entrepreneurship. *Commitment to ethics, personal and organizational goals, and worthy teams and organizations. *Curiosity, which is a basis for continued learning, fresh approaches, development of new technology or innovative applications of existing technology and new endeavors. *Honesty and integrity ----telling the truth and keeping one's words. *Optimism to face challenges and setbacks, recognizing the power inherent in vision, commitment, planning, persistence, flexibility and teamwork. *Respect for and tolerance of the rights, values, views, property, possessions and sensitivities of others and *Thoroughness and self-discipline in keeping with the public health, safety and welfare implications for most engineering projects and the high degree of interdependence within project teams and between teams and their stakeholders.

Table 1.5: Domains of Knowledge, Skills and Attitudes (Quoted herein (in parts) from the Vision Report of ASCE[14])

To quantify the extent of employability or unemployability of graduate civil engineers in India or elsewhere is indeed a very tough task in view of the wide areas of activities involved in the construction industry. There is a lot of misleading data relating to employability percentages. Therefore, in this discussion, quantifying this data on the basis of many reported ones (mostly by individual organizations for all categories of engineers) has not been relied upon. Instead, the results of Graduate Aptitude Test in Engineering (GATE) have been considered to be a better basis for judging the quality of fresh engineers in India. Therefore, table 1.6 has been prepared.

Year	Total appeared	Total qualified	% of qualified
2023	5,17,000(Appx.)	1,00,000(Appx.)	18%
2022	5,97,030	1,12,678	18.80%
2021	7,11,542	1,26,813	17.80%
2020	6,85,000	1,78,780	18.80%

(a) For all branches of engineering.

Year	Total appeared	Total qualified	% of qualified
2022	1,36,285	1,00,000	17.80%
2021	1,15,270	---	17.50%
2020	1,25,974	NA	NA
2019	1,45,064	NA	NA

(b) For the branch of civil engineering only.

Table 1.6: Results of Gate (India) Based on References[15 & 16]

Table 1.6 (a) shows that about 18% of total candidates appearing in GATE qualify every year in all disciplines. On the other hand, in civil engineering alone, as shown in Table 1.6 (b), about the same, i.e. 18% of the candidates qualify every year. The GATE is considered to be the most appropriate examination to measure the aptitude of fresh engineers in respect of 'knowledge' relating specifically to the clear understanding of the basic principles of engineering, which form the basis for acquiring the skills required in any domain of the engineering profession. The poor performance of fresh graduates to the extent of only around 18%, the minimum qualifying marks (out of 100) being very low, as shown in table 1.7, is a clear demonstration of the poor quality of fresh engineering graduates coming out of the technical institutes of the country. If the candidates appearing in GATE from institutes like IITs, IIITs, NITs, etc., are separated from the total number of candidates who appeared, as shown in table 1.6, the above-noted qualified percentage will appreciably come down. Against this situation, there are some examples of 4th and 6th-semester students (from some top institutes like IITs, NITs, etc.) qualifying in GATE. Therefore, the contention of many surveys (conducted by many organizations) to the effect that only 10 to 20 percent of fresh graduates are employable cannot be totally ignored. According to another source[16], the employability of civil engineering graduates was 26.5% in 2020. The obvious reasons attributable to this situation of employability of fresh engineers are the appreciable gaps existing in them in areas of 'knowledge, skills and attitudes', some of which have been briefly stated above. Narrowing this gap not only among the fresh engineers but also among the younger generation of practising engineers is, indeed, the greatest challenge to the modern-day construction industry.

Year	General	OBC	SC/ST/PwD**
2022	30.4	27.3	20.2
2021	29.2	---*	---*
2020	32.9	29.6	21.9
2019	28.2	25.4	18.8
2018	26.9	24.2	17.9

*Data not available, **Person with disability*

Table 1.7: Gate Qualifying Cut-Off Marks[15] in Civil Engineering

An approach to meet this challenge has been attempted below. A discussion on the broad approach brings in the roles played so far or to be played now by many stakeholders such as students, guardians, teachers, management of institutes (private or government), approval or accreditation bodies for technical institutes and all the stakeholders of the construction industry. An impartial discussion on the broad approach to meet the challenges confronting the construction industry (placing the country in the 70th position among 141 countries of the world with respect to the quality of infrastructures[9]) will naturally involve the roles played by all those stated above. In fact, the roles played by them are interrelated, as far as the approach to be followed for meeting the challenges is concerned. *Having been in the profession for about 59 years, partly in technical institutes (under both government and private sectors) as a teacher and partly in the construction industry as the project supervisor, project manager and project consultant, the author develops a sense of hesitation for writing on this complex issue in view of the wide involvement of different stakeholders (as mentioned above) in the system of technical education. Eventually, he (the author) decides to write, being wide open for correction in case of mistakes, if any.* For the convenience of a fruitful discussion on this approach, two secondary sub-heads have been chosen as:

- Educational level in the technical institutes and
- Professional level in the construction industry.

1.5.3. Level in the Technical Institutes

At the level of imparting (by the teachers) and acquiring (by the taught) technical education (in civil engineering), all efforts need to be directed towards facilitating the development of personal attributes: knowledge, skills and attitudes (as briefly stated in Table 1.5). Civil engineering has now become a global profession. Today, a civil engineer is expected to grow and become at some stage 'the master' in some of the different areas of the profession. As noted in the Vision for Civil Engineers[14], a civil engineer has to serve *'competently, collaboratively and ethically as master'* in one or more of the different roles to be played by a civil engineer during his professional life. It is absolutely impossible to become a master in any one or more of the professional domains at the institutional level. However, the basics of 'knowledge, skills and ethical values' have to be delivered/acquired in educational institutes. It is in this context that the roles played by different stakeholders of technical education (with reference to civil engineering) come into the forefront of the discussion on gaps existing with respect to these qualities, resulting in the poor employability of fresh graduates.

The expansion of engineering education covering all disciplines was phenomenal during the last few decades. As stated in the research paper[17], the private sector accounted for only 15% of the total intake in engineering (in all disciplines) in 1960. However, this percentage increased to 86% of the total enrolment by 2019. The major portion of the unemployable fresh graduate engineers (in all disciplines) are apparently produced by these institutes (barring a few private institutes of repute), though a certain portion thereof being from poorly run state-government level institutes as well. The institutes in the private sector are self-financed and are heavily dependent on capitation fees. The poor enrolment percentage, particularly in civil engineering, as discussed earlier, has eventually impacted the quality of education in these institutes, leading to the poor percentage of employability to the extent noted above. The financial constraint caused by the poor enrolment resulted in a poor 'teacher-student ratio', a poor 'lab infrastructure', 'poorly paid teachers,' etc., creating thereby an adverse impact on the desired quality of technical education with respect to knowledge, skills and ethical values (as discussed above). The approach to meet the challenges created by poor employability of fresh products demands a greater role to be played by each of the main players of technical education, namely the concerned governments, statutory bodies (controlling the process of technical education), the promoters of private institutes, the teachers and the students. The role of guardians/parents comes in, particularly with respect to the selection of an appropriate institute for their wards.

Many policies and guidelines set by AICTE, according to initial approval and renewal of approval to technical institutes, are in place. To what extent these policies and guidelines are strictly followed by all the institutes (particularly under private sectors) has today become a question of great concern in view of the extent of unemployability, as reflected above. A number of actions for strict enforcement of these guidelines appear to be absolutely necessary and may feasibly be taken as well. Some of these actions are briefly discussed below.

The first action, which is apparently necessary, is regarding institutes having enrolment below 50% of approved intake capacity. As discussed earlier, there are many institutes, mostly under the private sector, in this category. This is now possibly the time for AICTE to review this type of discipline to be followed by measures such as 'closure of relevant discipline' or 'reduction of intake capacity' for stopping the adverse effects on the quality of products, given rise to by various factors referred to earlier. The adoption of online applications for renewal of approval (not followed by physical inspection in many cases) has apparently created a scope for manipulation of data (particularly by some promoters treating education purely as profit-earning units) relating particularly to 'teacher-student ratio', 'proportion of teachers at different levels (i.e. Assistant Professor, Associate Professor and Professor)', 'lab infrastructure,' etc.

The accreditation granted by NBA to different disciplines of engineering in India is a highly appreciable and desirable measure for improving the quality of fresh engineering graduates. A detailed analysis of institutes having this accreditation in the country is not available. Apparently, there are many institutes that do not possess the mandatory requirements, even for inviting NBA to inspect for grants of accreditation to individual disciplines. The necessary measures for making this accreditation mandatory appear to be the call of the day in view of the poor employability of fresh engineering graduates.

The salient aspects, such as innovation, research, skill, etc., are the topics very often discussed appropriately in different forums. The basic need for the growth of these qualities is, indeed, a deeper understanding of engineering principles and their basic applications within the limits of the modern-day stock of knowledge in engineering and technology, including those codified on the parts of the fresh engineers. The lack of this basic requirement is clearly indicated by the poor percentage of GATE-qualified candidates that have already been dealt with. Therefore, the basic approach to be adopted to meet the challenges relating to employability needs to be directed towards the strengthening of the hands of the teachers with respect to knowledge, skills and pedagogy. Barring the IITs, NITs, IIITs, some state-government institutes and a few top-ranking private institutes/universities, a lot more needs to be done with respect to the existing position of teachers in many of the institutes (mostly under private sectors). The problems relating to teachers in engineering institutes primarily relate to non-payment of salaries (as specified by the law of the land), non-conformity to the specified 'teacher-student ratio', engagement of teachers on a contractual basis, non-existence of terms and conditions for the future security of teachers, etc.—to name only a few. These problems (fully or partly) are there in most of the institutes under private sectors. This is where the ethical values on the parts of the management and other stakeholders of technical education count. The only way to address this challenge is to ensure the strict enforcement of policies and guidelines of both AICTE and NBA and also those of the newly constituted NEP. An ideal atmosphere for attracting talented young people to the profession of teaching in technical institutes has to be created even in the technical institutes under private sectors so that the gaps existing in the capabilities of faculty and quality of pedagogy get narrowed down.

Secondly, in recognition of the poor employability of fresh engineers to the extent of around 20% (as analyzed above), the primary emphasis has to be laid on measures necessary for reducing the gaps existing in knowledge and skill, as required on the parts of the faculty of the concerned discipline (in this case civil engineering) in light of the requirements for today's construction industry (some of these requirements already discussed above). One of the recommendations made by the AICTE Committee[12] to this effect may be mentioned. It goes as: *"Competencies of the faculty need to be developed, especially in the areas of new age technologies and research through rigorous faculty development programs. Training of existing teachers at teachers training institutes, using quality improvement programs (QIP) and using IIT/NIT faculty and infrastructure are some of the immediate interventions we recommend."* In fact, this type of program has been in operation for a long time for government institutes. *(The author of this article got benefitted by undergoing a Technical Teachers Training Program in IIT, Kharagpur in the period 1968-71, including the completion of his post-graduate degree (M. Tech) in the first two years as a govt-deputed teacher from Jorhat Engineering College, Assam).* However, most of the teachers of technical institutes in the private sector are not exposed to this type of program, which is against the fact that the majority of teachers of these institutes do require this type of facility. The feasibility of enforcing this type of training program, even in institutes under the private sector, needs to be looked into by the AICTE.

Another recommendation of the AICTE Committee[12] relating to the quality improvement of teachers appears to be highly appreciable and is considered necessary, particularly for technical institutes in the private sector. This recommendation goes as: *"Also, we may have to seek more technology interventions, such as MOOCS, to circumvent some of the constraints with faculty shortage and the quality of pedagogy."* MOOCs (Massive Open Online Courses) include different disciplines, including many areas of civil engineering. The e-DX MOOCs (e-DX being a platform providing MOOCs) provide a number of certification courses even relating to the construction industry (in addition to many open courses), which are internationally valued today.

The task of providing the basics of 'knowledge and skills' to budding engineers does require capable trainers (obviously the first category being the faculty). Therefore, the teachers are expected to be well aware of the skills necessary for the modern-day construction industry, for which the exposure of the faculty (particularly the young ones) to industry becomes the basic necessity. It is in this context that the 'institute-industry' partnership in an effective way comes into play. What this effective way should be is an area in which there have been a number of discussions held and recommendations made by different forums.

The necessity of an 'Industry-Institute partnership' (also called an 'industry-academia partnership') is discussed with reference to undergraduate programs of engineering colleges since the topic in hand relates to the employability of graduate engineers in the construction industry. The first step consists of signing an agreement between an industry and an institute/university for effective cooperation between the two, with the basic objective of producing graduate engineers who can become employable in the construction industry. Keeping this basic objective in mind, the areas of mutual support to each other need to be duly identified for inclusion in the partnership agreement. As normally thought of, the major area of cooperation between industry and academia should include scientific research activities and the adoption of the results thereof to solve real problems of the industry. However, this major area has not been considered necessary for the undergraduate programs of the institutes responsible for the production of the major portion of unemployable graduate engineers, as discussed earlier. The majority of institutes falling into this category are obviously those in the private sector, as discussed earlier. On the other hand, for taking care of the problems of the construction industry through scientific research, there are many institutes such as IITs, some NITs, some top-ranking private institutes/universities, SERC, CBRI, CRRI, CWPRS, etc., in India. In this context, a few words taken from the Abstract of a paper from ASCE Library[17] may be quoted as: *"The degree to which construction engineering graduates are prepared to perform well in practice can be enhanced by effective industry-university cooperation on such matters as the construction education mission and objectives, curriculum, course content, faculty qualifications and development, resources, co-ops* and internships and other issues." (*The meaning of co-op programs in an institute is the option of completing a course in a longer period. A period of one or two years, as decided upon, will be in excess of the normal period of four years required for the degree. The excess period is utilized in industry to gather practical experiences.)*

Based on the broad guidelines, as reflected above, the agreement between the industry and the institute/university, as required, needs to be signed and executed effectively. As far as the undergraduate courses in civil engineering and the construction industry are concerned, two areas of cooperation between the two partners (institute and industry) appear to be of utmost necessity. These areas are:

- *Area 1* (Faculty Development with respect to knowledge and skills necessary for the construction industry): A mechanism needs to be developed through a partnership agreement. A feasible way is to send a faculty member to the industry for a certain period, and at the same time, a competent engineer with adequate experience may also be brought in for a certain period to teach subjects requiring industry experience.
- *Area 2* (Students' Internship): The students need to be given extensive exposure to the construction industry through compulsory internship programs. The provision of practical training does exist in the undergraduate courses. Its

effectiveness has to be enhanced substantially through industry-institute partnerships.

The AICTE has been taking a number of actions in respect of industry-academia partnerships. In 2017, it made the internship (in some semesters of the undergraduate course) mandatory, and in addition, a thrust is being laid on start-ups to be incubated in the institutes. A detailed discussion on start-ups incubated in the institutes through industry-institute partnerships is avoided herein since the area, as stated above for inclusion in the agreement of industry-institute partnership, appears to be more effective in respect of efforts directed at enhancing the employability of graduate engineers in the construction industry. In this connection, a few recommendations made by the AICTE Committee[12] may be quoted as:

- *Analytical tools should be used to understand the impact of various teaching methods and identify the best method of executing coursework and apprenticeship. Tightly integrate apprenticeship with pedagogy.*

- *Apprenticeship should be made mandatory in industry (in some ways, it exists but needs rigorous implementation) and progressively mandatory in educational institutions (starting with 25% to 100% in five years).*

As far as the employability of graduate engineers in the construction industry is concerned, the industry-institute partnership needs to be developed with priority on the aspects of internship and faculty development (with respect to requirements of the construction industry), as stated above. Today, in most of the states of India, many construction projects are being executed. The partnerships with project management authorities (both government and public or private sectors) need to be developed specifically with respect to student internship and faculty development, as stated above. The present duration and timings of the internship (for students) need to be reviewed to enhance its effectiveness. In addition to the internship, a culture of sending students to construction projects, even for their minor and major projects, needs to be developed through industry-institute partnership agreements. For example, the case of the construction of an Extradosed PSC Bridge over River Brahmaputra connecting Guwahati and North Guwahati, including Viaduct and Approaches may be cited. Image 1.3, given below, shows the use of many modern techniques and technology for this bridge. *(An extradosed bridge employs the principles of both the girder bridge and cable-stayed bridge).* We, the civil engineers, including the budding ones, can learn a lot about modern construction technology by studying the design and construction aspects of a bridge of this kind.

Image 1.3: Some Constructional Aspects of Guwahati—North Guwahati Bridge (Images Taken From Systra[18])

The institutes in and around Assam may enter into a partnership agreement with the PWD, Govt. of Assam with respect to the internship of graduating engineers and for exposure of faculty to the construction industry. This is just an example.

Regarding knowledge relating to understanding the basic principles of engineering, two important aspects, the evaluation systems (for internal marks) and examination systems (for theory marks), need to be reviewed in light of parameters reflecting on the employability of fresh graduates. The aspect of open-book examination in some of the subjects, such as design papers, construction management papers, etc., appears to be necessary for encouraging students to pursue a deeper understanding of fundamentals. The degree courses in civil engineering carry a substantial portion of internal marks (to the extent of 40% of the total marks). Therefore, the quality of the evaluation system for internal marks has a significant bearing on the quality of products.

These are, therefore, areas demanding frequent review and scrutiny by competent bodies.

Another aspect that has a great impact on employability has been considered to be the quality of students joining the institutes (at entry level), particularly the institutes under the private sector, which produce the majority of unemployable graduate engineers. The criteria of minimum qualifying marks, as laid down by AICTE, are adopted by all institutes (under government or private sectors). The question arises as to whether a student with 40% or 45% marks in PCM (which are the minimum qualifying marks for reserved and general categories, respectively) for civil engineering has the required knowledge in basic sciences in view of the present standards of marks in (10+2) level. A review of the qualifying marks by AICTE appears to be necessary in light of the present scenario of the employability of graduate engineers.

While concluding the discussion on this sub-head *(Educational level in the technical institutes)*, it may be re-emphasised to the effect that all efforts, some of which have been discussed herein, need to be directed towards the reduction of gaps in knowledge, skills and attitude so that the employability of graduate engineers gets enhanced in the construction industry.

1.5.4. Professional Level in the Construction Industry

As stated earlier, for a fresh graduate engineer, it is impossible to acquire all the knowledge and skills required by the modern-day construction industry at the level of entry into the industry. Acquiring knowledge and skills, including attitudes, is a continued process in the professional career. Whether the ideal professional atmosphere for ensuring this 'continued process' exists in India or not is a highly debatable topic, particularly in view of the poor quality of construction, as evidenced by its 70th position of India among 141 countries of the world with respect to the quality of infrastructures[9].

The basic problem in the construction industry in India arises from the fact that the profession of engineers in India has not yet been regulated through an Act of the country. An article entitled *'Draft Professional Engineers' Bill, 2019 yet to Become an Act'* appears in the last Chapter of this book. It has been now more than 50 years since the initiation of the draft Engineers' Bill. However, to date, the Bill has not become an Act. The reasons for the delay in enactment of this Bill (the final draft being ready in 2019) are beyond understanding in view of the fact that similar Acts are there for professions like doctors, architects, chartered accountants, etc. A huge portion of the national budget is being spent in the construction industry. The delay in enacting the bill is, to a great extent, responsible for many of the problems of the construction industry, such as improper utilization of funds, poor quality of construction, delay in execution, corruption, etc. The most appreciable part of the Final Draft Engineers Bill consists in the fact that the bill (if enacted) will create a compulsion among the engineers for 'the Continued Professional Development (CPD)' apart from strengthening the hands of the engineers of the construction industry in fighting the odds created by the moral degradation of the society as a whole.

The young engineers joining any project implementation unit, may it be a government department or any other agency such as project management companies (public or private), need initial training on knowledge and skills, as required in the relevant areas of work done by the employing agency. For this purpose, the departments or companies need their own training units with qualified master trainers. Apparently, there are provisions of this type in some of the employing organizations. However, there is a need to strengthen these training units in light of the requirements of the modern-day construction industry, which emphasize continued professional development. In addition, the employing organizations need to develop a mechanism for encouraging and facilitating the engineers employed by them to pursue the process of 'Continued Professional Development' in the relevant domains of their (engineers') activities.

1.6. Concluding Remarks

As well recognized by now, there is a shortage of skilled workforce also. Engineers can contribute immensely through the above-noted training institutes to the development of the workforce, as required by their own organizations for the execution of construction projects. In this case, the engineers will have to contribute as trainers. A detailed discussion on the skill development of the workforce required for the construction industry has been avoided in this chapter since the main objective of this article has been to present a discussion on the employability of graduate engineers in the construction industry. This chapter concludes with an excerpt from The Vision for Civil Engineering[14] that goes as: *"Proud of its legacy, the global civil engineering community cannot rest on its laurels. Public Health, safety, and welfare require giving even more attention to infrastructure and the environment."*

Chapter 2 | Seismic Vulnerability of Structures: A Strong Warning to India

2.1. Introduction

The extent of damage to life and property caused by earthquakes is known from the major contemporary earthquakes of Latur, Gujarat and Manipur. Assam faced a major earthquake in 1950 with a magnitude of 8.6 on the Richter Scale, which had an impact as far as Tibet, leading to an estimated loss of 4800 lives. As per recent statistical predictions, a major earthquake similar to the one of 1950 is due anytime in the North Eastern Region of India, one of the six highly seismic zones of the world identified by the International Workshop on Strong Motion Instrumentation, held in Honolulu in 1978. The earthquake zoning map of India has duly considered the North Eastern Region as the most severe earthquake-prone zone with the highest zone factor of 0.36.

In keeping with the objectives of the Yokohama Strategy for Safer World adopted at the UN-sponsored World Conference in 1994, all earthquake-prone countries in the world are focusing on the adoption of proactive measures for mitigation of earthquake damages. The Government of India and related agencies are making concerted efforts to mitigate damages likely to be caused by natural calamities such as earthquakes, floods, cyclones, and droughts. In accordance with the same, the Building Materials & Technology Promotion Council under the Ministry of Housing & Urban Poverty Alleviation, Government of India, published the Vulnerability Atlas of India19 pertaining to Earthquake, Windstorm and Flood Hazard Maps and Damage risk to Housing.

The Vulnerability Atlas, however, does not identify the vulnerable structures in specific terms. What it gives is an Earthquake Hazard Map (showing faults, thrusts, and earthquakes of magnitude greater than or equal to 5) and a district-wise distribution of houses based on predominant materials such as roof and wall and the level of damage risks. For the mitigation of earthquake damages in vulnerable structures, the basic approach lies in the appropriate identification of these structures. This in itself is a huge task, which can only be carried out by experts with requisite technical knowledge in areas such as planning, structural design, construction technology, construction materials, etc.

In any vulnerable region, the approach will be uniform as far as the aspect of identification is concerned. The owners of vulnerable buildings include the Government (Centre and State), semi-government organisations, private organisations and individuals. Since earthquake damages may affect vulnerable buildings, the owners should initiate the identification process of such vulnerable structures in time, as duly stressed upon by the Government of India.

A structure is considered to be vulnerable when the reserved strength available in it is inadequate to take the effects of earthquake forces. The knowledge of earthquake technology has advanced considerably, with many aspects being codified in different countries and in India by the Bureau of Indian Standards (BIS). Additionally, the construction techniques and construction materials have developed significantly. Therefore, the interventions (Retrofit Measures) required in structures vulnerable to earthquake forces are possible and cost-effective in view of the increase in life to be achieved with the proper implementation of intervening measures.

The priority for identification of vulnerable structures to be followed by intervention has to be fixed on the basis of the importance factor of the structures. The structures, such as heritage structures, bridges, public buildings, educational buildings, water-supply installations, power-supply installations, etc., deserve the utmost priority.

The vulnerability of structures against resistance to earthquake forces may accrue for a number of reasons. The correct assessment of the reasons leading to the deficiencies is a prerequisite to the formulation of appropriate retrofitting measures. The different studies conducted on structures that collapsed or were severely damaged due to past earthquakes suggest that many of the damaged ones were non-engineered structures with several deficient areas.

Many engineered buildings also got damaged or collapsed on account of faulty design and/or faulty construction, overloading, etc.

In many of the buildings, overloading is caused by a change in the type of use. A building designed as a residential one, when used for commercial purposes, is subjected to a significant increase in both dead load and live load. This type of overloading is a common phenomenon in urban centres.

The effectiveness of retrofitting measures is fully dependent on the correct assessment of the deficiencies in a vulnerable structure. Modern technology has aided the development of a number of tools and techniques for condition assessment, which broadly include non-destructive tests, intrusive tests (Core test, in-situ shear test, Bond test and test of masonry prisms) and numerical modelling techniques. The deficiencies to be assessed may be global or local. Based on the assessment of the deficiencies, the retrofit measures have to be worked out.

The study of damages caused by earthquakes has identified the collapse of many structures on account of foundation failures. Therefore, the investigation of the existing foundation of vulnerable structures forms a major aspect in the formulation of retrofit measures. Many modern methods are available today for strengthening soil and foundation, and these may be judiciously taken as recourse in the formulation of retrofit measures.

Based on the fact that the earthquake forces on a structure are caused by ground motion, modern technology has developed some techniques for the reduction of earthquake forces. This technique is called the Base Isolation. This technique consists of creating a joint between the superstructure and the substructure to allow for relative movement. On the other hand, the earthquake forces are a function of the mass and height of the structure. The reduction of mass, particularly in upper levels, results in the reduction of earthquake forces.

In the state of Assam, there are many historical and heritage structures. In the case of these structures, special care has to be taken in the formulation of retrofitting measures by giving due consideration to the heritage value of the structure. Archaeological reconstruction may also be adopted in case of heritage structures being damaged beyond the stage of incorporation of retrofit techniques.

The prediction of earthquakes with regard to specific dates, times and locations has not been possible so far. In view of this position, the adoption of appropriate retrofit measures for existing vulnerable structures on the one hand and the strict adoption of earthquake-resistant design and construction for new structures on the other are of paramount importance for earthquake-prone zones like northeastern regions.

2.2. Structural Damages Caused by Earthquake

2.2.1. General Analysis

The two countries—Turkey and Syria, were hit by two earthquakes on 6.2.23. The magnitude of the first one was M 7.8, while that of the second one was M 7.5. The death toll has been more than 50,000 as of 25.6.23. This led to tremendous human suffering. About 1,60,000 buildings collapsed or were badly damaged in the quake. According to the United Nations Development Program (UNDP), 1.5 million people are now without a permanent shelter in the earthquake-hit zone[20]. A feel of the structural damages may be had from image 2.1 (taken from the internet).

Image 2.1: Damages of Super Structures [148]
Source: https://www.breakingnews.ie/world/19-killed-as-strong-earthquake-hits-turkish-coast-1027504.html

A critical study of different photographs available on websites on the internet reveals the following two broad areas:

- Failure of superstructures, including the failure of soft-storey and
- Failure of the substructure, including over-turning.

The technical discussion on these two areas will be taken up at a later stage of this chapter. Image 2.1 shows the failure of the superstructure. A typical image (taken from the internet) of the failure of substructures, including turning, is shown in image 2.2.

Image 2.2: Foundation Failure[149]
Source: https://www.bgs.ac.uk/discovering-geology/earth-hazards/earthquakes/

The general study of the images reveals the fact that most of the damaged buildings were built in violation of basic principles of design and construction in earthquake-prone zones. This observation brings in the aspects of earthquake zoning maps, regulatory bodies controlling design and construction and standards followed in these two countries (Turkey and Syria). A perusal taken with respect to these aspects has led to the following facts.

Both the countries—Turkey and Syria are in earthquake-prone zones. Earthquake zoning maps are also available. In addition, government Building Standards and bye-laws are also in existence.

The United Nations sponsored a project called "The Global Hazard Assessment Program." This was a multi-year project and ended in 1999. This project led to the development of the Seismic

Hazard Map of the World. This map identifies 20 regions of seismic activity around the globe. Turkey and Syria are covered in these regions.

In these two countries, as in the case of other seismic regions, there are seismic codes, which are claimed to be of global standard. In addition, there are other building rules relating to the responsibilities of the constructor, regulatory bodies, etc. Against this situation of controlling measures being in place, the collapse of buildings resulting in tremendous loss of lives and properties raises a lot of questions. A political answer to some of these questions is contained in a statement[21] made after the quake by Turkey's President, Recep Tayyip Erdogan, which goes as: *"not possible to be prepared for such a disaster."*

However, a technical answer to some of these questions consists in the fact that, in view of the availability of the appreciable amount of seismic knowledge today, the extent of disaster caused by the collapse of buildings could have been reduced greatly if not averted totally.

The zoning maps of the world are primarily based on historical data of past earthquakes. The magnitudes of past earthquakes in different earthquake-prone countries are utilized to prepare the earthquake zoning maps for the world as well as for individual countries. The top 10 earthquakes in the world[22] and the top 10 earthquakes in India[23] in terms of magnitudes are indicated in table 2.1.

World*		India**	
Name of eathquake	Magnitude	Name of earthquake	Magnitude
Valdivia Earthquake (1960)	*9.5*	*Indian Ocean (2004)*	*9.1--9.3*
Great Alaska Earthquake (1964)	*9.2*	*Kashmir (2005)*	*7.5*
Sumatra Earthquake (2004)	*9.1*	*Bihar and Nepal (1934)*	*8.7*
Tohoko Earthquake (2011)	*9.1*	*Gujrat (2001)*	*7.7*
Kamchatka, Russia Earthquake (1950)	*9.0*	*Kangra (1905)*	*7.8*
Mouli (Chile) Earthquake (2010)	*8.8*	*Latur (1993)*	*6.4*
Equador-Columbia Earthquake (1906)	*8.8*	*Assam (1950)*	*8.6*
Rat Islands Earthquake (1965)	*8.7*	*Assam (1897)*	*8.1*
Assam-Tibet Earthquake (1950)	*8.6*	*Uttarkashi (1991)*	*6.8*
Sumatra Earthquake (2012)	*8.6*	*Koynanagar (1967)*	*6.5*

**Data taken from website[22], **Data taken/from website[23].*

Table 2.1: Top Earthquakes of the World and India
(Prepared by the Author on the Basis of Data Given in Websites[22, 23])

The building standards prepared in different countries take into account magnitudes like the ones noted above. In India, we have the earthquake codes of practice *(published by BIS, such as IS 1893)* and related explanatory handbooks, wherein the seismic zoning map of our country is available. The basic principle of the design and construction of structures consists of ensuring safety not only under normal loads but also under the most severe earthquakes. As such, a building, properly planned, designed, constructed and maintained with due regard to the related codes and standards, is not expected to collapse and kill people to the extent evidenced by the Turkey-Syria earthquakes. It is of interest to note in image 2.1 (given above) that there are some buildings which did not collapse. The same situation was observed even in India after the Gujarat, Latur and Manipur earthquakes. These observations clearly indicate the lapses in the roles of planners, designers, constructors, and law-enforcing agencies (regulatory bodies). In addition, these observations are indicative of a huge gap between the availability of seismic knowledge today and its application to the construction of buildings at large. It is truly in this context that "A STRONG WARNING TO INDIA" has been added to the title of this chapter.

Out of the four seismic zones of India, Zone IV is the most severe earthquake-prone one. It includes parts of Jammu and Kashmir (Kashmir valley), the Western part of Himachal Pradesh, the Eastern part of Uttarakhand, Kutch in Gujarat, part of Northern Bihar, all north-eastern states of India and the Andaman and Nicobar Islands. These parts of India, the north-eastern region, in particular, have many vulnerable structures. No assessment of vulnerable structures under different sectors is in the public domain so far. Therefore, the recent damage to buildings in Turkey and Syria needs to be treated as another strong warning in addition to the warnings given earlier by the earthquakes of Gujarat, Latur and Manipur. We, all concerned with the construction industry in India, have to look into all aspects bearing on the safety of our structures—building structures in particular. For a brief discussion on these aspects, the following broad areas have been chosen:

- Lack of awareness among stakeholders of the construction industry, Lack of understanding of available seismic knowledge (standardized) on earthquake-resistant structures and
- Lack of strict enforcement of laws and guidelines of regulatory bodies for the construction of buildings.

2.2.1.1. Lack of Awareness among Stakeholders of the Construction Industry

The stakeholders of the construction industry broadly include the planners, the designers, the supervisors, the builders, the contractors and the owners. The first three stakeholders are technical persons (architects, engineers, and diploma engineers), while the builders and the contractors may or may not be technical persons with formal technical education. On the other hand, a huge group of skilled, semi-skilled and unskilled workforce is associated with the construction industry. The owner is a wide term that involves government sectors, public and private sectors and individuals. An earthquake-resistant structure is an end product intended to provide safety under all situations of loading, including the one caused by occasional earthquakes in the identified earthquake-prone zones. For the achievement of this intended purpose during the intended period of life of the structure, the active participation of all the aforementioned stakeholders is necessary. This participation needs due respect to the absolute necessity of avoiding the total collapse of a structure, particularly a building structure, thereby avoiding the loss of lives and properties, as seen after the earthquakes of the recent past, may it be that of Turkey-Syria or may those be of Gujarat, Latur or Manipur in India. The extent of the damage caused by all these earthquakes clearly indicates the lack of adequate awareness among the stakeholders about the necessity of earthquake-resistant buildings. It is in this context that efforts have to be made by all concerned to create awareness about utilizing the available seismic knowledge in the construction of earthquake-resistant structures. How to create this awareness among the stakeholders is indeed the question today. An attempt has been made herein to find some answers to this question.

To start with, this aspect of creating the required awareness, a statement made immediately after the Turkey earthquake of 2011 by the then Prime Minister of Turkey, Recep Tayyip Erdogan[24] may be referred to. He blamed the *"Municipalities, constructors and supervisors"* for their *'negligence'* that resulted in shoddy construction leading to loss of lives. The term 'negligence' needs to be deeply analyzed. This term may be interpreted to involve two aspects: firstly, the lack of appropriate awareness about available seismic knowledge and, secondly, the lack of moral responsibility towards the society at large. Therefore, the essence of all efforts to be made to create awareness among the stakeholders lies in these two major elements.

With respect to the first element, the stakeholders need to know that the seismic knowledge, as made available to the construction industry through different codes and handbooks, ensures that:

- An earthquake-resistant structure suffers no damages to structural elements under minor earthquake,
- An earthquake-resistant structure may suffer only repairable damages to structural elements under moderate earthquake and
- An earthquake-resistant structure may suffer major damages to structural elements without collapse, even under a strong earthquake.

The code[25] of BIS states: *"The structures designed as per this standard are expected to sustain damage during strong earthquake ground shaking".* How to create this awareness among the different stakeholders is indeed a crucial aspect. To facilitate a systematic discussion on this aspect, the stakeholders have been broadly looked upon as the ones falling under two groups: (i) the non-technical group and (ii) the technical group. The non-technical group (the owner, the contractor, the builder and the workforce) has to depend on the technical group for the required expertise in planning, design and supervision of the construction of earthquake-resistant structures. On the other hand, the technical group (the planner, the designer and the supervisor) has to play the expected role effectively with adequate knowledge of the construction of earthquake-resistant structures. This approach ought to be the essence of creating awareness among the stakeholders. In the present scenario of the construction of structures—particularly in the case of building structures, the adoption of this approach appears to be missing to a great extent. There are different reasons leading to this situation, a discussion of which has been outside the scope of this article. However, a detailed discussion on the aspect of awareness among the members of the technical group has been attempted under the next sub-head.

2.2.1.2. Lack of Understanding of Available Seismic Knowledge (Standardized) on Earthquake-Resistant Structures

While starting a discussion on this sub-head, a few words of a great engineer named E. Freyssinet, who wrote in the 'Foreword' of a book[26], may be quoted as: *"Those of my readers who have insufficiently reflected on the conditions in which technicians carry out their activities, or who are ignorant of them will perhaps be astonished at the importance which I attach to the moral side of technique. May I assure them that if, among the certitudes which I have acquired during a half-century of construction and research, there is one which is abundantly certain, it is that virtues of character—courage, probity, respect of and love for the task accepted—are infinitely more necessary to the engineer than those of intelligence, which is never more than a tool in the hands of a moral being."*

To plan, design and construct earthquake-resistant structures, the qualities referred to in the above-noted words of Prof. Freyssinet need to be cultivated right from the stage of budding as a member of the technical group, as defined in the preceding sub-head. The stage of budding obviously relates to the life of stay as a student in the technical institutes, which offer diplomas and basic degrees in engineering. The curriculum relating to moral values and seismic knowledge needs to be reviewed in light of the construction of earthquake-resistant structures. While doing so, a consideration needs to be given to:

- The set of technical persons taking care of supervision and management of the construction of structures and

- The set of technical persons taking care of the planning and design of these structures.

A major part of the products coming out of the institutes with a diploma or a basic degree take up the profession, as mentioned under set (i). On the other hand, the other set, as given under set (ii), takes up the profession of planning and design. The first set obviously needs a clear knowledge of structural details in conformity with the provisions of relevant codes of practice, including the basic knowledge of earthquake-resistant structures, while the second set needs a deeper knowledge of planning, designing and detailing of structures. It is in this context that the necessity of a review of the curriculum of these institutes has been strongly felt. A greater emphasis has to be placed on training the budding engineers in the construction of earthquake-resistant structures. After joining the profession, they are expected to play the role of mentors to create the required awareness among the non-technical stakeholders of the construction industry.

The lack of appropriate awareness about different aspects of planning, design and construction among some engineers, including diploma holders, engaged in the housing sectors is clearly demonstrated by the reasons found to be responsible for the collapse of buildings in the recent earthquakes *(dealt with in the technical part at a later stage of this discussion).* There is, therefore, an urgent need for measures to be taken to create awareness among this group. Some of these measures may be the culture of the necessary knowledge through organizing technical discussions in the form of seminars, workshops and training programs. A lead in this respect may be feasibly taken by the associations of engineers, departments dealing with housing sectors and also by technical institutions. Engineers and architects have to equip themselves so that they can play the role of mentors for the non-technical group of stakeholders in the construction industry.

A situation of conflicting attitudes between the two groups of stakeholders of the construction industry is noticeable, at times in appreciable measure. The conflicting attitude is basically accountable to a lack of mutual respect for the tasks performed by each of the two groups (non-technical and technical groups, as mentioned earlier). This attitude adversely affects the quality of construction. The different tasks to be performed by each of the stakeholders of a construction project with mutual respect for one another are dealt with in greater detail in Chapter V.

A chaotic situation of planning, design, and construction is imminent in the construction industry today due to expertise and experience in respective fields of activity. This is because of the fact that there is no legislation for the regulation of the profession of engineers through an Act of our country, as we have in the case of the professions, as mentioned earlier. The second point that comes after taking care of ensuring the intended purpose with safety relates to the aspect of ensuring the intended period of the life of a structure. It is in this context that the aspect of proper maintenance of a structure becomes important.

The earthquake safety of buildings is an area that should get due attention not only in urban development but also in rural development, as there have been a lot of reports of damage to houses in rural areas caused by the earthquakes of the past. This situation warrants necessary measures to create awareness among the rural population concerned with the construction of rural houses, including traditional houses.

2.2.1.3. Lack of Strict Enforcement of Laws and Guidelines of Regulatory Bodies for the Construction of Buildings

The discussion under this area may be initiated with reference to an observation made by the Honorable Supreme Court while giving the verdict[27] of the demolition of the Noida Twin Towers. *(Article 153 of the verdict)*. This observation goes as the Court *held that it was imperative for the public authority to not only demolish such constructions but also to impose a penalty on the wrongdoers involved. This lament of this Court, over the brazen violation of building regulations by developers acting in collusion with planning bodies, was brought to the forefront when the Court prefaced its judgment with the following observations:*

1. In the last five decades, the provisions contained in various municipal laws for planned development of the areas to which such laws are applicable have been violated with impunity in all the cities, big or small, and those entrusted with the task of ensuring implementation of the master plan, etc. have miserably failed to perform their duties. It is highly regrettable that this is so despite the fact that this Court has, keeping in view the imperatives of preserving the ecology and environment of the area and protecting the rights of the citizens, repeatedly cautioned the authorities concerned against arbitrary regularization of illegal constructions by way of compounding and otherwise.

The above-noted observation of the highest court of the country is indicative of the extent of poor enforcement of the laws and guidelines existing in the country for the regulation of construction in urban areas. In fact, this situation is responsible, to a great extent, for the growth of structures vulnerable to earthquake damage.

The lack of strict enforcement of the existing laws and guidelines has resulted in the growth of a huge number of non-engineered building structures (many of which are vulnerable to earthquake damage) and also of many vulnerable engineered buildings in urban areas. Let us all (the stakeholders) join our hands together to minimize the volume of vulnerable structures by paying due regard to the existing laws and guidelines of the regulatory bodies, on the one hand, and by honoring the seismic knowledge made available to us through different codes and handbooks on the other. The earthquake will always remain a threat to life and property in earthquake-prone regions. We have to learn to live with this threat by creating a safe shelter for ourselves, as conceived in the UN's Sustainable Development Goal No. 11, which goes as: *Make cities and human settlements inclusive, safe, resilient and sustainable.*

<u>2.2.2. Technical Analysis – A Damage in Superstructure</u>

2.2.2.1. Damages in Building Structures in General
Many footage of structural damages caused by the Turkey-Syria earthquake of February 2023, as available on the internet, along with some of the footage of structural damages caused by Indian

earthquakes of the past, have been studied from the perspective of structural engineering. A general observation of these footages suggests the following areas for a technical discussion on different factors resulting in structural damages caused by earthquakes:

- *Damages in super-structures:* There are primarily four types of the failure of super-structures. These are buildings having total collapse, buildings having partial collapse, buildings having damages to only non-structural elements and buildings collapsing due to failure of soft-storey.
- *Damages in sub-structures:* There are buildings with no foundation, leading to either complete or partial overturning. A technical discussion on all the above-noted areas of structural damage is attempted under the subsequent subheads.

2.2.2.2. Buildings Having Total Collapse

The portion marked as A in the representative footage shown in image 2.3 shows the total collapse of a number of buildings. The details of these buildings with regard to age and structural system are not available. The visual study of the totally collapsed-ones does confirm that they were not earthquake-resistant. It is not known whether these buildings were engineered or non-engineered. In either case, non-adoption of even the basic principle of seismic design is clearly evident. The basic principle consists of the adoption of an appropriate load path with appropriate connections between respective structural elements. This situation was observed even in cases of buildings that collapsed during the past earthquakes in India. With respect to the load path, the code of BIS[28] states: *"The structure shall contain at least one rational and complete load path for seismic forces from any horizontal direction so that they may transfer all inertia forces in the building to the foundation."*

Image 2.3: A Representative Footage of Total Collapse of Buildings of Turkey[150]
Source: https://zeenews.india.com/world/turkey-syria-earthquake-deadliest-quakes-in-two-decades-claim-over-24000-lives-2572031.html

On the other hand, building blocks marked as 'B' and 'C' in image 2.3 show no sign of even minor damages (not to speak of partial or total collapse), despite the fact that they stand at the same site as the one at which the collapsed-ones were located. This situation demonstrates the appropriate adoption of the available seismic knowledge in the design and construction of these two blocks (B and C). The 'negligence' or 'ignorance' on the part of those involved in the construction and maintenance of the buildings in the portion marked 'A' is easily understandable. The lives of many would have been saved if the available technology for seismic evaluation and strengthening of vulnerable structures had been adopted in time.

2.2.2.3. Buildings Having Partial Collapse

A representative footage of a building having partial collapse in the last Turkey-Syria earthquake is shown in image 2.4. The right part of this building suffered partial collapse primarily because of the failure of a number of joints between the beam and column. These joints are indicated in the image by circles. This building indicates a structural system, which is apparently a framed structure. As evident, some of the columns failed, apparently due to inadequate lateral stiffness of the bay concerned. It is interesting to note that the left bay of this block appears to have adequate lateral stiffness due to the presence of a good infilling wall. It may be noted that the infilling wall appreciably increases the lateral stiffness of a frame. This contribution of infilling wall has been taken into account in the latest revision of IS code[25].

Image 2.4: A Representative Footage of Building[151] Having Partial Collapse of Turkey. A Similar Situation of Partial Collapse of Buildings Was Observed Even in Cases of Indian Earthquakes of the Recent Past.
Source: https://www.livehindustan.com/photos/international/turkey-earthquake-rescue-workers-and-residents-in-multiple-cities-searched-for-survivors-1-7733019

A representative footage of the partial collapse of a building in Imphal in the earthquake of 2016 (Magnitude 6.7) is shown in image 2.5. The primary reason for this partial collapse has been the failure of the joints, as shown within circles.

Image 2.5: A Representative Footage of Partial Collapse of
A building of Manipur in 2016 Earthquake[152]
Source: https://www.firstpost.com/india/manipur-earthquake-death-toll-rises-to-
eight-govt-announces-compensation-2571184.html

The detailing of beams and columns in a reinforced concrete framed structure is the most important consideration for providing adequate toughness and ductility. These two properties are of absolute necessity for enabling these structural elements to take up extensive inelastic deformations and dissipate seismic energy appropriately. This aspect of structural detailing appears to have been completely ignored in the buildings having either total or partial collapse, as shown in images 2.3, 2.4 and 2.5. The engineers involved in the design and construction of the buildings shown in the above-noted footage (if at all these were engineered ones) were apparently ignorant of these aspects. The available seismic knowledge does include these aspects.

In India, the BIS code[29] deals with Ductile Detailing of Reinforced Concrete Structures subjected to seismic forces. Many deficiencies were observed in the performance of reinforced concrete structures, which were designed and detailed as per IS 4326: 1976 during the past earthquakes in India. Based on these deficiencies, the earlier edition of IS 13920 was revised, and the revised one[29] was then published. Many salient aspects of the design and detailing of reinforced concrete structures have been incorporated into the revised version of this code. Some of these aspects include: *geometric constraints on cross-sections of flexural members, minimum and maximum reinforcement limits, explicit requirements for detailing of longitudinal reinforcements in beams at joint faces, splices and anchorage requirements, detailing of transverse reinforcements in beams, etc.*

A lot of footage (as available on the websites) of buildings having either total or partial collapse in the earthquakes of Turkey-Syria and those of Gujarat, Latur and Manipur in India are indicative of deficiencies with respect to many areas of structural detailing, as briefly dealt with in the preceding para. It is in this context that a greater emphasis has to be laid on the creation of the required awareness, as dealt with already. In contrast to this situation, the buildings marked as "B" and "C" in the footage of Turkey shown in image 2.3 indicate the proper utilization of available seismic knowledge relating to the design, detailing and construction of earthquake-resistant buildings. These two buildings have shown no sign of damage, even in an earthquake of M 7.8. Similar examples are found in India, too.

The discussion presented above obviously raises a question as to whether the buildings constructed before the present state of seismic knowledge are safe against earthquakes or not, presuming that they were constructed in conformity with the then-available seismic knowledge. Obviously, an answer to this question may be given by an appropriate vulnerability assessment of old structures, as per the guidelines of BIS28. The priority with respect to this aspect needs to be given to the buildings that have a higher importance factor.

2.2.2.4. Buildings Having Damages to Only Non-Structural Elements

A footage of a building having damages (including collapse) of non-structural elements is shown in image 2.6. The elements that are not involved in the load path conceived in the adopted structural system are called non-structural ones. The common examples are parapet walls, infilling walls (if their contribution to lateral stiffness is not accounted for in design), and other architectural, mechanical or electrical components that are permanently installed.

Image 2.6: Damages to Non-Structural Elements in a Building in Last Turkey-Earthquake[153]
Source: https://www.gettyimages.co.uk/photos/turkish-earthquake

The non-structural element carries its self-weight only, and self-weight is transferred to the supporting structural element. Therefore, the connection between the non-structural and structural components becomes important for avoiding the collapse of the former. Because of the poor connection of the parapet wall to the supporting frame element (roof beam in this case), the masonry parapet wall provided in the portion marked 'A' in image 2.6 collapsed out-of-plane under the lateral pressure caused by the earthquake. As shown in the image marked 'B', a masonry infilling wall (unreinforced) got crushed or cracked and fell out-of-plane. An infilling wall may be subjected to either cracking or crushing (under in-plane lateral pressure) or cracking due to bending caused by out-of-plane lateral pressure. The first situation of cracking and crushing because of in-plane lateral pressure is evident in the infilling wall marked 'C' in image 2.6. Though the masonry infilling wall was apparently adopted in this case as a non-structural element, it became a structural element since it was subjected to in-plane stresses (tensile along one diagonal and compressive along the other) under the action of lateral force created by the earthquake along the in-plane direction. This is precisely why the recent revision of the BIS code[25] incorporated the contribution of unreinforced masonry infilling walls towards the lateral stiffness of a framed structure. This footage is indeed a clear demonstration of this phenomenon.

In view of the possible collapse of masonry parapet walls under lateral forces (as stated above), alternative measures, such as providing light railings with galvanized iron pipes, have been adopted in some cases. *(In some of the buildings designed by the author, this has been very effective).* This system yields two major benefits:

- It reduces the weight and
- It facilitates the connection with the supporting structural element.

2.2.2.5. Buildings Collapsing Due to Failure of Soft-storey

A representative footage of a building collapsing on account of the failure of a soft-storey in the Bhuj (Gujarat) earthquake of 2001 is shown in image 2.7. A lot of footage of buildings having a failure of the soft storey has been found on the internet, even in the case of the recent Turkey-Syria earthquake. However, the one shown in image 2.7 has been taken because no visible damage has been observed in storeys above the soft storey of the ground floor.

Image 2.7: Failure of Soft Storey of a Building in Bhuj Earthquake of 2001[154]

This situation is indicative of two important aspects:

- The lateral strength available in the top four storeys was adequate to take the lateral forces caused by the earthquake of magnitude 6.9 and
- The lateral strength available in soft storey (ground floor) was obviously inadequate.

This was indeed the broad deficiency resulting in partial collapse, as indicated by the image. The structural system adopted in this building is obviously a reinforced concrete moment-resisting frame. Then, the question is: What elements have been responsible for the adequate lateral strength of the top four storeys? An apparent answer to this question consists in the presence of infilling walls placed in the frames of top storeys in the direction of seismic forces. A masonry-infilling panel in tight contact with a frame around its full perimeter is called a shear infill, as defined in BIS code[28]. In this case, the shear infills present in the upper four storeys have been the elements contributing to the lateral stiffness along the direction of seismic forces caused. Therefore, the primary reason for the failure of the soft storey in this case may be the absence of diagonal bracings, shear walls, or shear infills. This resulted in inadequate lateral strength against seismic forces as caused. On the other hand, the maximum base shear is caused in the lowest storey. This situation amply demonstrates the failure on the part of the designer to take care of the required lateral stiffness against seismic forces in the soft storeys by appropriately placing a shear wall or shear infill or diagonal bracings in the soft storey.

In the urban areas of India, there are many buildings with vulnerable soft storeys, which are likely to collapse in the way shown in image 2.7 under the situation of a strong earthquake. An example of an Apartment Building in Guwahati city in Assam has been briefly dealt with at a later stage of this chapter *(under subhead 2.6).*

2.2.3. Technical Analysis: Damages in Substructure

2.2.3.1. Buildings Having Failure of Foundation Leading to Complete Overturning

A lot of footage of foundation failure in the earthquakes of Turkey-Syria and Bhuj (Gujarat) have been critically looked into. It has been found difficult to ascertain the specific reasons leading to the failure of the foundation of a particular building. This is possible only on a detailed site investigation. However, an attempt has been made herein to deal with some aspects of the failure of the foundation in relation to some of the footage.

There are a series of standards internationally available on the design and construction of foundations of structures for all types of foundations, such as shallow, deep and special foundations. In India, too, we have a number of codes of practice concerning foundations. The basic BIS code[30] deals with the general requirements of the design and construction of foundations in soils. All other codes relevant to different types of foundations are duly mentioned in this basic code. To what extent these standards are honoured in the construction industry is an obvious question led to by a huge number of foundation failures of structures as reflected by the available footage of structural damages seen on different websites.

A research paper[31] by A. Srivastava et.al has dealt with different aspects of failure of foundations including some preventive and remedial measures. It was stated in the Abstract of this paper: *'The paper reviews different failure modes of foundations such as (i) Drag down & heave, (ii) Lateral movements, (iii) Load transfer failures, (iv) Vibrating effects, (v)Floating & water level changes, (vi) Design & Construction errors, (vii) Earthquakes, (viii) Uplift forces, (ix)Slope instability/landslide, etc. Also discussed are several remedial measures with case studies to overcome and prevent these failures to stabilize soil using ground improvement techniques'.* (Interested readers may please refer to this paper for details on each area).

A brief discussion on different factors bearing on foundation failures in earthquakes is attempted herein. A footage of complete overturning of a building structure appears in image 2.2. This footage indicates complete overturning without visible damage to the superstructure. The building in this footage was intact before the earthquake occurred last February in Turkey. This proves that the building overturned on account of the earthquake forces. The major reasons for failure on account of earthquakes are well-identified[31]. The salient reasons are – (i) Ground failures (or instabilities due to ground failures), (ii) vibrations transmitted from the ground to the structure, (iii) Ground cracking, (iv) Liquefaction, (v) Ground lurching, (vi) Differential settlement, (vii) Lateral spreading and (viii) Landslides. There are different kinds of literature treating all these aspects in greater detail. A detailed discussion of these areas is outside the scope of this book. However, an attempt is made herein to deal with some aspects relating to the failure of foundations, as observed in the construction industry in general and in the northeast region of India in particular.

The major area requiring the attention of all concerned is the geotechnical investigation for the design of foundations. Two major problems with respect to geotechnical investigation are very often observed. The first one is the design of a foundation without a report of a due geotechnical investigation. There are many cases of even engineered buildings for which foundations are designed without geotechnical investigation. The second problem relates to the quality of geotechnical investigation, even if there is a report of this investigation. There have been cases of faulty reports of geotechnical exploration, even for some structures taken up at this end for structural design. The basic reason for a situation of this type may be attributed to ignorance of the consequences of a foundation design based on 'no geotechnical investigation' or on 'faulty geotechnical investigation report', to be led to in the event of an earthquake, as well evidenced in many of the available footages of structural damages in the earthquake. The principles of geotechnical investigation are well-set in BIS code[32]. These principles need to be adhered to, for the purpose of which the ethical values on the part of those responsible for this investigation play a significant role.

The footage given in image 2.2 shows the case of the complete overturning of a building. On the other hand, the footage given in image 2.8 shows the case of partial overturning coupled with pounding. It is difficult to identify the specific reasons for this without a detailed physical inspection. However, the apparent reasons for overturning may be attributed to differential settlement and/or liquefaction if the structures concerned were not on land-slope (thereby eliminating the possibility of landslides). Presuming that the foundations of these buildings were stable under the inertia loads (DL + LL), the overturning occurred due to the differential settlement induced by the earthquake. Generally, there are three factors for earthquake-induced differential settlement of buildings on natural subsoil. These factors are wave-type seismic ground motion, the property and distribution of soil layers below the building, and the weight distribution of the building and foundation[33].

Image 2.8: Footage Showing Partial Overturning and Pounding of Buildings of Turkey[155]
Source: https://www.punjabkesari.com/explainer/north-india-trembled-due-to-earth-shaking-know-why-earthquake-occurs-and-all-the-questions-related-to-it

On the other hand, as stated above, the overturning might have been caused by soil liquefaction as well, which a phenomenon is commonly observed in large earthquakes. In the 1950 earthquake of Assam (Magnitude 8.6), there were many locations of soil liquefaction. The footage given in image 2.9 shows a clear case of this phenomenon. Fortunately, there were no structures on that site.

Image 2.9: A Footage Showing Liquefaction in Assam- Earthquake of 1950[156]
Source: https://kihikila.in/ki-hikiba/history-stories/the-great-earthquake-of-1950/#google_vignette

A significant amount of work was done in the last few decades to understand the phenomenon of liquefaction and its hazards to structures. Today, we have the technology developed for the evaluation and mitigation of liquefaction hazards. There is a lot of literature and standards available today. The BIS code[25] includes a *'simplified procedure for evaluation of liquefaction potential'.*

As seen in image 2.8, the two buildings present the case of partial overturning and the case of pounding. Pounding (the portion marked as 'B') is a phenomenon of two adjacent buildings impacting during the earthquake excitation, mainly due to insufficient distance (the portion marked as 'A' in the image). The desired distances between two adjacent buildings to avoid the pounding are dealt with in BIS codes[25] and[28]. On the other hand, in the footage shown in image 2.8, it is not definitely known whether the portion marked 'B' is a pounding accountable to insufficient separation-distance between the two buildings or to the collision between the two buildings.

The modern concept[28] of 'Supplemental Damping and Isolation' is being used for tall buildings in different countries, including India. The basic principle of "base isolation" consists of separating the base (foundation or substructure) from the superstructure so that the seismic energy transferred to the superstructure (on account of ground motion caused by the earthquake) gets substantially reduced. This reduction leads to the requirement of lesser lateral stiffness of superstructure than that required otherwise. This is a specialized area, and therefore, the utilization of this concept in buildings does require the engagement of specialists.

2.3. Role of Civic Bodies in Mitigation of Earthquake Damages in Vulnerable Structures of Urban Areas (This article was published in the Assam Tribune on 25.09.2020)

2.3.1. General

The structures existing in different cities and towns of the country are under the control of civic bodies like Municipal Corporations, Councils, Municipality Boards, Town Committees, among others. These civic bodies regulate new construction activities within their respective jurisdiction. However, the regulatory aspects of new construction are outside the scope of this article. Different factors pertaining to the mitigation of earthquake damages in the existing structures are briefly discussed herein.

The earthquakes of the recent past, such as those in Latur, Gujarat and Manipur, have already shown the extent of loss of life and property. An earthquake of the type of 1950 with a magnitude of 8.6 in NE Region is due anytime. Therefore, the civic bodies of our region have reasons to rise to the occasion. The intervention in existing structures vulnerable to earthquake damage has been a known proactive action followed internationally. Even in India, the Government of India has started taking actions in this direction. This is evident from a recent project taken up by the Government of India named National Seismic Risk Mitigation Programme under the aegis of the World Bank.

2.3.2. A Broad Approach

Immediate attention to the adoption of mitigation measures is necessary in view of the fact that:
- There are many unauthorized structures violating the rules and regulations well laid down in bye-laws, as applicable to the respective cities and towns and
- There are many structures (mostly buildings) vulnerable to

earthquake damages.

Therefore, the primary role to be played by civic bodies lies in taking appropriate measures to identify unauthorized structures as well as structures vulnerable to seismic risks. The unauthorized structures are normally vulnerable.

Identifying the unauthorized ones is apparently simple; it requires a survey to be conducted by the civic authorities. Once duly identified, appropriate actions may be taken for regularization within the limitations of the relevant bye-laws or for demolition.

The identification of vulnerable structures will obviously need the services of experts with specialized knowledge in areas which include planning, structural design, testing of materials, construction techniques, etc. The civic bodies may engage a competent team with the requisite expertise for the identification of all the existing structures within their jurisdiction. A list of vulnerable buildings may then be prepared along with the names of the owners, which will include Government (State and Centre), Semi-Government Organisations, Private Organisations and Individuals. This task, though challenging, is feasible under the guidance and assistance of the State Disaster Management Authority, empowered by the Disaster Management Act of the country.

Once the list of vulnerable structures is prepared, intervention measures, which will basically be the incorporation of Retrofit Measures or Reconstruction, will have to be decided upon. The choice of the appropriate intervention measure in a particularly vulnerable structure may be identified by the experts, as mentioned earlier. The cost necessary for the implementation of retrofit measures may be substantial. At times, it may run into the range of 50 to 70 percent of the cost of new construction. However, the implementation of technically sound retrofit measures will ensure a life equal to that of a new structure. In view of the likely damages to be caused by an earthquake, the civic bodies may take regulatory measures for the implementation of retrofit measures or reconstruction for vulnerable structures on the strength provided by the Disaster Management Act.

The active participation and cooperation of all categories of the owners of the structure is an absolute necessity in view of the major thrust now being internationally laid on the mitigation of earthquake damages in earthquake-prone countries. The NE Region happens to be one of the six severe-most earthquake-prone zones of the world.

The actions initiated by the government of Assam and some other northeastern states relate to heritage structures and government structures vulnerable to earthquake damage. However, there are a huge number of vulnerable structures in our cities and towns under the ownership of semi-government organizations, private organizations and individuals. These structures in relation to hazards likely to be caused by an earthquake of great, major or strong magnitude (great for magnitude above M 8.0, major for magnitude in the range of M 7 to 7.9 and strong for magnitude in the range of M 6.0 to 6.9) deserve equal attention. The loss of life and property in the event of the occurrence of earthquake damage to this category of structures will be huge.

The civic bodies of our region are expected to rise to the occasion before a great earthquake of the type of 1950 hits us. In 1950, we did not have so many tall structures housing the huge population as we have today. It requires a concerted effort from all stakeholders to act towards mitigation of earthquake damages in vulnerable structures, thereby avoiding a likely situation of human tragedy, as led to by the earthquakes of the past.

2.4. A Modern Concept (EEWS) for Reducing Loss of Life and Property in Earthquakes

2.4.1. General

The loss of life and property on account of earthquakes has been a challenging issue for a long time, and it is a well-recognized world over now. Scientists and engineers have been engaged in the formulation of different measures to reduce the extent of loss of life and property. According to an assessment, during the last four decades (1970-2017), the earthquakes caused over a million deaths around the world. There have been continuous efforts directed towards the reduction of loss of life and property in case of all types of natural calamities, including earthquakes. The salient of these efforts is the Sendai Framework for Disaster Risk Reduction (2015-2030) (Known as Sendai Framework), which was approved by the UN General Assembly following the 2015 UN World Conference on Disaster Risk Reduction. This Framework has set seven global targets[34] to be achieved by 2030. Four of these targets have been set for 'Substantial Reductions', which are—*(a) Reduce global disaster mortality, (b) Reduce the number of affected people globally, (c) Reduce direct economic loss in relation to GDP and (d) Reduce disaster damage to critical infrastructure and disruption of basic services.* On the other hand, the other three targets set for 'Substantial Increases' are – *(e) Increase the number of countries with national and local disaster risk reduction strategies,(f)Substantially enhance international cooperation with developing countries and (g) Increase the availability of and access to multi-hazard early warning systems* (EWS).

2.4.2. Warning System

The area chosen for a discussion herein has been limited to target (g), i.e. 'increase the availability of and access to' warning system for substantial reduction of only earthquake hazards (not for warning systems for other natural hazards such as those caused by flood, tsunami, wind, etc). Therefore, the specific area chosen for a discussion relates to Earthquake Early Warning Systems (EEWS), which are now being adopted internationally as a modern concept for substantial reduction of earthquake hazards. The adoption of EEWS has a positive effect to a substantial extent on four targets set by the Sendai Framework for substantial reductions, as stated above.

The development followed by the adoption of EEWS has been necessitated by the failure to scientifically predict an earthquake. The basic elements of a scientific prediction are—(a) the date and time, (ii) the location and (c) the magnitude. So far, a prediction based on these basic elements has not been possible[35]. A prediction of this type is unlikely in the foreseeable future, too. In view of this scenario of earthquake prediction, the international effort, as evidenced by the Sendai Framework, has been directed towards the adoption of EEWS in seismic regions around the world.

The basic principle on which the development of EEWS is based consists of the properties and characteristics of seismic waves created by the occurrence of an earthquake. The seismic waves basically are of two types: (a) Body Waves and (b) Surface Waves. Body waves are of two categories: primary waves (P-waves) and secondary waves (S-waves). The primary waves are compressional and longitudinal in nature. These pressure waves (P-waves) travel faster through the earth's core (after getting generated at the hypocentre). On the other hand, the secondary waves (S-waves) are transverse in nature, and they travel at a speed lesser than that of P-waves through the Earth's crust, as in the case of P-waves. P-waves are non-destructive, while the S-waves are destructive.

There are several types of surface waves, the two most common types being the Rayleigh Wave and the Love Wave. Surface waves travel just below the surface of the earth at a speed slower than that of body waves (S-wave) and are the most destructive. These properties of seismic waves clearly indicate that the P-wave is the first to reach the seismograph station (Data Processing Centre) located nearest to the epicentre, followed then by S-waves and thereafter, the surface wave reaches. There is a time gap (interval) between the reaching times of the P-wave and the surface wave at the Data Processing Unit. This time gap constitutes the basic principle of the development of EEWS. This time gap (interval) generally ranges between 60 and 90 seconds[36] depending on the depth of the hypocentre, the distance of the Data Processing Centre from the epicentre and the magnitude of the earthquake.

Obviously, the locations (delivery centres) to which the alert notification will be served have to be appropriately connected to the Data Processing Centre, and those locations have to be equipped with all necessary items (with necessary Apps, etc.) for blowing the alarm (or otherwise). The whole process of data analysis (at the Data Processing Centre), issuing of warning notice (by the Data Processing Unit) and giving the warning, i.e. blowing the siren or otherwise (at the delivery centre), is automated and takes some seconds. Therefore, only a few seconds (maybe a few seconds to a minute) after the issue of warning may be left for the arrival of the actual shaking. Obviously, a question arises as to what protective measures may feasibly be taken for the reduction of loss in respect of life and properties and other associated damages likely to be caused by the earthquake. A broad answer to this question is contained in the statement: *Even a few seconds' warning provides enough time to take protective measures*[36]. Some of these protective measures may include – (a) Persons inside the buildings may protect themselves by dropping, covering or holding on, (b) Traffic may avoid moving onto the bridge and into tunnels, (c) The trains may stop, (d) Aircraft may avoid landing, etc. These are only a few of the broad guidelines. The disaster management agencies concerned with a particular location where EEWS is installed will have to prepare a list of protective measures in consultation with the manufacturer of the system, depending on the type of infrastructure of the location.

G. Cremen *et al.* gave an account of the recent position of EEWS as of 2020 in an article[37]. As stated in that article, *'These systems are currently operating in nine countries, and are being/have been tested for implementation in 13 more.'* In respect of India, as stated by A. Kumar et al.[38]: *'For earthquakes originating from the central Himalayas, such a system can provide tens of seconds of warning to the adjoining plains and Delhi can get as much as 70s of warning time. A successful EEWS, in the event of 7 + magnitude earthquake from the central Himalayas, can save millions of live.'*

The relevance of the adoption of EEWS for India is obvious and is covered in the target (g) of the targets of the Sendai Framework, as stated earlier. The country's first EEWS (in the form of a Mobile App developed by IIT, Roorkee) was installed in Uttarakhand[39] in 2021. 'This App will give early warning of earthquakes 30-40 seconds before the earthquakes for which 64 sensors have been installed in the entire state.' The National Disaster Management Authority (NDMA), Government of India, initiated a project in association with the World Bank for the installation of EEWS in a number of states.

Research works aimed at the refinement and further development of earthquake early warning systems, including performance evaluation of those already installed in different countries, are going on in different corners of the world. Let us hope, by 2030, the target, as set by the Sendai Framework, that the seismic regions of the world, including India, will have enough EEWS in place so that the extent of damages to life and property caused by earthquakes gets reduced substantially.

2.5. An Approach to Retrofitting of Structures Vulnerable To Earthquake Damages

2.5.1. General

Extensive damages to structures are caused by earthquakes in all earthquake-prone zones of the globe. A few of the extents of damages caused by the earthquakes of the past are evidenced by the structures shown in image 2.10 (a), (b) and (c).

Image 2.10 (a), (b) & (c): Structures Damaged by Past Earthquakes in India [157, 158]
Sources: Image 2.10 (a):
https://www.facebook.com/permalink.php/?story_fbid=860976847363818&id=23003
1747125001
Image 2.10 (b): https://www.firstpost.com/india/manipur-earthquake-death-
toll-rises-to-eight-govt-announces-compensation-2571184.html
Image 2.10 (c): https://www.firstpost.com/india/manipur-earthquake-death-
toll-rises-to-eight-govt-announces-compensation-2571184.html

There is ample evidence similar to those shown in image 2.10 of structural damages around the world. In India, too, the whole of the land mass is prone to earthquakes *(as indicated by the zoning map given in image 2.11). The zoning map is associated with the 1964 MSK Intensity Scale[25]. According to NDMA Guidelines[40]*, about 80% of India's population lives in areas under seismic zones V, IV and III, thereby indicating the fact that a huge majority of the Indian population lives under earthquake risks.

Image 2.11: Earth Quake-Zonning Map India (Taken Form BIS Code[25])

Against this scenario of earthquake risk, there are many structures vulnerable to earthquake damage today, more so in urban and semi-urban areas where the density of structures of this type is very high. The loss of life and property has also been immense in the past earthquakes. A picture of the extent of human casualties and building collapsed during the past earthquakes in India has been given by NDMA[40], as shown in table 2.2.

Year	Name of Earthquake	Human Casualties	Buildings Collapsed
1988	Bihar-Nepal Border	1,004	2,50,000
1991	Uttarkashi	768	42,400
1993	Killari	8,000	30,000
1997	Jabalpur	38	8,546
1999	Chamoli	100	2,595
2001	Bhuj	13,805	2,31,000
2005	Kashmir	~ 1,500	4,50,000

Table 2.2: Human Casualties and Buildings Collapsed
(Prepared by the Author Based on Data of NDMA[40])

The need for proactive measures for reduction in the extent of loss accountable to structural damages caused by earthquakes has been internationally stressed pursuant to the objective of Yokohama Strategy for a Safer World, adopted at the UN-sponsored conference of 1994. There are, in fact, many proactive measures in place. There are two types of buildings which can be retrofitted. One is the type of buildings already damaged partly by earthquakes, and the other one is the type of those vulnerable to earthquake damage. However, the scope of this discussion has been limited only to the 'retrofitting' of vulnerable buildings, an approach that is being internationally practised. The adoption of this approach has been absolutely necessary because the prediction of the earthquake with regard to specific date, time, and location has not been possible, as already stated earlier.

The extensive magnitude of damages caused by earthquakes elsewhere very often creates in the minds of the general public a question as to whether the related technology has failed us. The obvious answer to this question is a clear 'No' because, as observed *(under subhead 2.2.2),* many of the structures close to the damaged ones survived with no sign of appreciable effects of earthquake forces. It is indeed the failure on the part of those involved in the construction and maintenance of the damaged structures to utilize appropriately and adequately the related technology made available to us through codes of practice, handbooks, guidelines, etc., in the field of planning, design, construction and maintenance of earthquake-resistant structures. Many studies conducted internationally on damaged structures suggest deficiencies in planning, design, detailing, and quality control during the construction and maintenance of structures. These deficiencies are observed in both the new and existing structures in variable measures. The author had the opportunity of incorporating retrofits into both of these two types of structures. Therefore, a broad approach for proactive measures is needed to ensure earthquake-resistance covers both the new and the existing structures. The scope of this discussion has been limited to the approach to be adopted for proactive measures (retrofitting) only for existing building structures. As suggested by NDMA[40], the two broad steps involved in the process of retrofitting are to – *'undertake preliminary seismic assessment'* and *'perform detailed seismic assessment to determine seismic retrofit option'*. These two broad steps are technically covered in a greater detail in the BIS code[28]. Therefore, the discussion of the approach for adopting retrofit measures is taken up in this discussion under the subheads[28]: Identification of Structures to be Retrofitted, Vulnerability Assessment, Design of Retrofit Measures, Working Out of Cost Involved, Justification for Incurring the Cost of Retrofit and Execution of Retrofit Measures.

2.5.2. Identification of Structures to be Retrofitted

2.5.2.1. Preliminary Evaluation

2.5.2.1.1. General

The first task is to identify the structures that need to be considered for retrofitting. There are many buildings apparently vulnerable to earthquake damage. As far as urban areas are concerned, all these buildings are under the relevant statutory bodies. However, the owners come under different categories, namely: state government, central government, public sector, private sector, etc. The responsibility of identification obviously lies with the respective owner. However, in India, the NDMA, under which different SDMAs function, conducts different measures for the mitigation of disasters, including those accountable for earthquakes. As reported by NDMA[41], the earthquake-disaster risk indexing of 50 cities of India *(falling in seismic zones III, IV and V)* was done. Three basic parameters, earthquake hazard, vulnerability and exposure, were taken into account while assessing the indices, which were classified as *'High'*, *'Medium'* and *'Low'*. These indices primarily facilitate the identification of cities where detailed evaluation of structures is necessary for taking up proactive measures to reduce earthquake damages, apart from creating awareness among different stakeholders about the importance of earthquake-resistant structures in general.

Based on the Guidelines[28, 42] of BIS, the phases of works involved in the process of evaluation (both preliminary and detailed ones) are briefly discussed below. The different phases of activities involved in preliminary evaluation are given in figure 2.1.

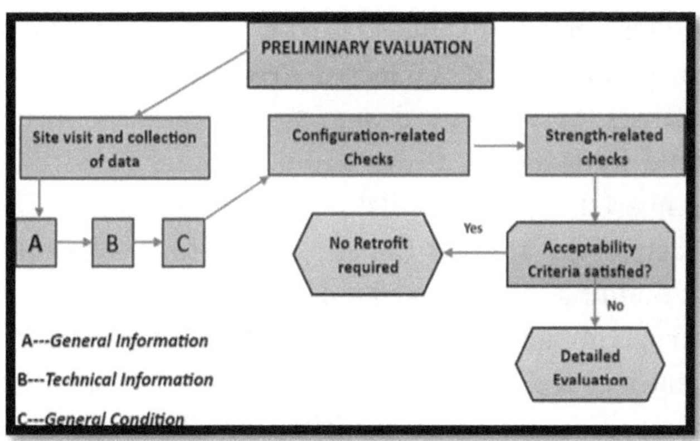

Figure 2.1: Flowchart Summarizing Preliminary Evaluation Process

2.5.2.2. Site Visit and Collection of Data

The visit to the site of the building under consideration has to be conducted by a team under the leadership of a structural engineer with experience bearing on both construction and design. The purpose of this site visit is to collect a series of information and data about the building. The accuracy of information and data collected at the site will reflect on the correctness of the decision to be taken *'for or against'* the retrofitting on the one hand and, on the other, on the techniques to be adopted for retrofits in case of a decision in favour of retrofitting. Therefore, a judicious formation of the team for site visits is of utmost necessity. The information and data to be collected broadly include the areas discussed below under the subheads[28]: *General Information, Technical Information and General Conditions.*

- *General Information:* The information relating to the year of construction, overall dimensions (both horizontal and vertical), site conditions (such as sewage system, drainage system, the orientation of the building, site plantation, etc.), type of use, nature of occupancy, etc. have to be gathered and duly noted.

- *Technical Information:* This phase is vital in respect of identifying a building for retrofitting. The error/omission committed with respect to the collection of information and data might lead to a wrong decision. It is in this context that knowledge, experiences, and ethical values on the part of the team engaged in this phase are absolutely important. The first information to be collected from the owner relates to drawings of concept design and structural design, which should be available if the building under investigation is an engineered one. If available, all the drawings need to be collected, and then at the site, it has to be checked whether the building on the ground corresponds to the size and internal arrangements indicated in the drawings. The deviations, if observed, will be duly noted. In addition, the soil investigation report, if available for the site of the building, needs to be collected from the client. In case the drawings are not available *(which is normally the case with many of the vulnerable buildings),* all measurements necessary for the preparation of plans for all floors, including the position of columns, elevations and cross sections, sizes of different elements (both structural and non-structural elements), type and depth of foundation will be taken and recorded duly at the site. The gaps, along with the height of adjacent buildings, will also be duly recorded for looking into the aspects of pounding and falling hazards.

- *General Conditions:* The general conditions of materials, such as concrete, steel, brickwork, etc., will be physically observed. Subsequently, the properties and strength of the same are ascertained through the conduct of non-destructive tests, as applicable. If the soil investigation report is not available or if it (if available) is very old or not reliable, the soil investigation at the site will have to be conducted, and a report will have to be prepared. The visible damages, such as cracks, leakages, dampness, pilling off, etc., on all elements (both structural and non-structural) will also be duly recorded. All architectural features, including the location of infilling walls, which are likely to impact the earthquake performance of the building will also be duly noted. Other conditions to be noted include geological site hazards, foundation conditions and any other construction anomalies.

The information and data collected under this phase of the site visit should invariably be adequate to yield all aspects necessary to ascertain the structural and architectural systems of the building so that all technical considerations to be made subsequently (to be discussed under the next subhead) are facilitated.

2.5.2.3. Configuration Related Checks

All activities under this subhead are carried out by structural engineers with adequate knowledge and experience in planning, design and construction. The first task is to identify the load path of the building on the basis of the data and drawings *(collected or prepared)* as discussed under the preceding subhead. Based on the identification of the load path, the structural system, i.e. whether the building under consideration is a framed structure or a masonry structure, is identified. As stated earlier, the discussion herein is limited to buildings with a Reinforced Concrete Framed System[28, 43]. If a masonry structure has to be dealt with, the factors to be duly considered will be broadly based on guidelines [43] of BIS.

For a framed structure, the salient parameters[28] to be critically looked into as per BIS code[28] are—*Load path, Redundancy, Geometry, Week Storey, Soft Storey, Vertical Discontinuities, Mass, Torsion, Adjacent Buildings, Short Columns and Mezzanines/Loft/ Subfloors.* With respect to load path, it has to be ascertained whether there is at least one well-defined load path in each of the horizontal and vertical directions. The vertical load-resisting system is required for the transfer of vertical loads to the foundation, while the horizontal load-resisting system is required for transferring the horizontal load caused by the earthquake/wind to the vertical load-resisting system. There should not be irregularities beyond the limitations suggested in the code[28] *(clause 6.4)* regarding the above-noted parameters. The consideration of gap in respect of adjacent buildings is an important consideration as defined in the code[28] *(clause 6.4.9).* The torsion to be caused by an earthquake is another important consideration based on the difference between the storey mass centre and the storey stiffness centre. The redundancy, as recommended in code[28] provides alternate load paths and additional strength and stiffness, which are beneficial for resisting substantially the lateral forces likely to be caused by occasional loads such as earthquakes, wind, blasts, etc. The different aspects of the weak storeys and/or soft storeys have to be critically looked into since there have been many examples of complete/partial collapse of buildings during earthquakes of the past, basically on account of these weak storeys.

2.5.2.4. Strength-Related Check

The strength-related check involves:

- Determination of modified demand lateral force,
- Shear stress check in columns and walls and
- Axial stress check in moment frame columns *(clause 6.5 of code[28]).*

These checks have to be based on the *'Evaluation Criteria'* given in the BIS code[28] *(clause 5).* The basic parameters on the basis of which different checks have to be based include: (i) Lateral Load Modification Factor (LLMF) and (ii) Modified Material Factor (MMF). These two parameters are evaluated on the basis of the information and data collected during the phase of *'site visit and collection of data'.* The LLMF is given by LLMF = (RUL /DUL)$^{0.5}$, RUL and DUL remaining useful life and designing useful life of the building (under consideration), respectively.

It is internationally accepted that *'a higher level of risk of life loss'* needs to be ensured for existing buildings. The LLMF is adopted to achieve this objective by reducing the lateral force by adopting this factor so that the cost of retrofitting[44] becomes economical. Different parameters necessary for calculating seismic forces, such as seismic zone, building type, response reduction factor, etc., will be based on BIS code[25]. However, as recommended by the code[28], the value of LLMF will not be taken less than 0.7 in any case. On the other hand, the strength capacities of different components of the building will be evaluated on the probable material strengths based on field and/or laboratory tests (as discussed in the preceding phase). The probable strengths so determined (or obtained otherwise from original building documents) will be modified by the Knowledge Factor (as given in Table 1 of code[28]). With these factors, the lateral loads on the frame will be calculated, and the following checks will be carried out:

- *Modified Demand Lateral Force:* The approximate and quick checks will be carried out to compute the strength and stiffness of the building components with the adoption of conventional methods of analysis. The seismic base shears and storey shears will be computed as per code[28] and modified on the basis of computed LLMF (described above).

- *Shear Stress Check for Reinforced Concrete Frame Columns:* The average shear stress to be computed as per the equation given in Clause 6.5.1 of the code[28] for column should be within the permissible limits as specified in the said clause. In case shear walls (either concrete or masonry) are there, the shear stress in the shear walls will be checked as given in Clause 6.5.2. However, in the case of reinforced concrete masonry infilled walls, the shear stress check will be governed by Clause 6.5.3.

- *Axial Stress Check in Moment Frame Columns:* The compressive axial stress in the columns of moment frames at base due to overturning forces alone will be calculated with the equation given in Clause 6.5.4 of the code[28]. It should not exceed 0.25fck.

2.5.2.5. Acceptability Criteria (For Preliminary Evaluation)

Based on the preliminary evaluation (covered under subheads site visit and collection of data, configuration-related check and strength-related check), it has to be decided as to whether the building under evaluation needs retrofitting or not. As given in Clause 6.6 of the code[28], a building that satisfies all the checks made during preliminary evaluation is not recommended for retrofitting. However, if any one of the following conditions (Clause 6.6 of the said code) applies to the building under preliminary evaluation, it (the building) then is recommended for a *'Detailed Evaluation':*

- *The building fails to comply with the requirements of the preliminary evaluation;*
- *The building is 6 storey and higher;*
- *The building is located on incompetent or liquefiable soils and/or located near (less than 15 km) active faults and/or inadequate foundation details; and*
- *The building has inadequate connections between primary structural members, such as poorly designed and/or constructed joints of pre-cast elements.*

2.5.3. Detailed Evaluation

2.5.3.1. General

The flowchart summarizing the different steps involved in the phase of detailed evaluation of a building is presented in figure 2.2 (prepared on the basis of code[28]). The building for which the preliminary evaluation, as covered under subhead 2.5.2.1, has been completed is now taken up for detailed evaluation since it has failed to meet the requirements of the acceptability criteria. A structural model for the lateral load-resisting system with the existing conditions *(as noted during preliminary evaluation)* is developed and then analyzed with the help of either the Equivalent Static Method or the Response Spectrum Method of linear dynamic analysis based on the code[25]. The objective of this analysis is to compare the probable strength of lateral load-resisting elements with those of the expected seismic demands. The probable strengths, as determined from the conventional methods, have to be modified by the use of the knowledge factor (described earlier). In addition, the lateral forces for analysis will be modified with the adoption of the modification factor as discussed under preliminary evaluation to ensure a higher level of risk of life loss for existing buildings.

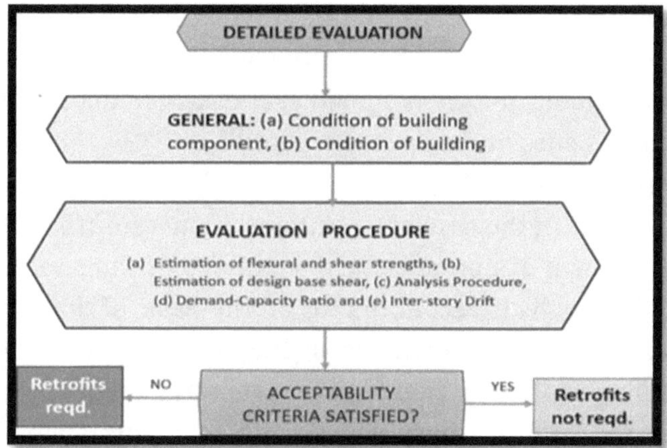

Figure 2.2: Flowchart Summarizing the Steps for Detailed Evaluation

2.5.3.2. Condition of the Building Components

The existing conditions of the building components are examined physically to identify the presence of any indicator of deficiency. At this stage, the structural engineer concerned should revisit the site of the building and recheck the data already collected with reference to the general conditions of different components of the building. It is, in fact, the stage at which the existing dry strengths of the materials of the building components have to be ascertained through appropriate field tests, including non-destructive tests *(as stated earlier under preliminary evaluation).* Extreme care has to be taken to collect the same with well-calibrated tools and equipment.

- *Deterioration of Concrete:* The concrete in all the vertical and lateral load-resisting elements of the building needs to be thoroughly checked to identify the portions showing any sign of deterioration, such as spalling, water penetration, cracks, etc. The portion of spalling (if any) leads to a reduction in the bond area between the rebar and its surrounding concrete. On the other hand, corrosion in rebars occurs due to moisture coming in contact with rebars through the cracks, leading to a reduction in the cross-sectional area of the rebar concerned.

- *Cracks in Boundary Columns:* Cracks and crushing in the concrete of outer columns indicate the locations of weak zones of the outer columns, which are subjected to reversal of bending stresses under lateral displacements accountable to lateral forces caused by earthquakes. As per the BIS code[28], there should not be diagonal cracks wider than 3 mm in the columns encasing the masonry infill.

- *Masonry Units:* There are a number of masonry units, especially in the case of a reinforced concrete-framed building in the form of non-structural elements. If the contribution of infilling walls is accounted for on the basis of the concept of a diagonal strut, as included in BIS code[25], then obviously the infilling wall, too, becomes a structural member. In all the masonry units, there should not be any visible sign of deterioration of masonry.

- *Masonry Joints:* Mortar joints in masonry units are commonly found to have shortcomings in the form of gaps, poor quality of mortar, the poor quality of workmanship, thereby adversely affecting its capacity to resist out-of-plane forces. The best way to perform an in-situ test is to see that no portion of the joints can be easily scraped away by hand with the help of a metal scraper.

- *Cracks/Crushing in Infilling Walls:* It has been an established fact[25] that the infilling walls in a framed building have a great contribution to the lateral stiffness of the building. Therefore, there should not be any sign either in the form of a diagonal crack or crushing of masonry at any of the corners (of the masonry infilling panel). The presence of either the diagonal crack or the crushing at conners will naturally weaken[45, 46] the concept of a diagonal strut on the basis of which the design criteria[25] is based.

2.5.3.3. Condition of the Building Materials

A clear knowledge of the present-day strength of materials is a basic necessity for the detailed evaluation of the building. Therefore, as stated earlier, the present-day strength of materials has to be evaluated *'using on-site non-destructive testing and laboratory analysis of samples'* (Clause 7.1.2 of code[28]). Some of the commonly performed non-destructive tests47 are given in Appendix IIA.

2.5.3.4. Evaluation Procedure

The evaluation procedure, as described in BIS code[28], consists of the steps briefly discussed below.

- *Estimation of Probable Flexural and Shear Strengths:* Based on the section properties and material properties *(as determined in the preceding steps)* of different elements of the lateral force-resisting system, the probable flexural and shear strengths of the critical sections and joints are estimated with the help of the conventional methods with due regards to the relevant codes of practice. The material strengths to be adopted in the estimation need to be modified with the appropriate knowledge factor, as discussed earlier.
- *Estimation of Design Base Shear:* Based on the BIS code[25], the base shear is evaluated. The lateral loads considered have to be modified by the LLMF *(as discussed earlier)* for the reduced useable life of the building. As given in code[25], the value of this factor is 0.67 against the minimum value[28] of 0.7.
- *Analysis Procedure:* The analysis procedure, discussed under the subhead 'General' above, is adopted for the analysis of the lateral load-resisting system with the modified base shear as calculated under the preceding subhead. The objective of this analysis is to evaluate the member actions for the critical components of the vertical load-resisting system. The component stiffness shall be computed on the basis of some rational procedure. Table 2 of code[28] gives some effective

stiffness values.

- *Demand–Capacity Ratio:* The analysis performed, as stated in the preceding para, gives the values of member actions required. Thereafter, the demand values obtained are compared with the corresponding capacities of the critical sections of the load-resisting system components to look at the acceptability criteria.

- *Inter-Story Drift:* The story drift is defined as the relative movement (in the lateral direction) of two adjacent stories, i.e. the lateral movement of one floor relative to the floor immediately below it. On the other hand, the Drift Ratio (DR) is the ratio of story drift to the height of the corresponding floor. The story drift limitations must satisfy the conditions of the BIS code[25]. The story drift and Drift Ratio (DR) are briefly described in Figure 2.3.

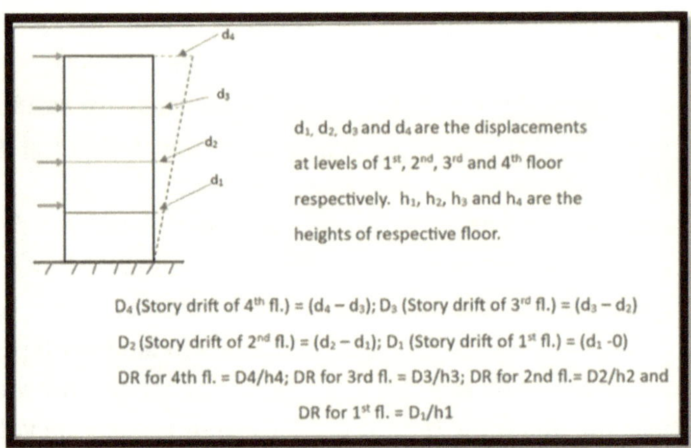

Figure 2.3: Story Drift and Drift Ratio

2.5.3.5. Acceptability Criteria

As given in the code[28], a building is considered to be acceptable (i.e. it does not require retrofitting) when either of the following two conditions are satisfied along with the *'Supplemental Criteria'* (discussed below) as applicable to the type of building under consideration:

Except for a few elements, all critical elements of the lateral force-

resisting elements have strengths greater than computed actions and drift checks are satisfied. The engineer has to ensure that the failure of these few elements will not lead to loss of stability or initiate progressive collapse. This needs to be verified by a non-linear analysis, such as pushover analysis, carried out up to the collapse load. The 'Supplemental Criteria' primarily relate to issues[44] of ductility and energy dissipation.

- *Ductility and Energy-Related Evaluation:* The issues of ductility and detailing relate to some special features affecting the capacity of the lateral load-resisting system. These features are specific to each building type. In this discussion, the features relating to the reinforced concrete framed building only are briefly stated. The different aspects of ductility and detailing are dealt with in Clause 7.4 of code[28] and also explained in greater detail in the IITK—GSDMA Guidelines[44]. These aspects broadly relate to the shear capacity of frame members, the connection between column and foundation, strong column/weak beam, beam reinforcements, column-bar splices, beam-bar splices, column-tie spacings, stirrups spacings, joint reinforcing, stirrup and tie hooks, etc.

The buildings failing to meet the acceptability criteria are obviously vulnerable to earthquake damages leading to partial or complete collapse *(in the event of an earthquake of moderate to strong magnitude)*. These are the buildings that need seismic strengthening, which is achieved through planning, design, and execution of retrofit measures. The planning and design of the appropriate retrofit measures will have to be obviously based on the type and degree of deficiencies as duly identified during the process of Detailed Evaluation.

2.5.4. Design of Retrofit Measures (Seismic Strengthening)

2.5.4.1. General

Around the world, there are a number of research papers, guidelines and standards dealing with the seismic strengthening of buildings vulnerable to earthquake damage. The salient ones for this purpose in

India have been the BIS code[28] and the NDMA Guidelines[40]. In addition, the IITK—GDMA Guidelines[44] and the publication by IIT, Roorkee[43] also deal with the different aspects of retrofit measures. The structural engineers in India have to follow the guidelines, as given in BIS code[28] and NDMA guidelines[40]. The appropriate retrofit measures may be planned, designed and executed only by those who fundamentally understand the basic structural actions caused by the lateral earthquake forces on the one hand and, on the other, the evaluation procedures (both preliminary and detailed), as discussed above. The basic objective of adopting the strengthening measures is to bring the vulnerable building to a level at which all the acceptability criteria (as discussed under detailed evaluation) are satisfied so that the collapse and overall instability of the structure are avoided. There are a number of options for retrofit measures. An attempt has to be made to plan and design the cost-effective retrofit measures only. The major areas requiring seismic strengthening in a reinforced concrete framed building are briefly discussed below.

2.5.4.2. Seismic Strengthening Options and Strategies

The different phases[28] involved in the whole process of strengthening a vulnerable building are summarised in figure 2.4. The choice of different options and strategies available is based on the extent of understanding of the deficiencies existing in the building under consideration with respect to lateral strength or stiffness and lateral displacement or ductility. As stated earlier, the two load paths, the vertical load transferring system (the moment resisting frame in this case) and the horizontal load transferring system (the diaphragm), must be free from any irregularity/discontinuity. Any irregularity or discontinuity, if found to exist, will have to be taken care of with the help of modification or the addition of retrofitting elements in the areas as necessary. In addition, all the elements of both the vertical load-resisting system and the horizontal load-resisting system must have adequate strength with ductility and proper connections to the respective load-resisting system.

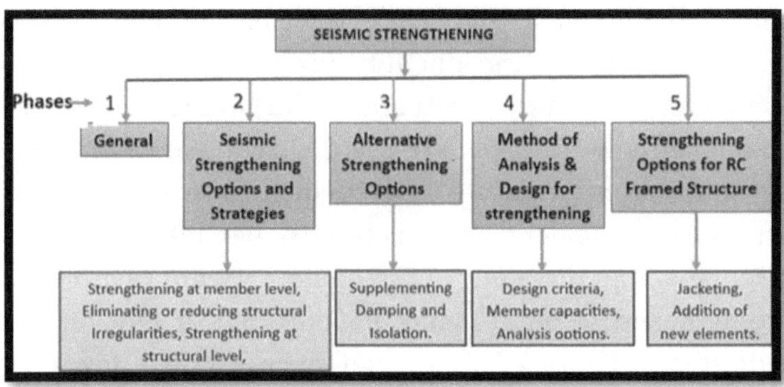

Figure 2.4: Chart Summarizing Phases Involved in Seismic Strengthening

The basic requirement for adopting the appropriate retrofitting measures is a conceptual understanding of the structural actions produced in the structural members of the load-resisting systems under both the vertical loads (mostly inertia loads) and the lateral loads (earthquake forces). In a framed structure, the critical zones in the vertical load-resisting system are schematically shown in figure 2.5.

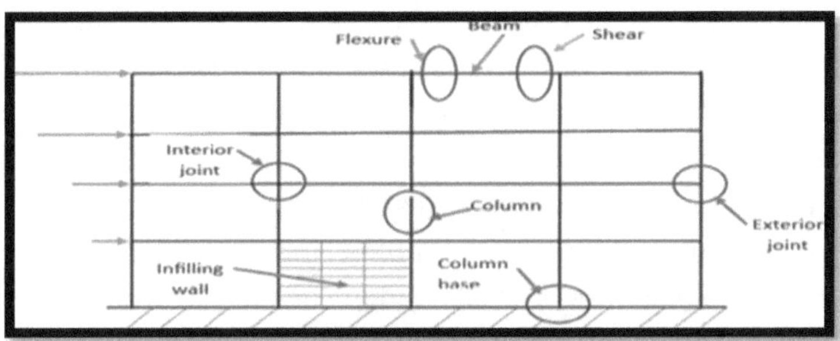

Figure 2.5: Critical Zones of a Moment Resisting Frame under Lateral Loads

As suggested in the code[28], there are three broad areas for incorporating retrofitting measures, namely: *'Strengthening at Member Level'* (i.e. at local level), *'Eliminating or Reducing Structural Irregularities'* and *'Strengthening at Structural Level'* (i.e. at global level). These three areas are briefly discussed below.

- *Strengthening at Member Level:* A building may have adequate strength and stiffness at the global level. However, there may be some components that have deficiencies with respect to strength, stiffness, and ductility (as identified during detailed evaluation). In such a situation, the strengthening of these components with respect to the deficient aspects will be done by adopting appropriate and adequate retrofitting measures. The salient elements and zones to be duly considered for strengthening the deficient members (with respect to both strength and ductility) may include only a few of the ones indicated in figure 2.5. They may include only a few *(since the strengthening at member level is taken up only for the system having no deficiency at the global level)* of beams, columns, beam-column joints (both exterior and interior), the connection of column to the foundation, infilling wall, short column, etc.

The beams under lateral loads have two critical zones for flexure and shear, as shown in the figure. The flexure zone is critical, as it is subjected to reversal of bending stresses and, therefore, needs special care to provide adequate strength in both the faces of the section *for the deficient beam only*. On the other hand, the shear zone in the right end of a beam (when lateral force acts from left to right, as shown in the figure) is likely to be critical (when combined with that of vertical loads) and may result in brittle shear failure[43] on account of heavy diagonal tension. Depending on the extent of deficiencies, retrofitting measures such as jacketing of the beam with adequate longitudinal reinforcement at both the faces and stirrups may be adopted.

The column presents a complex interaction mechanism of structural actions under lateral loads. The structural actions[43] are axial force, shear, flexure and bond. The failure mode led to under-lateral loads due to a deficiency with respect to any/or more of these actions, which has been broadly discussed in the Retrofitting Strategies[43]. Appropriate retrofitting measures to eliminate the respective deficiency/deficiencies are adopted on the basis of a clear understanding of the action (s) leading to the same (deficiencies). Even to eliminate deficiencies in a column, the obvious choice of retrofitting measures is jacketing, as in the case of a deficient beam. Another zone of possible deficiency consists of beam-column joints. The exterior beam-column joint (Figure 2.5) is more likely to become deficient in the case of inadequate lateral reinforcements. If the beam reinforcement is inadequate, there is a possibility of slip leading to a diagonal crack in the joint. Such a shear crack will naturally reduce the stiffness of the building under lateral force. Since there is no global deficiency in respect of strengthening a building at member level, it is unlikely that there will be beam-column joint deficiency. *(Even if there is one, obviously, the joint jacketing has to be taken as a recourse to enhance the joint capacity).*

- *Eliminating or Reducing Structural Irregularities:* The irregularities in buildings broadly come under two categories: vertical irregularities and plan irregularities. These irregularities have a tremendous impact on the seismic performance of a building structure. The existence of these irregularities substantially increases the seismic demands of other components. Therefore, the judicious removal of the existing irregularities is absolutely necessary before taking up strengthening measures for global deficiencies.

Vertical irregularities are primarily related to strength, stiffness, and mass and are mostly created by disruptions in load paths (both vertical and horizontal ones) and weak or soft storeys. For an appropriate corrective approach, measures such as the appropriate placing of shear walls/infilling walls/bracings are taken so far as vertical irregularities are concerned. At times, even the adjustment of dead load (particularly those of non-structural elements) may be necessary for achieving a reduction of seismic forces on the one hand and on the other, a reduction of the difference between the building's mass center and stiffness center (thereby reducing the extent of overturning moment).

The plan irregularities are corrected by providing seismic gaps between various parts to make independent parts of regular plan geometry, and care is being taken to provide adequate gaps to avoid the possibility of pounding.

- *Structural Level Strengthening (at Global Level):* It is taken up only for the building for which more than a few critical components have been found to be deficient with respect to strength and ductility. The purpose of strengthening at the global level is to reduce the overall displacement demand to the limit as required by the acceptability criteria with the adoption of available options (as discussed in a subsequent subhead). While doing so, some other elements may become deficient regarding strength. These elements will be strengthened further (obviously at member level).

2.5.4.3. Alternative Strengthening Options

Alternative strengthening measures have been developed in the recent past and are currently in use in India only in a few buildings, apparently one in Gujarat and one in Delhi. These options are based on the principles of *'Base Isolation'* and *'Supplemental Damping'* *(Energy Dissipation)*.

- *Base Isolation:* The principle of base isolation consists of separating the superstructure from its foundation. The earthquakes create ground motion that is responsible for creating high seismic demands (with respect to both strength and stiffness) on different elements of the lateral force-resisting systems. In the case of high seismic demands (to avoid partial or total collapse), the cost of retrofitting conventional types of measures (as discussed in the preceding phases) becomes very high. Under such a situation, particularly for buildings like hospitals, powerhouses, communication centres, etc., the base isolators are adopted to restrict the transfer of vibration (accountable to ground motion) to the structure, thereby reducing the seismic demands of the superstructure at both member level and global level. There are different types of base isolators, such as Elastomeric (rubber) bearings, lead rubber bearings, High-damping rubber bearings (HDRB), etc. The design and selection of an appropriate type have to be based on site-specific requirements.
- *Supplemental Damping:* The buildings with relatively high flexibility are liable to be subjected to high seismic demands under earthquake forces. The retrofitting of this type of building with conventional measures becomes very costly.

Under this situation, the adoption of the technique of supplemental energy dissipation in the superstructure of a building is being encouraged nowadays. Many control devices, such as viscous fluid dampers, viscoelastic dampers, friction dampers, and tuned mass dampers, are being adopted internationally to reduce the seismic demands in the superstructures of buildings. The cost incurred on this account is likely to be offset by the cost required to take care of the seismic demands of the undamped superstructure. However, for the cost-effective adoption of the devices for energy dissipation dampers, it has been stated in the paper48 by Y. T. Chen et al. – *'careful selection of dampers and their tactical placement for maximum efficiency becomes important, and these considerations have been an active area of research in recent years'.*

2.5.4.4. Methods of Analysis and Design for Strengthening

The three aspects of this phase (Phase 4 in Figure 2.4) are discussed below.

- *Design Criteria:* The design criteria for designing the retrofits in a vulnerable building are the same as those dealt with in the acceptability criteria adopted for the evaluation process (*discussed earlier (as given in Clause 5 of code[28]*).
- *Member Capacities:* The member capacities for all elements of the retrofitted load-resisting systems of the building should not be less than the seismic demands required during the process of detailed evaluation. (Clause 5 of the code[28]).
- *Analysis Options:* The options available to a structural engineer for the earthquake analysis of a building are: *Equivalent Static Analysis, Response Spectrum Analysis, Linear Dynamic Analysis, Non-linear Static Analysis* (also called *Push over Analysis)* and *Non-linear Dynamic Analysis.* The choice of the appropriate option has to be made by the engineer depending on the complexity of the structure including geometry. The non-linear static analysis, which is the push-over analysis (referred to in the preceding discussion of

detailed evaluation), is considered to be an improvement over linear static or dynamic analysis since this method allows for the inelastic behaviour of the structure. However, as suggested by code[28], the structural engineer concerned may choose the method adopted during detailed evaluation.

2.5.4.5. Strengthening Options for RC Framed Structures

The strengthening options for the frames of a framed building are broadly covered under two categories28: Jacketing and the Addition of new structural elements. A brief discussion of different options under each of these two categories is presented below.

- *Jacketing:* The most popular option is jacketing, a technique adopted for confining the reinforced concrete in beams, columns, joints and foundations. The different types of jacketing are reinforced concrete jacketing, steel profile jacketing and steel encasement or wrapping with FRPs (Fiber Reinforced Polymers). The members found to be deficient in detailed evaluation may be judiciously jacketed for enhancing strength, stiffness or ductility. The Code[28] and other publications[43, 44, 49] have dealt with different technical aspects of jacketing, including FRPs. The author (of this book) strengthened all the columns *(suffering deterioration such as spalling, cracks and crushing primarily on account of poor concrete and poor workmanship)* of the ground floor *of* a three-storey residential building with reinforced concrete jacketing successfully about 35 years back when there was a dearth of guidelines (as we have today). Interestingly, in that building, all the columns of the other two floors were perfectly intact, showing no sign of deterioration. Therefore, it is indeed an absolute necessity for engineering judgement to adopt the appropriate technique for strengthening a member in relation to the deficient aspects.

- *Addition of New Structural Elements:* There are a number of new elements that can be adopted judiciously to enhance the strength and stiffness of a framed building. The most commonly adopted one is the reinforced concrete shear walls.

The different aspects of providing the shear wall between columns are given in code[28]. Another type of new element recommended by code[28] is steel bracing, which can be added to existing concrete frames. The design criteria for steel bracings are dealt with in the code. In addition to these two main types of new elements, there are other types of new elements[43] such as infilling walls and wing/buttresses, the addition of which enhances the strength and stiffness of an existing reinforced concrete frame under lateral forces. For the adoption of these new elements in an existing structure, the technical aspects as covered in code[28] and other publications[43, 44] need to be followed.

2.5.5. Working out the Cost of Retrofits

The cost of the retrofits to be implemented in a vulnerable structure is the final product of the long exercise carried out, as discussed under the preceding subheads of this chapter. This is the cost on the basis of which the owner will decide whether to implement the retrofit measures or go for a new construction. Therefore, as stated earlier, the structural engineer concerned has to design the most cost-effective option of possible sets of options available for retrofitting on the one hand and, on the other, to work out the cost thereof in the most realistic manner for the location of the structure concerned. The realistic working out of cost needs a number of considerations, such as rates of items covered by the government Schedule of Rares as applicable to the location (for the scheduled items of works), appropriate rates for non-scheduled items of works (based on appropriate rate-analysis), due accounting of costs to be involved for cleaning, stress-relieving measures such as propping during all phases of execution, etc. The working out of the total cost of retrofit measures has to be based on the due inclusion of all expenses to be involved in the complete implementation of the retrofitting project.

2.5.6. Justification for Incurring the Cost of Retrofits

To justify the cost of retrofitting for a particular building is a complex issue, as the cost of retrofitting is dependent on the age of the building on the one hand and, on the other, on the extent of deficiencies existing today in light of the requirements of strength, stiffness and ductility, as demanded by the modern codes of practice governing design and construction of an earthquake-resistant structure. The complexity emerges basically from the fact that the cost-benefit analysis of a particular set of retrofitting measures cannot assign a monetary value to the lives to be saved in the event of an earthquake. Even today, the topic of cost-benefit analysis of retrofit measures is a hot area of research internationally. However, the broad guidelines given by NDMA[40] present a general basis for the owners to make a choice between the retrofits and the reconstruction of the vulnerable building. This basis (in terms of the cost of retrofitting as a percentage of the cost of reconstruction) is given in table 5 of the NDMA Guidelines[40].

Above all, the investment incurred in the implementation of judiciously designed retrofit measures in a vulnerable building has to be looked upon as the one for proactive measure absolutely necessary for the safety of the property in addition to ensuring a safe roof to live or work under even in the event of an earthquake.

2.5.7. Execution of Retrofit Measures

Once the project of retrofitting a vulnerable building has been finalized, the stage of implementation comes in. The execution of different items of work has to be carried out under the supervision of an engineer who understands the retrofitting scheme in detail from the perspective of impacts likely to be created on the building during the stage of execution. For example, the case of strengthening a beam element by jacketing may be taken. Before the start of the work, all measures, such as proper propping of the structural elements transferring load to it (the element under strengthening) to release stress on it (the beam under strengthening), need to be taken. The adoption of the propping system, in this case, becomes absolutely important for avoiding damage to other elements of the load-resisting system. Therefore, the engineer supervising the retrofitting project must have adequate knowledge of both quality control and safety aspects. On the other hand, the contractor selected for the purpose is expected to have experience in executing similar works. Since there is a dearth of contractors appropriately experienced in work retrofitting, even a contractor having no similar experiences may also execute the work under the constant and strict guidance of the site engineer, who has to take the responsibility of execution under the constant and clear guidance of the designer of the retrofitting scheme. In the case of the adoption of modern options such as base isolation or dampers, the parties specialized in these areas should be directly involved in their installations.

2.6. Concluding Remarks

The efforts and time required to identify structures vulnerable to earthquake damages to be followed by design and implementation of appropriate retrofits to make them earthquake-resistant are immense, as it has been evident from the different phases of work involved in the whole process discussed in this chapter. In fact, building a new earthquake-resistant building apparently requires a lesser extent of effort and time than that required for retrofitting a vulnerable one. However, a huge volume of vulnerable buildings exists in India today. As observed by NDMA[40]: *Over 95% of fatalities in past earthquakes in India occurred in non-engineered houses and structures.* Even in cases of engineered buildings as well, there does exist a number of vulnerable buildings basically on account of two basic reasons, the first one being the fact that many of the engineered buildings were designed and constructed before the upgradation of the latest codes governing earthquake-resistant design and construction. The second reason is the erroneous design and construction. Therefore, adopting retrofitting measures in vulnerable buildings as priority-proactive measures for mitigating earthquake damages needs no overemphasis.

A deficiency with respect to lateral stiffness commonly exists in the soft storey (mostly used as parking space) of many of the buildings in urban and semi-urban areas of India. These buildings are obviously vulnerable to earthquake damage, even under moderate to strong earthquakes. Immediately after the Assam Earthquake of April

2021 (moment magnitude of 6.00), the author had to visit a building that suffered damages only in the soft storey. It was found that all the exterior columns developed crushing/cracks of concrete at both the top and bottom ends in the soft storey. Interestingly, there was no sign of even minor damages anywhere in the upper storeys. This was a clear demonstration of deficiency with respect to necessary lateral stiffness in the soft storey. Immediate strengthening measures, either with shear walls or bracing, were advised. This type of measure in the weak storey needs to be taken as soon as possible since it does not involve a long process of vulnerability assessment and has a substantial cost. This type of immediate proactive measure will go a long way in reducing the possibility of total collapse of a building having a weak storey.

The proactive measures for mitigating earthquake damages to vulnerable structures include several actions, as summarized in figure 2.6.

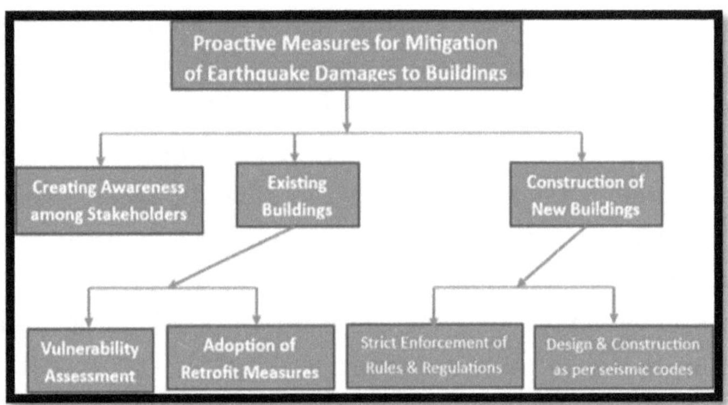

Figure 2.6: Summarized Proactive Measures for Mitigation of Earthquake Damages to Buildings

The retrofitting is a proactive measure for existing buildings only. Therefore, it is absolutely necessary to adopt proactive measures, even for new ones, so that the stock of vulnerable buildings in the country does not increase. The first action towards this end consists of strict enforcement of rules and regulations, laws and codified seismic knowledge for earthquake-resistant design and construction.

Chapter 3: Urbanization in India and Its Challenges with Specific Reference to North East Region

3.1. Introduction

The urban population in the world has been increasing at a rate, as reflected by the growth chart appearing in figure 3.1. It was only 34% of the total population in 1960. It has been increasing on a regular basis, and eventually, the balanced condition of the rural and urban population of the world (i.e. an equal share of the population between the urban and rural world) was reached in 2007 (as shown in the figure). Thereafter, the urban population started exceeding the rural population of the world, reaching the percentage of 57% of the total world population in 2023. If this average trend of growth of urban population continues for the next 50 years, the world will get urbanized by around 2075 to the extent of around 73% of the total population, thereby pushing the world into a pool of a series of serious issues.

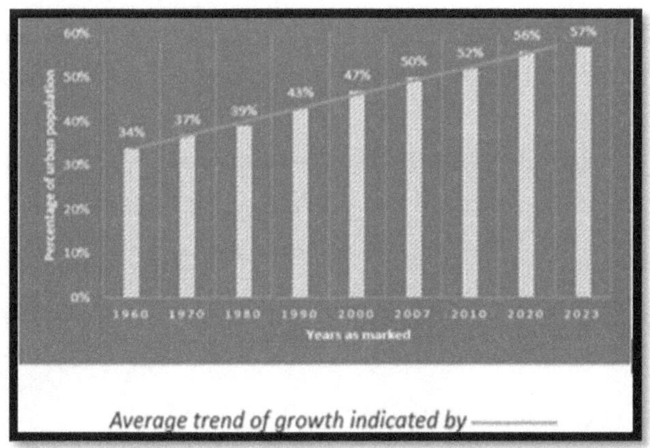

Figure 3.1: Growth of Urban Population in the World from 1960 to 2023 (Prepared by Author on the Basis of Data Given by World Bank[73])

The trends, promises and challenges of urbanization are being widely discussed all over the world by different institutions, including the UN. In fact, the intensities of these parameters vary country-wise. Basically, urbanization is the result of the migration of the rural population to urban areas. There are a number of factors responsible for this migration. These factors are defined by many in the world as *Push Factors (factors forcing people to leave rural areas)* and *Pull Factors (factors attracting rural people to urban areas)*. The push factors[74] commonly include the challenges in rural areas, such as:

- Limited employment opportunities accountable to farming mechanization and environmental factors,
- Lack of adequate income and appropriate living conditions,
- Inadequate access to basic resources such as water, healthcare, education, etc.

Similarly, the pull factors include employment opportunities, better living standards, better education facilities, better healthcare services, etc.

The speed and scale of urbanization, as reflected in figure 3.1, have contributed immensely to the growth of GDP of different countries. As per WB[75], the urbanization has contributed more than 80% of the global GDP. However, urbanization, to this extent, has created a series of challenges today. These challenges[75] are: *"Meeting accelerated demand for affordable housing, viable infrastructure including transport systems, basic services, and jobs, particularly for the nearly 1 billion urban poor who live in informal settlements to be near opportunities."*

The situation of urbanization in India with specific reference to the states of NER has been dealt with in this chapter under a number of subheads.

3.2. Growth of Urban Population in India

3.2.1. Growth of Urban Population

The present scenario of haphazard growth of urban areas in India in general and in the North-East Region, in particular, has given rise to major issues with respect to sustainable development. For a better appreciation of the different challenges faced by the process of urbanization in our country today, it is necessary to have a clear picture of the nature of the growth of our population—both rural and urban. The DESA[50] of the United Nations has given a clear picture of the population growth of the world. Table 3.1 gives the historical growth of the population (Rural and urban) of India from 1970 to 2024, along with its Global Ranks (in total population) held in the respective years. An analysis of this table leads to the following observations:

Year (Col.1)	Total Population* (Col.2)	Share of world Pop (%)(Col.3)	Urban Population (Col,4)	% of Urban Pop** (Col.5)	Global*** Rank(Col.6)
2024	1,441,719,852 (0.92%)	17,.76	53,03,87,142	36.8	1
2023	1,428,627,663 (0.81%)	17.76	51,82,39,122	36.3	1
2022	1,417,173,173 (0.68%)	17.77	50,63,04,869	35.7	2
2020	1,396,387,127 (0.96%)	17.81	48,30,98,640	34.6	2
2015	1,322,866,505 (1.29%)	17.81	42,90,69,459	32.4	2
2010	1,240,613,620 (1.45%)	17.76	38,07,44,554	30.7	2
2005	1,154,638,713 (1.73%)	17.61	33,44,79,406	29	2
2000	1,059,633,675 (1.90%)	17.23	29,13,50,282	27.5	2
1995	964,279,129 (2.07%)	16.79	25,55,58,824	26.5	2
1990	870,452,165 (2.21%)	16.37	22,22,96,728	25.5	2
1985	780,242,084 (2.29%)	16.05	19,03,21,782	24.4	2
1980	696,828,385 (2.25%)	15.68	16,09,41,941	23.1	2
1975	623,524,219 (2.26%)	15.32	13,25,33,810	21.3	2
1970	557,501,301 (2.20%)	15.09	10,93,88,950	19.6	2

*The figures within bracket indicate the percentage of yearly change in the total population inclusive of both the rural and urban, **Percentage of urban population in respect of total population, ***Global rank in the world population in the respective year.

Table 3.1: Historical Growth of Population of India
Prepared by the author on the basis of data given by United Nations[50]

- **Observation 1:** India became the country with the highest population in the world in 2023, with a total population of 1,428,627,663. Till 2022, it was in the second position, next to China. Our country today shares 17.76 Percent of the world population (Column 3 of the table). The population as of July 2024 has been 1,441,719 852, the yearly increase being 0.92% over 2023 (Column 2 of the table).

- **Observation 2:** The urban population in India has been rising from 10,93,88,950 (19.6 Percent of the total population) in 1970 to 53,03,87,142 (36.8 Percent of the total population as shown in Column 5) in 2024. The increase in urban population (in terms of percentage of total population as shown in Column 5) from 19.6% in 1970 to 36.8% in 2024 (July) clearly shows the decrease in rural population from 80.4% in 1970 to 63.2% in 2024, indicating thereby the regular migration of rural population to urban areas.

Observation 1 and observation 2 reflect the present position of both the urban and rural population of our country (as of 2024). However, for an effective discussion of urbanization issues, a clear idea of the projected population for the future becomes necessary. An analysis of the data of DESA, UN50 leads to the following additional observations:

Year (Col.1)	Total Population* (Col.2)	Share of world Pop (%)(Col.3)	Urban Population (Col.4)	% of Urban Pop** (Col.5)
2025	1,454,606,724 (0.82%)	17.76	54,27,42,539	37.3
2030	1,514,994,080 (0.82%)	17.73	60,73,41,981	40.1
2035	1,567,802,259 (0.69%)	17.66	67,54,56,367	43.1
2040	1,611,676,333 (0.55%)	17.54	74,43,80,367	46.2
2045	1,645,863,187 (0.42%)	17.38	81,17,49,463	49.3
2050	1,670,490,596 (0.30%)	17.2	87,66,13,025	52.5

*The figures within bracket indicate the percentage of yearly change in the total population.

**Percentage of urban population in respect of the total population of the corresponding year.

Table 3.2: *Projected Growth of Population of India Up to 2050 (Prepared by the Author on the Basis of data of United Nations[50])*

- **Observation 3:** The projections for population have been given for the years 2025, 2030, 2035, 2040, 2045 and 2050, as shown in table 3.2. As projected, the population of India will go on increasing from 1,454,606,724 in 2025 to 1,670,490,596 in 2050. The urban population will also go on increasing from 37.3% in 2025 to 52.5% in 2050 (Column 5 of the table), indicating thereby that the rural population will go on decreasing from 62.7% in 2025 to 47.5% in 2050.

- **Observation 4**: The country's share of the projected world population has shown a downward trend from 17.76% in 2025 (same as in 2024) to 17.20% in 2050. However, India will continue to be the country with the world's highest population till 2050.

- **Observation 5**: As reflected clearly by Observation 3, more than half of India's total population will be living in urban areas by 2050.

The changing structure of the human population, as reflected well by the above-noted observations, suggests many challenges confronting the country today in the process of urbanization. The basic approach to be followed towards meeting the challenges is briefly covered in the words of Dr. Kumar[51]: *'We must rethink, reimagine and re-establish the very purpose and approach towards planning cities and towns in India.'*

The major challenge is the increasing rate of migration of rural populations into urban areas. The primary reasons for this migration are obviously better scopes of business, employment and education in cities and towns. To counteract the ill effects of the increase of urban population to such an extent, as stated in Observation 2 and Observation 3 (as given above), the basic approach consists of the adoption of ways and means based on modern tools, techniques and technology (3Ts), globally available today for the development of both the rural and urban areas, keeping in view the present and the projected population- structure of our country, as well reflected by the five observations mentioned above. It is in this context that there is a need for the synergy of rural and urban development (an aspect to be taken care of by the Town and Country Planning Departments). However, the discussion herein will be confined to issues concerning urbanization alone.

3.2.2. Challenges Facing Urbanization

As per Census 2011[51], the urban system of India is classified as shown in figure 3.1. The definitions are given in Appendix – IIIA.

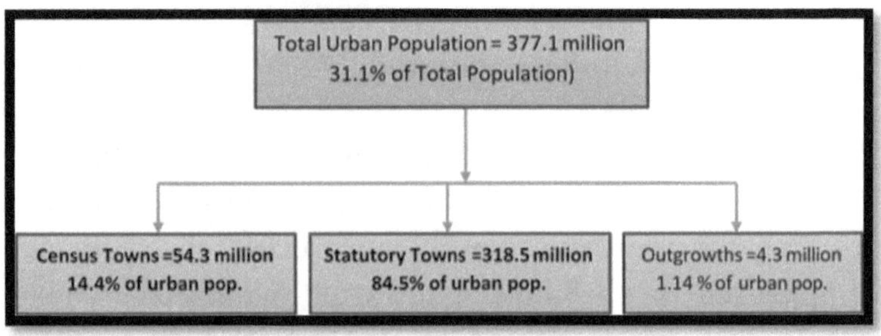

Figure 3.1: Classification of Urban System of India as Per Census, 2011

There is, in addition, a size-class distribution[51] of towns as Class I (with a population of one lakh and above), Class II (with a population of 50,000 to 99,999), Class III (with a population of 20,000 to 49,999), Class IV (with a population of 10,000 to 19,999), Class V (with a population of 5,000 to 9,999) and Class VI (with a population less than 5000). In view of the increase of urban population to today's level (as indicated in Observation 2), the revision of this size-class distribution appears to be necessary.

The Annual Report[52] of MoHUA, Govt. of India, has noted: "*Urban Development is a State subject, and the Seventy-fourth Constitutional Amendment Act, 1992 has delegated many functions to urban local bodies. The government of India, however, plays a coordinating and monitoring role and also supports various housing programs, urban livelihood missions and overall urban development through Central and Centrally Sponsored Schemes.*" Therefore, the Urban Local Bodies (ULBs) are primarily responsible for urbanization.

The ULBs are elected by the citizens of a statutory town or a city. Therefore, indirectly, the citizens are responsible for different activities of the ULBs. The basic questions are: *Do we (the citizens) elect competent and dedicated members of ULBs? Are the ULBs aware of the issues confronting their respective cities or towns? Are they aware of the issues that will develop gradually with the increase in urban population, as projected above? Do they (ULBs) have an idea about the rate of migration of the population from rural areas to their respective cities or towns? Do they follow the broad guidelines set by MoHUA? Do they take advice and assistance from the National Institute of Urban Affairs (NIUA) as and when required? Do they have adequate and competent technical manpower? Do they have a master plan?* For appropriate answers to questions of this type, the discussion between the citizens and ULBs from time to time is an absolute necessity. It is strongly noted by NITI Aayog[51]: *"The platforms for citizen participation, and their awareness about the process of urban planning and development are limited. There is a perceptible communication gap between planning agencies and the people, who are the ultimate beneficiaries."* Urban citizens, being socially conscious, will be legally and morally right to ask for the platforms for their participation.

Our cities and towns, on account of lack of due attention, have developed a lot of stress and strains over the years. It is stated by NITI Aayog[51]: *"Issues like lack of availability of serviced land, traffic congestion, pressure on basic infrastructure, extreme air pollution, urban flooding, water scarcity and droughts are not merely a reflection of infrastructural shortcomings in the cities. These issues indicate a deep and substantial lack of adequate urban planning and governance frameworks."* Therefore, the major challenges emerge primarily from (a) a lack of adequate planning and (b) a lack of appropriate governance frameworks. Both of these aspects are distinctly dealt with by NITI Aayog [51].

With respect to a lack of adequate planning, the following two observations of the Advisory Committee of NITI Aayog[51] are indicative of the haphazard development of many of the towns of our country:

- About half of the statutory towns are expanding without any master plan to guide their growth and infrastructural investment.
- About two-thirds of census towns do not have master plans to guide their spatial growth.

Therefore, the most important step in the process of modern urbanization consists in the development of the master plan. The citizens of these towns have a role to play in this respect. The measures for the creation of development policy awareness among the citizens need to be taken up by different institutional bodies. On the development of this awareness among the citizens, the ULBs (in case of statutory towns) and others responsible for management (in case of census towns) will come under pressure to go for master plans and to adopt development activities in a planned manner. A detailed discussion on many other technical aspects and problems relating to appropriate governance frameworks has been covered in the Final Report of NITI Aayog[51].

The level of urbanization is not uniform over different states of India, as given in a table in the Handbook of Urban Statistics[53]. This table was prepared on the basis of the 2011 Census when the Indian urban population was 31.14%. However, this percentage has gone up to 36.8% (Table 3.1— Column 5). However, the table in the handbook[53] clearly indicates the variation in the level of urbanization among the different States/UTs of India, the lowest and the highest being 0.03% (in Himachal Pradesh) and 97.25% (in Chandigarh), respectively, against India's average of 31.14% in 2011. The levels of urbanization in the states of NER and the Annual Exponential Growth Rate (AEGR), as prepared from the data given in the handbook[53] are given in table 3.3.

States	Percentage of urban population			AEGR	
	1991	2001	2011	1991—2001	2001—2011
Arunachal Prad.	12.80	20.75	22.94	7.49	3.31
Assam	11.08	12.90	14.10	3.29	2.46
Manipur	27.52	26.58	29.21	1.31	3.70
Meghalaya	18.60	19.58	20.07	3.24	2.71
Mizoram	46.10	49.63	52.11	3.33	2.60
Nagaland	17.21	17.23	28.86	5.11	5.10
Sikkim	09.10	11.07	25.15	4.93	9.42
Tripura	15.30	17.06	26.17	2.61	5.66
India	25.73	27.82	31.14	2.73	2.7

Table 3.3:   Level of Urbanization and Annual Exponential Growth Rate for the States of NER (Prepared by the author on the basis of data of the handbook[53])

An analysis of table 3.3 reveals a few important facts at the level of urban population of NER in 2011. Firstly, the level of urbanization is the highest in Mizoram (52.11%, Column 4) among the states of NER; it is appreciably higher than India's average level of 31.14%. Secondly, the level of urbanization in the remaining states is lower than India's average (Column 4), with Assam being the state with the lowest level of urbanization at 14.10%. This table deals with the level of urbanization only on the basis of population based on the 2011 Census. It may be noted with great concern that a correct assessment of the level of urbanization on the basis of the present population in the absence of the new Census (which has yet to come after 2011) cannot be made. In no way does this level reflect the quality or standard of urbanization. Even in the case of sustainable development goals, dealt with in Chapter IV, no composite indices relating to urbanization state-wise except for the 56 cities of the country have been available. However, a publication[54] (by O. P. Malhotra et al.) has dealt with the Urbanization Index computed on the basis of 25 indicators for all the States/UTs of India *(as given in Table 37—page 95 of the publication[54]).* Figure 3.2 gives the index scores along with the ranks for the states of NER. The index scores of figure 3.2 indicate the standard (quality) of urbanization. The lowest and the second lowest ranks have been held by Manipur and Assam, respectively. The highest rank among the states of NER has been held by Mizoram, with an urbanization index score of 62.2 (Figure 3.2). The standard of urbanization in the states of NER may be gauged by a comparison of the indices of the states of NER with those of the high-ranking states of India. These high-ranking states are (with index scores being shown within brackets) Goa (66.5), Kerala (66.0), Haryana (56.6), Maharashtra (53.9) and Karnataka (51.4).

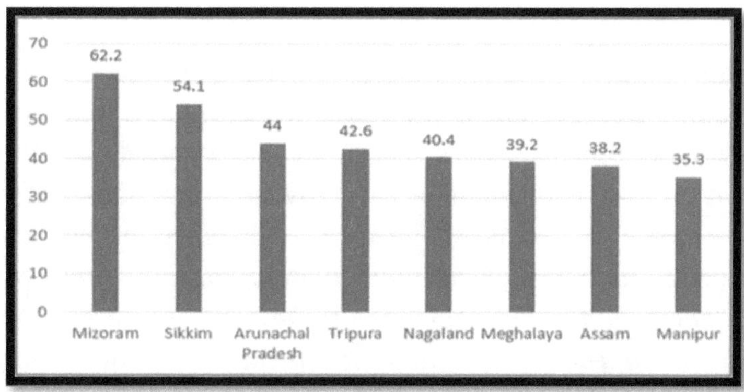

Figure 3.2: Urban Index for the States of NER in Order of Ranks (1 to 8) Among the Eight States (Prepared on the Basis of Data from the Publication[54])

The economic growth of our country is primarily dependent on the extent of qualitative development of urban areas. It is observed by MoHUA[52]: *"Today, urban India contributes 65% to India's GDP, which is estimated to rise to 70% by 2030'.* Against this positive aspect of urbanization, let us have a look at the issues created by the high rise in urban population (as discussed above). It is indicated by the Urbanization Indices[54] and also by the Annual Report[52] of MoHUA that the basic urban services like water supply, sewerage and drainage network, solid/liquid waste management facilities, citywide roads, public transport, and public safety systems like street lighting and pedestrian pathways have not been adequately developed or increased to match the increase in urban population. In addition, the supply of land and housing has also been a major problem. Many of the Sustainable Development Goals of the United Nations have been set for addressing many of these urban issues. If the issues, as stated, are not addressed appropriately at this stage, our country will not be in a position to derive the positive contribution of urbanization, particularly in view of the projected growth of the urban population by 2050 (as reflected by Observation 5 noted above). The Ministry of Housing and Urban Affairs, Government of India has been taking a series of schemes[52, 53] for addressing the issues of urbanization. Some of these schemes are discussed below.

3.3. The Flagship Missions of Government of India

3.3.1. General

The issues of urbanization in India are manifold. Some of these issues were briefly discussed under the preceding subheads. In appropriate recognition of these issues, NITI Aayog created a Managing Urbanization (MU) Division[55]. This Division *'provides data-based policy inputs for making India's urbanization manageable, economically productive, environmentally appropriate, and equitable. It offers advice and policy guidance to key stakeholders involved in urban planning, development, and management'.* The question arises as to whether the state governments, local bodies, and other stakeholders, including the citizens of urban areas, consult the MU

Division in a timely and adequate manner in terms of planning, formulation, and implementation of various urban projects.

Many experts working in the field of urbanization have put their knowledge together under the banners of NITI Aayog and the Ministry of Housing and Urban Affairs, Government of India[51, 52, 53, 55]. Based on their data and advice, the Government of India has been taking up a series of flagship schemes[53] to address the challenges confronting urbanization. These schemes have been formulated basically with the objective of improving primarily *(a) the indicators on access to basic amenities* and *(b) the socio-economic indicators* in urban areas. The discussion herein is limited to basic amenities in urban India. The indicators considered by MoHUA[53] as determinants of quality of urban life (in respect of basic amenities only) have been: (i) households with safe drinking water, (ii) households with electricity, (iii) households with latrine and (iv) households with septic tank/flush. There are socio-economic indicators as well. However, these economic indicators are outside the scope of this analysis. The flagship schemes of the Government of India relating to 'basic amenities' in urban India include: Smart Cities Mission, Swachh Bharat Mission, Atal Mission for Rejuvenation and Urban Transformation (AMRUT, AMRUT 2.0), Pradhan Mantri Awas Yojana (urban), Deendayal Antyodaya Yojana, National Livelihoods Mission (DAY-NULM), National Heritage City Development and Augmentation Yojana (HRIDAY), NERUDP Schemes and Real Estate (Regulation and Development) Act, 2016. A brief discussion on some of these schemes with specific reference to the states of NER has been attempted herein.

3.3.2. Smart Cities Mission (SCM)

The core elements of a smart city, as given by MoHUA[56] are adequate water supply, assured electricity supply, sanitation including solid waste management, efficient urban mobility and public transport, affordable housing, especially for the poor, robust IT connectivity and digitalization, good governance, especially e-governance and citizen participation, sustainable environment, safety and security of citizens, particularly women, children and the elderly and health and education.

The allocation of 100 smart cities was made to States/UTs on a basic principle[57]. The share of smart cities among the states of NER has been two (Pasighat and Itanagar) for Arunachal Pradesh, one (Guwahati) for Assam, one (Imphal) for Manipur, one (Shillong) for Meghalaya, one (Aizawl) for Mizoram, one (Kohima) for Nagaland, two (Namchi and Gangtok) for Sikkim and one (Agartala) for Tripura. Different projects for each smart city that were selected have been formulated. The lists of projects for each smart city are available in Smart Cities Mission of MoHUA[58]. For example, the list of projects finalized for Guwahati is given in Appendix IIIB. The progress details as of 20.03.2023 for the smart cities of NER (prepared on the basis of data given by the Standing Committee[59]) are given in table 3.4. The SCP costs appearing in the 2nd column of this table relate to the costs of the projects planned for the respective cities of NER. The total SCP cost (2nd column) for the whole of the NER cities works out to *Rs. 16,554.18 cr.*, which is 8.154% of the total costs *(Rs. 203021.37 cr.)* of all the projects planned for 100 smart cities in India.

Cities*	SCP Cost(Cr)	Financial Progress(Cr)		No. of Projects	No. of Projects
		GoI FR**	State MSR***	Planned	completed****
Itanagar(AR)	1343.00	243.00	61.61	80	7(8.75%)
Pasighat(AR)	1535.00	245.00	51.77	64	12(18.75%)
Guwahati(AS)	2256.00	294.00	244.80	185	9(4.86%)
Imphal(MN)	1523.00	245.00	20.00	50	9(18.00%)
Shillong(ML)	1039.00	294.00	55.00	96	1((1.04%)
Aizawl(MZ)	2053.01	196.00	106.88	105	7(6.67%)
Kohima(NL)	1661.25	318.50	30.00	101	27(26.73%)
Namchi(SK)	921.56	318.50	25.00	24	12(50.00%)
Gangtok(SK)	2234.00	292.00	29.94	224	6(2.68%)
Agartala(TR)	1988.36	453.25	78.31	26	62(238.46%)
TOTAL(INDIA)	203021.37	36561.16	32149.34	7821	5343(68.32%)

*Figures within bracket indicate states in short forms----AR for Arunachal, AS for Assam, MN for Manipur, ML for Meghalaya, MZ for Mizoram, NL for Nagaland, SK for Sikkim and TR for Tripura
**FR--Fund Released, ***MSR--Matching Share Released, ****Figures within bracket indicate Completion Rate (Projects completed/Projects planned) in %.

Table 3.4: Progress-Details of Projects for Smart Cities of NER as on 20.03.2023 (Prepared By the Author Based on Data of the Standing Committee[59])

This table clearly reflects the level of up-to-date progress of works *(as of March, 2023)* of smart cities of NER, as shown by the Completion Rate (CR) in the percentage of 'completed projects

(Column 6) to projects planned (Column 5)'. The best progress of works has been achieved by Agartala with a CR of 238.46% among the smart cities of NER, indicating thereby the fact that the number of completed projects (62) has been appreciably more than the projects planned (26). However, the State MSR for Tripura has been appreciably less *(only 78.31 cr. against GoI FR of 453.25 cr., as shown in the table).* The up-to-date progress for all the remaining cities of NER has been poor, with the respective CR (Column 6) being less than the average India CR of 68.32%. The achievements of progress for Itanagar (8.75%), Guwahati (4.86%), Shillong (1.04%), Aizawl (6.67%) and Gangtok (2.68%) have been alarmingly poor. This situation absolutely needs a critical analysis by the concerned Project Management Consultants (PMCs) for the greater interest of the state in general and the citizens of the smart cities in particular.

Top five smart cities		Bottom five smart cities	
Cities*	CR(%)	Cities*	CR(%)
Kakinada (Andhra Pradesh)	720.00	Amaravati (Andhra Pradesh)	0.00
Devanagere (Karnataka	433.30	Shillong, Meghalaya	1.00
Belagavi (Karnataka)	414.90	Gangtok (Sikkim)	2.70
New Town--Kolkata West Bengal)	410.00	Guwahati, Assam	4.90
Lucknow (Uttar Pradesh)	366.70	Karimnagar (Telengana)	6.50

Respective states are mentioned within brackets.

Table 3.5: The Top 5 and Bottom 5 Performing Smart Cities of India (Prepared by the author on the basis of data of Indiaspend[60])

The names of the top 5 and bottom 5 smart cities among the 100 smart cities of the country are given in table 3.5. A comparison of the performance of the states of NER (as reflected in table 3.4) with that of the top five states of the country (as reflected in table 3.5) indicates the extremely poor performance of the former (NER states). The performance of Agartala, being the best in NER, has also been far below that of the top 5 smart cities (table 3.5). On the other hand, three of the smart cities of NER, namely Shillong (4th lowest), Gangtok (3rd lowest) and Guwahati (2nd lowest), have come in the bottom five performers of the country, as shown by table 3.5. It is of interest to look into the performance of the smart city of Guwahati, particularly in view of the facts that: (i) It is the largest city of NER with a strategic location in the region and (ii) It has the SCP cost of Rs. 2256.00 cr., which is, in fact, the highest one among the states of NER *(Column 2 of table 3.4).* The projects planned for Guwahati (Smart City), appearing in Appendix—IIIB, include some important ones such as the Borosola Beel Project, Mora Bharalu River Project, Area Based Development Project, Bharalu River Project, Brahmaputra River Front Project, Deepar Beel Project, Pan City, ICT Project on Public Transport System, Bus-stop wholly developed on BOT Model and Improvement of Road/Foot Path/Traffic Junction on PPP Mode. The progress achieved as of March 2023 has been extremely poor, with a Completion Rate (CR) of only 4.90%, as indicated in tables 3.4 and 3.5. Obviously, a question arises as to what reasons have been responsible for such a deplorable state of activities relating to the smart city of Guwahati. Basically, the PMC concerned has to critically analyze the situation and find remedial measures at the earliest, since the extended time[61] for completion of all works for smart cities has been March, 2025.

Therefore, it is in this context that there must now be an open discussion between PMCs and citizens with the objective of resolving issues (such as land, labour, etc.) that are causing so much delay in completing the projects planned. The citizens, including the engineers, have a great role to play since the benefits to accrue on completion are meant for them. The citizen forums, Engineers' Forums, etc., may organize discussions with respective PMCs since less than a year is left now before the expiry of the extended time for completion. All concerned (particularly the citizens) need to extend constructive support and pressure for timely completion. The failure to complete in time will give rise to a number of issues, such as a crisis of funds, cost escalation, and uncertainty about the implementation of the remaining planned projects (like the ones shown in Appendix – IIIB only for Guwahati). All the PMCs of NER smart cities have to take up necessary measures for completing the planned projects.

3.3.3. Atal Mission for Rejuvenation and Urban Transformation (AMRUT, AMRUT 2.0)

AMRUT has been a very important Mission in the process of urbanization in India. It was launched by the Government of India in June 2015 in 500 cities across the country. All the ULBs with population of one lakh or more (as per Census 2011), all other capital cities of States/UTs, all the HRIDAY cities, identified cities to hill states, islands and tourist destinations and on the stem of main rivers[53] have been covered under this scheme (500 cities). The total outlay provided for this mission is Rs. 1,00,000 crore, including the central assistance of Rs. 50,000 crore, spread over a period of five years from FY 2015-16 to 2019-20. The most important aspect of this scheme is the flexibility provided to the concerned States/UTs to appraise, improve and implement. The responsibility of the central government consists of approving the State Annual Action Plans (SAAPs) and then releasing the central assistance. The proportion of central assistance is - (a) one-third of the project cost for cities with a population of more than 10 lakh and (b) 50% of the project cost for cities with a population of one lakh or more. This mission, if implemented with full dedication by the ULBs, will improve urban living immensely, as clearly demonstrated by the excerpt[53], which goes as: *"Besides creating basic infrastructure, the Mission also has a reform agenda spread over a set of 11 reforms comprising 54 milestones to be achieved by the States/UTs over a period of four years. These reforms broadly cover e-governance, a single window for all approvals, establishing a municipal cadre, achieving at least 90% billing and collection of taxes/user charges, developing at least one park for children every year, establishing a maintenance system for parks and playgrounds, credit rating of ULBs, implementing model building bye-laws and audit of energy and water, etc. The States/UTs are incentivized for reforms implemented in the first four years of the Mission."*

There are 12 cities[62] spreading over the states of NER as: Arunachal Pradesh (Itanagar), Assam (Dibrugarh, Guwahati, Nagaon and Silchar), Manipur (Imphal), Meghalaya (Shillong), Mizoram

(Aizawl), Nagaland (Dimapur and Kohima), Sikkim (Gangtok) and Tripura (Agartala). As stated in the 18th report of Standing Committee[59], this Mission was extended till March 2023, including the addition of a new scheme named AMRUT 2.0. The city-wise performance, as of the termination date of March 2023, could not be located. However, the progress made by these cities of NER, as available in the handbook[53] of MoHUA, is shown in table 3.6, which demonstrates the extremely slow progress made by the cities of NER in the implementation of projects of this Mission.

States	No. of Cities	SAAP Size* appd.	CA* committed	CA* Released	Total Ucs received*	DPRs to be approved*
Col. 1	Col. 2	Col. 3	Col. 4	Col. 5	Col. 6	Col. 7
Arunachal Pradesh	1	140.25	126.22	92.57	66.14	25
Assam	4	657.14	591.42	139.29	47.32	316
Manipur	1	180.31	162.28	99.84	93.27	0
Meghalaya	1	80.14	72.12	74.04	0.89	75
Mizoam	1	140.14	126.22	80.86	76.48	1
Nagaland	2	120.22	108.19	33.17	14.34	49
Sikkim	1	40.06	36.06	11.21	10.65	11
Tripura	1	148.25	133.48	40.16	14.95	12
India	**	77,640.02	35,989.70	17,167	10,166.50	2,794.00

*Values are in Rupees Crore, **For all the 500 cities, CA stands for Central Assistance

Table 3.6: Progress of Project Implementation for the Amrut Cities of NER, As of March, 2019 (Prepared by the Author on the Basis of Data of the Handbook[53])

Table 3.6 gives the status of project implementation as of the first part of 2019, almost three years after the launch of AMRUT MISSION. A critical analysis of table 3.6 leads to the following observations:

- **Observation 1:** All the SAAPs (Column 3) for the entire Mission period were approved in the first three years itself. The total project value for the entire NER works out to Rs. 1506.51 crore, which constitutes 1.94% of the total project value of India of Rs. 77,640.02 cr. The average project cost (per city) for 500 cities is Rs. 155.28 cr. against the same value for NER cities, being Rs.125.54 crore only.
- **Observation 2:** The percentage of DPR yet to be approved

(Column 7) is 17.8% for Arunachal Pradesh, 48.1% for Assam, 0.0% for Manipur, 93.6% for Meghalaya, 0.7% for Mizoram, 40.8% for Nagaland, 27.5% for Sikkim and 8.1% for Tripura against the corresponding all India figure of only 3.6%. The same figure for all the states of NER together works out to 32.5%, which is much higher than the all-India figure of 3.6%, indicating thereby the fact that all the states of NER except Manipur and Mizoram were far behind (in the proportion as noted above), as of March 2019.

- **Observation 3:** Another important aspect reflected by table 3.6 is the submission of the utilization certificates for the amounts of CA released (% of the ratio of Column 6 to Column 5 of the table). The percentages of the amount for which the utilization certificates were submitted as of March 2019 were 71.4% for Arunachal Pradesh, 34% for Assam, 93.4% for Manipur, 1.2% for Meghalaya, 94.6% for Mizoram, 43.2% for Nagaland, 95% for Sikkim and 37.2% for Tripura against the all-India average of 59.2%. Evidently, the performance of Assam, Meghalaya, Nagaland and Tripura was not satisfactory, appreciably behind the all-India average of 59.2%.

The above-noted observations have clearly indicated, in general, the poor performance of the states of NER up to March 2019. AMRUT has indeed been a great mission towards the development of basic infrastructure in the selected cities and towns of India in the sectors of water supply, sewerage and septage management, storm water drainage, green spaces and parks, and non-motorized urban transport. In addition, this mission has included a set of Urban Reforms and Capacity Building. However, in many of the selected cities, the progress of implementation of the projects of this mission has not been up to the expectation, as evident from the analysis presented above with reference to the selected cities of NER. The MoHUA has duly provided the central assistance as committed. Against this assistance, many of the selected cities have apparently failed to complete the projects of this mission in time. There are many examples of the selected cities suffering from poor water supply and poor drainage of storm water. A glaring example is the suffering of the citizens of Guwahati City due to these two aspects. It is, therefore, time for the citizens to be aware of these schemes on the one hand and, on the other, to extend their constructive participation and cooperation in the implementation of the projects of this type of great mission of the central government. In addition, the role to be played by the engineers, in particular, is clearly imminent.

AMRUT was extended to achieve its objective and subsumed[63] under AMRUT 2.0 till March 2023. Since it was subsumed under AMRUT 2.0, a detailed status of the projects under AMRUT by the end of March 2023 could not be located at this end. There is no information about the States/UTs failing to complete the projects of AMRUT Mission by the end of March 2023. However, as noted in the guidelines[64], the States/UTs failing to complete the AMRUT projects by the end of March 2023 will have *to complete the remaining ones from their own resources.* AMRUT 2.0 was launched in October 2021. As stated in the Operational Guidelines[64], this Mission (AMRUT 2.0) has the provision for providing 2.68 crore new water tap connections to all in about 4,800 statutory towns in the country. In addition, it has the provision to get universal household coverage of sewerage/septage services in the 500 AMRUT cities through 2.64 crore new sewer connections. Other components of this Mission include rejuvenation of water bodies, green spaces and parks. The total outlay[64] for AMRUT 2.0 is Rs. 2,99,000 crores. This outlay includes about Rs. 22,000 crores marked for the then-ongoing projects of AMRUT Mission only for two years (FY 2021-22 & FY 2022-23). The time set for the completion of the projects of the AMRUT 2.0 Mission is 5 years, ending in FY 2025-26. This mission is highly appreciable with respect to urbanization since it has (in addition to the objectives briefly stated above) a strong reform agenda[64] with a focus on *strengthening urban local bodies and the water security of the cities.* In addition, it (AMRUT 2.0) has a Sub-Scheme on Formulation of GIS-based master planes for 675 Class-II towns with a population of 50,000-99,999 with a tentative outlay of Rs. 631.13 crore. As reported by PIB[65], the funds of Rs. 76.00 crores have already been released to 18 states covering 550 towns as of July 2024. The statutory towns covered by this Sub-Scheme under AMRUT 2.0 in the states of NER are shown in Appendix—IIIC. These towns are in addition to those covered by Amrut Cities. The distribution of a total number of 77 statutory towns in the NER has been 5 for Arunachal Pradesh, 37 for Assam, 5 for Manipur, 6 for Meghalaya, 2 for Mizoram, 5 for Nagaland, 1 for Sikkim and 16 for Tripura.

For the appropriate implementation of the Mission, MoHUA has put in place[64] a very strong institutional mechanism, as given in Appendix—IIID. The question is: To what extent are the different units of the well-conceived implementation mechanism at the national, state, and district levels committed to their respective responsibilities, as defined in the guidelines[64]? This commitment of the units is reflected in the progress made so far in the different projects of the Mission, particularly in view of the fact that the duration of the Mission is only up to 2025 –26.

Table 3.7 gives the status of the implementation of the projects under AMRUT 2.0 as of July 2024 for the states of NER. The total number of projects approved for India has been 8205 (Column 2), against which NER has a total share of 367 projects, a share of only 4.47% of the total for India. On the other hand, the total project cost approved for the 8 states of NER (Column 3) has been Rs. 2043.89 crore, 1.12% of India's total project cost of Rs. 1,82,569.26 crore. Against this situation of approved projects, the performance of the states on the approved projects is reflected by an analysis of Columns 3 and 5 of the table. The awarded projects constitute - 6.6% for Arunachal Pradesh, 48.5% for Assam, 2% for Manipur, 100% for Meghalaya, 21.04% for Mizoram, 0.0% for Nagaland, 42.64% for Sikkim and 94.68% for Tripura. These percentages may be compared against the average performance of all the 34 States/UTs of India, which works out to 42.35%.

States	Approved Projects		Awarded Projects		DPR,Tendering Stage	
	No	Total Projec Cost*	No	Total Project Cost*	No	Total Project Cost*
Col. 1	Col. 2	Col. 3	Col. 4	Col. 5	Col. 6	Col. 7
Arunachal Pradesh	19	185.02	10	12.24	9	172.78
Assam	59	961.97	36	466.65	23	495.32
Manipur	32	155.73	15	3.11	17	152.62
Meghalaya	1	121.00	1	121.00	0	0.00
Mizoram	166	157.78	4	33.19	162	124.59
Nagaland	64	218.90	----	---	64	218.90
Sikkim	8	49.41	4	21.07	4	28.34
Tripura	18	191.08	14	180.91	4	10.18
India**	8,205	1,82,569.26	4,065	77,317.40	4,140	1,05,251.87

*Values are in Rs. Crore, **Total for 34 States/UTs of India

Table 3.7: Status of Implementation of Projects under Amrut 2.0, as of July 2024 (Prepared by the Author on the Basis of Data Given PIB Release[65])

As far as the award of projects is concerned, the best performance has been achieved so far by Meghalaya (100%), though only one project costing Rs. 121 crore is involved. On the other hand, the worst performer (0.0%) has been Nagaland. In fact, this state has not awarded a single project out of 64 approved projects (Column 2 of the table). Tripura's performance (94.68%) has also been appreciable. The performance of Assam (48.5%) and Sikkim (42.64%) has been higher than India's average of 42.35%. The performance of the remaining states, i.e. Arunachal Pradesh (6.6%), Manipur (2%) and Mizoram (21.04%), has been below India's average. This position has been only with respect to the award of projects. Table 3.7 does not indicate the progress achieved regarding the awarded projects. However, even the position of awarded projects reflects the fact that most of the states have to take measures to increase the pace of progress. Many of the approved projects are yet to be awarded, as indicated by Column 7 of the table.

The units of the Implementation Mechanism at the state and district levels (Appendix—IIID) have to be more active now since only about one and a half years are left before the expiry of the duration of AMRUT 2.0. The elements[64] of the Reforms of this Mission include the one called the *'Information Education and Communication (IEC)'* having the following objectives:

- *To create awareness about practices for water conservation like rainwater harvesting, clean water bodies, groundwater recharge, intensive plantation, etc.*
- *To make people aware of municipal services, especially new water connections.*
- *To effect behavioural changes regarding optimum usage and minimize wastage of water.*
- *To inculcate a sense of ownership of water supply infrastructure among citizens.*
- *To enhance awareness about the creation of markets for treated used water in rural/peri-urban areas and*
- *To encourage potential investors to invest in PPP projects in the water sector through project profiles.*

The Operation Guidelines[64] has suggested a number of strategies and tools for the achievement of the above-noted objectives of IEC. However, in many states, adequate measures for executing the suggested strategies and tools do not appear to be on the ground. It is in this context that the role to be played by the citizens in general and the implementation units and agencies, including the engineers in particular, is of primary importance in due recognition of the fact that the different projects conceived in these missions (both AMRUT & AMRUT 2.0) will appreciably improve the Ease of Living Index for the cities of the country on their proper implementation.

3.3.4. Swachh Bharat Mission – Urban (SBM–U)

This mission was launched by the Government of India in October 2014 in due recognition of the great words of Mahatma Gandhi *(as stated in the Operational Guidelines[68]), which go as: 'Sanitation is more important than political freedom'.* The main objectives of the first part of SBM-U were: *(a) Achieving 100% Open Defecation Free (ODF) status, (b) Ensuring 100% scientific Solid Waste Management (SWM) and (c) Behaviour change through 'Jan Andolan' by 2nd October, 2019 in all statutory town.*

The first phase of this mission achieved success to a significant extent. The salient achievements include solid waste management and measures for ODF. However, based on the recommendation of NITI Aayog, this mission was further extended in 2021 as SBM-U 2.0 for a period of five years. The objectives[68] of this extended version of the mission have been:

- To make Urban India 'Garbage Free' with emphasis on issues such as source segregation, collection, transportation, and processing.
- To sustain the ODF status and prevent slippage by ensuring containment, transportation, and processing disposal of faecal sludge and wastewater.
- To focus intensively on IEC and behavioural change through citizen outreach, including capacity building and skilling of relevant stakeholders.

All projects under SBM-U 2.0 are being implemented by MoHUA through the States/UTs in all the statutory towns. As of now, the duration of this project comes to an end in October, 2026. The present status of the projects of this mission with respect to projects allocated and funds released under SBM-U 2.0 has been available in the PIB[70] (MoHUA) Release dt. 01 August, 2024. The projects allocated and the funds released by the Government of India so far to the states of NER, along with the corresponding values for all the States/UTs, appear in table 3.8. However, utilization of the funds released to the states so far could not be ascertained at this stage. As evident from this table, Assam has the highest project allocation *(Rs. 503.5 cr.)*, followed by Nagaland *(Rs. 158.88 cr.)* amongst the states of NER. Other states of the region have relatively smaller allocations. This variation is understandable since the fundamental principle[71] adopted for the allocation of funds under SBM-U has been the weightage to (i) the ratio of urban population of the State/UT to the total urban population and (ii) the ratio of number of statutory towns in each State/UT to the total number of statutory towns. The major aspect with respect to the fund released is its utilization.

States of NER	Projects allocated (Rs. Cr.)	Fund Released (Rs. Cr.)
Arunachal Pradesh	129	28.73
Assam	503.5	82.02
Manipur	96.2	14.79
Meghalaya	67.3	16.79
Mizoram	82.5	14.84
Naga Land	158.88	40.17
Sikkim	19.4	4.03
Tripura	85.3	15.34
India (Total)	32,609.99	5,555.02

Table 3.8: Projects Allocated & the Fund Released as of August 2024 under SBM-U 2.0 (Prepared by author on the basis of data from PIB[70], Delhi)

An account of the progress of works with respect to IHHL and CT/PT, as of December, 2023, has been available from the answer[71] to a Lok Sabha question. Table 3.9 shows the progress of works with respect to IHHL and CT/PT in the states of NER. An analysis of this table reveals a number of important observations with respect to both the objectives (IHHL & CT/PT) of the mission. These observations are briefly discussed state-wise below. This analysis is based on the average performance of all the States/UTs (total no. being 35) of India, with total targets for India being 58,99,637 for IHHL and 5,07,587 for CT/PT. Against these targets, the respective achievements have been 63,06,979 (for IHHL) and 6,36,826 F (for CT/PT). Therefore, India's achievement percentages have been 106.9 % and 125.46% for IHHL and CT/PT, respectively—indeed an appreciable performance on an all-India average. The state-wise analysis for NER has been based on the average performance of all the states/UTs in India.

States of NER	Individual Household Latrine		Community/Public Toilets	
	Targets	Constructed	Targets	Constructed
Col. 1	*Col. 2*	*Col. 3*	*Col. 4*	*Col. 5*
Arunachal Pradesh	12,252	9,743	387	89
Assam	75,720	78,214	3,554	3,356
Manipur	43,644	40,148	620	581
Meghalaya	5,066	1,604	362	152
Mizoram	16,441	12,607	491	1,324
Nagaland	23,427	20,448	478	238
Sikkim	1,587	1,527	142	268
Tripura	19,464	21,757	586	1,089

Table 3.9: Achievements of States of NER on IHHL and CT/PT, as of December,

2023 (Prepared by Author on the Basis of Data of India Environment Portal[71])

- *Arunachal Pradesh:* The performance of this state has not been satisfactory—only 79.52% and 23% have been achieved in IHHL and CT/PT, respectively—much less than the respective average achievements of India, noted above.
- *Assam:* Its performance has been appreciable with respect to IHHL—103.29% (Columns 2 & 3), though slightly less than the corresponding all-India average of 106.9%. On the other hand, its performance on CT/PT has been only 94.43% (Columns 4 & 5), significantly less than India's average of 125.46%.
- *Manipur:* Its achievements in both IHHL and CT/PT have not been good, 91.99% and 93.71%, respectively, which is much less than the corresponding average values of India.
- *Meghalaya:* Its performance has been disappointing, with achievements in IHHL and CT/PT being only 31.66% and 41.99%, respectively—much lower than the Indian average achievements.
- *Mizoram:* The performance of this state has not been good with respect to IHHL, with its achievement being only 76.68%, against the Indian average of 106.9%. However, its performance in CT/PT has been highly appreciable, 269.65% against India's average achievement of 125.46%.
- *Nagaland:* The performance of this state has been very poor, with achievements in IHHL and CT/PT being 87.28% and 49.79%, respectively, appreciably lower than the Indian average values.
- *Sikkim:* Its performance has been satisfactory, with achievements being 96.22% for IHHL and 188.73% for CT/PT.
- *Tripura:* Its performance in both the categories has been the best in NER, 111.78% in IHHL and 185.84% in CT/PT.

The states having the gaps, as reflected in the above-noted analysis, need to take up corrective measures before the expiry of the termination year of the mission. The status of the progress of works with respect to other objectives such as measures for *'ensuring functionality and maintenance'* of CTs/PTs, construction of *'Aspirational toilets'* in historic/tourist places, *'Urban Waste Management (UWM)'* etc., as of 2024, could not be ascertained in clear terms, since the works relating to these areas are in progress with the allocated fund, as reflected in table 3.8. Apparently, Central Assistance is provided for *'mechanized desludging equipment, sewage/septage treatment facilities and interception and diversion of drains',* as per the PIB Release[72]. Another important addition to SBM-U 2.0 has been the availability of a grievance redressal platform. For this purpose, an App called *'Swachhata App'* has been made available to the citizens of the cities.

The remaining flagship schemes of the Government of India, as mentioned under subhead 3.3.1, have not been included in this discussion. However, these schemes do contribute substantially to the process of urbanization in India.

3.4. Ease of Living Index in Cities of India:

3.4.1. Global Scenario of Living Index in Cities

Oxford Economics[66] published the Global Cities Index, 2024, for 1000 cities of the world. These 1000 cities covering over 30% of the world population in 2023 accounted for 60% of the global GDP. The overall scores and rankings were based on 27 indicators across five categories: economics, human capital, quality of life, environment and governance. The top 10 cities of the world based on the overall score are (Ranks and Scores being shown within bracket—the first figure for rank and the second one for score): New York, US (1, 100.0), London, UK (2, 99.4), San Jose, US (3, 98.5), Tokyo, Japan (4, 97.8), Paris, France (5, 96.3), Seattle, US (6, 95.8), Los Angeles, US (7, 95.4), San Francisco, US (8, 94.7), Melbourne, Australia (9, 94.6) and Zurich, Switzerland (10, 94.2). The total number of Indian cities included in the 1000 cities assessed by Oxford Economics for Living Index has been 90. The top 10 cities in this ranking are shown in table 3.10.

Cities	Ranks based on overall score	Ranks on individual categories				
		Economics	Human Capital	Quality of Life	Environment	Governance
Col. 1	Col. 2	Col. 3	Col. 4	Col. 5	Col. 6	Col. 7
Delhi	350	108	51	838	973	380
Bangaluru	411	171	179	847	727	380
Mumbai	427	169	126	915	812	380
Chennai	472	244	189	879	763	380
Kochi	521	259	560	765	790	380
Kolkata	528	166	392	884	919	380
Pune	534	386	181	897	713	380
Thrissur	550	326	698	757	581	380
Hyderabad	564	253	524	882	674	380
Kozhikode	580	392	607	783	620	380
New York (US)*	1	1	4	278	353	184
London (UK)*	2	7	1	292	197	72
San Jose (US)*	3	3	28	38	53	184

*Top three cities holding world ranks of 1, 2 and 3 are shown for facilitating a direct comparison of ranks held on individual categories with those of the top ten cities of India.

Table 3.10: Top Ten Cities of India in the List of Rankings of 1000 Cities of the World as Per Oxford Economics[66]. (Prepared by Author on the Basis of Data of Oxford Economics[66])

The ranks held by the top 10 Indian cities (Column 2 of table 3.10) indicate the poor standard of urbanization by international standards. The methodology adopted includes the distribution of weightage over the five categories: 30% for economics, 25% for human capital, 25% for quality of life, 10% for environment, and 10% for governance. A comparison of the ranks held by the top three cities of the world (shown in the last three rows of the table) with those of the top-ranking 10 Indian cities truly reflects the extent of the efforts to be put in with regard to different activities of urbanization under each of the five categories. For a better appreciation of the poor situation of urbanization in India, the position of the bottom-most five cities of India (out of 90 cities considered) in the ranking list, as given in table 3.11, may be analyzed.

The ranks held in each of the five categories, as shown by columns 3, 4, 5, 6, and 7 of table 3.11, are indicative of the deplorable conditions of Indian cities with respect to international standards. The remaining 75 (90-10-5) cities of India have ranks in the range of 581 to 981. The city of Guwahati, apparently the only city of NER included in the list of 1000 cities, has a rank of 770. This city has the ranks on individual categories as 492 for Economics, 548 for Human Capital, 934 for Quality of Life and 895 for Environment. The ranks held by this city on Quality of Life and Environment do speak of the worst situation under which the citizens have been living.

Cities	Ranks based on overall score	Ranks on individual categories				
		Economics	Human Capital	Quality of Life	Environment	Governance
Col. 1	*Col. 2*	*Col. 3*	*Col. 4*	*Col. 5*	*Col. 6*	*Col. 7*
Kanpur	982	864	914	953	985	380
Shahjahanpur	990	913	862	917	999	380
Bokaro	993	953	879	899	1000	380
Hardoi	998	992	973	946	974	380
Sultanpur (UP)	1000	998	982	960	989	380

Table 3.11: Bottom Five Cities of India in the List of Rankings of 1000 Cities of the World as Per Oxford Economics[66]. (Prepared by author on the basis of data of Oxford Economics[66])

3.4.2. Indian Scenario of Ease of Living Index in the Cities

The second edition[67] of the Ease of Living Index for 111 cities of India was published by MoHUA in March 2021. The first edition was published[53] in 2018. The cities considered for the Ease of Living Index (EoLI) include 49 cities with a Million+ population and 62 cities with less than a Million population. The main pillars, including the components of each pillar, are shown in figure 3.3. The weightage given to each pillar is also indicated in the figure. The national average score on the Ease of Living Index is 53.51. The rankings for the 111 cities are given in two categories: one for the cities with Million+ populations and the other for those with less than a Million population. The top-ranking five cities in each category and also the bottom-ranking five cities in each category are shown in table 3.12.

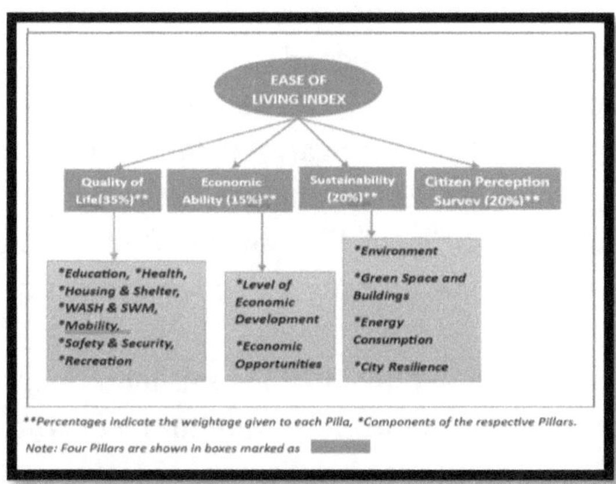

Figure 3.3: Pillars with Components for Computation of Ease of Living Index (Prepared by Author Based on the Ease of Living Index[67])

An analysis of table 3.12 reveals a number of salient points. Firstly, all the top five cities under each of the two categories have scores more than the average national score of 53.51. Secondly, no city from the NER occupies a place in the list of top five positions in either category. On the other hand, Guwahati is the only city from NER in the category of cities with a Million+ population. However, it finds a position only in the bottom five of this category with an all-India rank of 46th *(Column 1 of the table),* its score being less than the national average.

Top 5 cities with Million+ population		Top 5 cities with less than a Million Population	
Cities*	Scores	Cites*	Scores
Col. 1	*Col. 2*	*Col. 3*	*Col. 4*
Bangaluru (1)	66.70	Shimla (1)	60.90
Pune (2)	66.20	Bhubaneswar (2)	59.85
Ahmedabad (3)	64.87	Silvassa (3)	58.43
Chennai (4)	62.61	Kakinada (4)	56.84
Surat (5)	61.73	Salem (5)	56.40
Bottom 5 cities with Million+ population		Bottom 5 cities with less than a Million Populn.	
Amritsar (45)	49.36	Aligarh (58)	47.15
Guwahati (46)	48.52	Rampur (59)	46.88
Bareilly (47)	47.73	Namchi (60)	46.46
Dhanbad (48)	46.96	Satna (61)	45.60
Srinagar (49)	42.95	Muzaffarpur (62)	45.53

Figures within brackets indicate the ranks held by respective cities.

Table 3.12: *The Top and Bottom Five Cities in Ease of Living Index in Each Category (Prepared by author based on data of MoHUA[67])*

The analysis of this table further reveals that all the bottom five cities in both categories have scores less than the national average and that Namchi, being a city from NER (Sikkim), finds a position in the bottom five cities of the second category of the cities (Column 2 of the table) with a score of only 46.46. However, this score is higher than the one secured by Srinagar, which occupied the last position with a score of only 42.95 (Column 1) in the first category of cities. The total number of cities of NER, included in the 111 cities for the computation of the Ease of Living Index has been only 10, as shown in table 3.13.

A critical analysis of table 3.13 reveals a number of salient points bearing on the standard of urbanization in the northeastern region of the country. These points are briefly noted below:

- *Point 1:* The overall Ease of Living Indexes (Column 7) has been less than the national average of 53.51 for all the cities except Agartala, which achieved a score of 55.2.

- *Point 2:* The Ease of Living Indexes computed without including the impact of the pillar of the Citizen Perception Survey are given in column 5 of the table. These indexes (all being in the range of 20 to 30 only) are truly indicative of an extremely poor standard of urbanization in this part of the country with respect to the important pillars of Quality of Life (Column 2), Economic Ability (Column 3) and Sustainability (Column 4).

- *Point 3:* The scores for Economic Ability (Column 3) reflect very well the poor economic condition of all the cities of NER.

Cities of NER*	Quality of Life	Economic Ability	Sustain-ability	Ease of Living w/o CPS**	CPS**	Final Ease of Living***
Col. 1	Col. 2	Col. 3	Col. 4	Col. 5	Col. 6	Col. 7
Itanagar (AR)	51.19	1.39	40.95	26.31	75.5	48.96
Pasighat (AR)	51.71	4.14	40.51	26.82	73.2	48.78
Guwahati (AS)	43.65	8.63	48.31	26.23	74.3	46.46
Imphal (MN)	45.01	1.14	38.38	23.6	86.8	49.64
Shillong (ML)	43.64	4.74	56.53	27.26	81.3	51.65
Aizawl (MZ)	41.03	8.41	44.51	24.52	78.8	48.16
Kohima (NL)	50.06	0.55	46.87	26.98	76.3	49.87
Agartala (TR)	47.87	3.17	60.25	29.28	86.4	55.2
Gangtok (SK)	52.14	16.36	40.5	28.8	74.6	51.18
Namchi (SK)	42.03	15.69	46.8	26.42	66.8	46.46

*Respective states are given within brackets in short forms, **CPS for Citizen Perception Survey, ***Final Score includes the weightage of CPS

Table 3.13: Cities of NER with the Ease of Living Indexes—Both on Individual Pillars and Overall (Prepared by author on the basis of data of MoHUA[67])

The above-noted three points raise the question of why the region has failed to derive the benefits of many urbanization schemes launched by the Government of India. Some of these schemes have been discussed in this book. It is in this context that the contents of this table need to be constructively discussed by the state machinery engaged in developmental activities of the states of this region. For example, the developmental activities covered under schemes such as SCM, AMRUT, AMRUT 2.0, SDG, etc., may be critically analyzed by all concerned, including the citizens and engineers, and the improvement measures, if found necessary, may be initiated without delay. In fact, the very purpose of this discussion is to facilitate and encourage this type of critical discussion among all stakeholders in the process of urbanization in the country.

Many of the citizens of these cities are unaware of the reasons for their miseries of urban life, which are primarily caused by non-implementation or poor implementation of many of the projects funded by the Government of India, even to the extent of 90% of the project costs. It is in this context that the creation of awareness among the urban citizens becomes absolutely necessary through open discussions among the stakeholders, including the citizens so that the issues confronting implementation of different projects may be sorted out. The different Engineers' forums, social organizations, educational institutions, etc., may feasibly take the lead in this direction.

3.5. Concluding Remarks

The efforts made by the Government of India to improve the situation of urbanization in India have been encouraging in view of the implementation of different ongoing/completed schemes, as briefly discussed in this chapter. However, as of today, urbanization faces a number of challenges, some of which have been well-reflected in this discussion. The most serious challenges include delays in the implementation of different projects under different schemes, gaps in monitoring the progress of work, including quality control, delays in the preparation of DPRs, etc. These challenges have been quite apparent in the case of many of the states of NER. Another challenge is the lack of adequate awareness among the citizens of the urban areas about their responsibilities and participation in the process of urbanization, for which different schemes are now being implemented/formulated. Hardly any discussion among the citizens of cities on different issues/projects relating to urbanization is constructively held. It is more apparent in the case of the cities of NER. It is in contrast to the fact that the MoHUA has been encouraging this type of discussion/participation of citizens in the process of urbanization, as reflected in the discussion presented under missions such as AMRUT, SCM and SBM-U.

Many of the schemes dealt with in this chapter basically relate to the supply of drinking water, sanitation and hygiene. Substantial progress has been achieved in these areas. However, the fact remains to the effect that there are still many cities suffering in some of these areas. For example, the drinking water situation in the city of Guwahati (the biggest and the most strategic city in NER) may be mentioned. Despite the fact that it is one of the 100 smart cities in India, many citizens still lack public facilities for drinking water. They have to still depend on their own water-supply arrangement.

Many facilities under these three elements (Supply of drinking water, sanitation and hygiene) of basic necessities have been created. However, the aspect of sustainability and maintenance presents a major area for attention for which AMRUT & SBM have made adequate provisions, as discussed already. The ULBs concerned need to pay adequate attention to this aspect as well.

Independent studies/investigations in respect of sustainability and maintenance of different facilities already created under different schemes/missions need to be taken up by different bodies such as Citizen Forums, Technical Institutions (in the form of study projects), NGOs, Engineers' Forum, etc. All the facilities created must be sustainable to avoid the re-cropping of the issues.

Chapter 4 | United Nations' Sustainable Development Goals and Role of Engineers

4.1. Introduction

The United Nations General Assembly (UN-GA) in 2015 formulated a set of 17 Sustainable Development Goals (SDGs) or Global Goals, intended to be achieved by 2030. These SDGs are included in Agenda 2030 of the United Nations. The Sustainable Development Goals Report[76], 2023 states, *"Halfway to the deadline for the 2030 Agenda, the SDG Progress Report; Special Edition shows we are leaving more than half the world behind. Progress on more than 50 Percent of targets of the SDGs is weak and insufficient; on 30 Percent, it has stalled or gone into reverse. These include key targets on poverty, hunger and climate. Unless we act now, the 2030 Agenda could become an epitaph for a world that might have been."* The main objective of this discussion has been to identify the specific goals in which the engineers are expected to play the predominant role in the achievement of the targets as set. However, from a wider perspective, engineers, being responsible for the society as a whole, have a scope for contributing to all goals in variable measures. It is in this context that all the 17 SDGs, along with the number of targets set under each goal (total targets = 169), are stated below:

- SDG 1: End poverty in all its forms everywhere, *Targets—7,*
- SDG 2: End hunger, achieve food, security and improved nutrition and promote sustainable agriculture, *Targets—8,*
- SDG 3: Ensure healthy lives and promote well-being for all at all ages, *Targets—13,*
- SDG 4: Ensure inclusive and equitable quality education and promote lifelong learning opportunities for all, *Targets—10,*
- SDG 5: Achieve gender equality and empower all women and girls, *Targets—9,*

- SDG 6: Ensure availability and sustainable management of water and sanitation for all, *Targets—8,*
- SDG 7: Ensure access to affordably reliable, sustainable and modern energy for all, *Targets—5,*
- SDG 8: Promote sustained, inclusive and sustainable economic growth, full and productive employment and decent work for all, *Targets—12,*
- SDG 9: Build resilient infrastructure, promote inclusive and sustainable industrialization and foster innovation, *Targets—8,*
- SDG 10: Reduce inequality within and among countries, *Targets—10,*
- SDG 11: Make cities and human settlements inclusive, safe, resilient and sustainable, *Targets—10,*
- SDG 12: Ensure sustainable consumption and production pattern, *Targets—11,*
- SDG 13: Take urgent action to combat climate change and its impacts, *Targets—5,*
- SDG 14: Conserve and sustainably use ocean, sea and marine resources for sustainable development, *Targets—10,*
- SDG 15: Protect, restore and promote sustainable use of terrestrial ecosystems, sustainably manage forests, combat desertification, halt and reverse land degradation and halt biodiversity loss, *Targets—12,*
- SDG 16: Protect peaceful and inclusive societies for sustainable developments, provide access to justice for all and build effective, accountable and inclusive institutions at all levels, *Targets—12* and
- SDG 17: Strengthen the means of implementation and revitalize the global partnership for sustainable development. *Targets—19.*

A critical look at the goals and targets stated above clearly suggests the fact that the world will be a paradise to live in once the set targets are achieved in the truest sense of the terms. However, as per the report[76] prepared by the UN at the end of about 9 years since

2015, the year of setting the targets, the achievement is not truly encouraging. The report, in its introduction, observes: *"Under current trends, 575 million people will still be living in extreme poverty in 2030, and only about one-third of countries will meet the target to halve national poverty levels. Shockingly, the world is back at the level of hunger that had not been seen since 2005, and food prices remain higher in more countries than in the period 2015–2019. The way things are going, it will take 286 years to close gender gaps in legal protection and remove discriminatory laws. And in education, the impacts of years of underinvestment and learning losses are such that, by 2030, some 84 million children will be out of school and 300 million children or young people attending school will leave unable to read and write."* However, the pleasing truth is that the UN has set a "Road Map for Survival" for mankind, which consists of the seventeen set goals.

4.2. Position of India with Respect to Progress Made So Far

4.2.1. Position of India in Global Perspective

At this stage, it has been considered appropriate to look into India's position with respect to progress made towards the achievement of SDGs. According to SDR-2023[77], India's rank is 112. This rank relates to an overall score of 63.4 out of 100. India's rank has slightly improved over last year's rank of 120, though it lags behind its neighboring countries Bangladesh (rank—101), Nepal (rank—99) and Sri Lanka (rank—83). On the other hand, India's SDG Index score (63.4) is appreciably less than the regional average score of 67.2, the region being East and South Asia (as adopted by UN[77]). The performance of India in different SDGs is shown in figure 4.1.

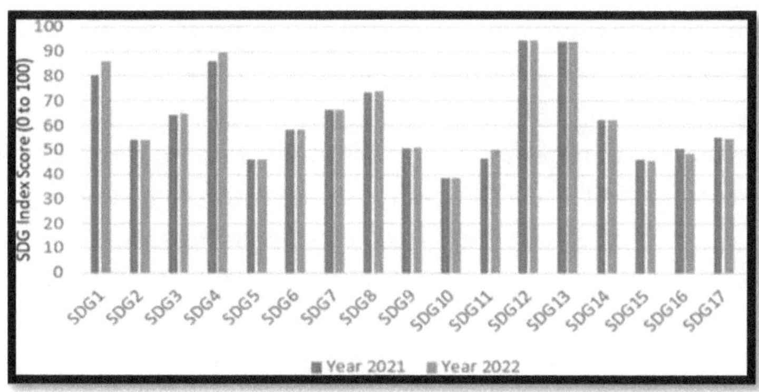

Figure 4.1: Chart Showing the SDG-Performance of India (Prepared by author on the basis of data given in SDR—2023[77])

As evidenced by the performance chart (Figure 4.1), India's performances in SDGs 12 and 13 have been excellent, with scores of 94.8 and 94.3, respectively (in 2022), against its average SDG score of 63.4. Similarly, its performances in SDGs 1 and 4 have also been appreciably good, with scores of 86.2 and 89.3, respectively. A comparison of the individual performances in the SDGs for the year 2022 (red-colored bars) with those of the corresponding SDGs for year 2021 (blue-colored bars) reflects clearly the fact that there has been no significant improvement in the performance of any of the SDGs over the preceding year (2021). As observed in SDR—2023[77], only SDGs 1 and 12 are on track with respect to SDG achievement. Challenges remain for SDGs 3, 4, 5, 6, 7, 8, 9, 14 and 17; significant challenges remain for SDGs 2, 11, 13 (stagnating—though the score is high) and 16 and major challenges (decreasing trend) are there for SDGs 10 and 15.

The SDSN (Sustainable Development Solutions Network), the world's largest knowledge network operating under the UN, conducts surveys on government efforts towards achieving the SDGs on a regular basis. The latest survey of SDSN[77], conducted for 74 countries, including India, reflects the fact that the Government of India needs to do a lot more to achieve the SDGs by 2030. The ranks for these 74 countries were based on three pillars: SDG Coordination, SDG Pathways (food systems, energy access and affordability, digital connectivity, education, jobs and social protection and climate change, biodiversity loss and pollution) and Multilateralism. India has been placed in the 66th position with a score of only 47.5.

In view of this situation, we are all concerned with the implementation of measures that are being/are to be taken with respect to achieving the SDGs, and we have to play our respective roles in a more effective way. It is in this context that engineers, having been major players in nation-building activities, have to rise to the occasion and play their roles more effectively.

The specific targets for the implementation that the engineers have to play a predominant role in are G6, G7, G9, and G11. A discussion on these goals from the perspective of the role to be played by engineers with reference to our country in general and the north-east region, in particular, has been attempted. While doing so, it has been necessary to look into the present status of the SDGs in India in general and in the states of the north-east region in particular. There have been many views and reports available on the internet regarding the status of SDGs in India. The Ministry of Statistics and Program Implementation (MoSPI) developed a National Indicator Framework (NIF) to monitor the progress of SDGs in India. According to the NITI Aayog's Annual Report[55], 2022-23, so far, three editions of the SDG India Index have been published:

- First Edition SDG India Index, 2018-19 – This report covered 13 goals out of 17 goals (leaving out goals 12, 13, 14 and 17), 62 indicators and 39 targets.
- Second Edition SDG India Index, 2019-20 – This report covered 16 goals, 100 indicators and 54 targets.
- Third Edition SDG India Index, 2020-21 – This report covered 16 goals (with a qualitative assessment of Goal 17), 115 indicators and over 70 targets.
- Fourth edition SDG India Index is now under preparation, as stated in the report[55]. As of today (31.05.24), the fourth edition has not been released yet by NITI Aayog.

4.2.2. Position of Indian States/UTs in Indian Perspective

The up-to-date position of the states/UTs of India based on the UN's report[76] is not available yet. The SDG India Index & Dashboard 2020-21 has been the latest one[78], being the third edition of SDG India Index, as released by NITI Aayog. Therefore, the position of the States/UTS of India has been analyzed on the basis of the data available in this report[78]. *(This analysis is subject to update on the availability of the fourth edition of the SDG India Index).* The States/UTs occupying the top 6 positions in India with respect to SDG Index Scores *(scores being shown within bracket)* are: Chandigarh (79), Kerala (75), Himachal Pradesh & Tamil Nadu (74), Andhra Pradesh, Goa, Karnataka & Uttarakhand (72), Sikkim (71), Maharashtra (70). These States/UTs have performed well, their index scores being above India's composite score of 66 (for 2020-21). On the other hand, the States/UTs occupying the bottom five positions are *(scores being shown within bracket):* Bihar (52), Jharkhand (56), Assam (57), Uttar Pradesh, Rajasthan, Meghalaya & Arunachal Pradesh (60) and Odisha (61), all scoring below India's composite score.

4.2.3. Position of North Eastern States in Indian Perspective

A deeper analysis of index-scores[78] reflects a disappointing situation for most of the north-eastern states. Four of the eight states (Assam—57, Meghalaya—60, Arunachal Pradesh—60 and Nagaland-61) are in the bottom five positions of the country. On the other hand, Sikkim is the only state in the NE region to have a position in the top five of the country with a score of 71. The other three states (Manipur—64, Tripura—65 and Mizoram—68) are in the middle positions. It is truly in this context that the engineers of India, in general, and those of the north-east region, in particular, have to play their role with a greater commitment to the main objective of the sustainable development goals.

A deeper understanding of the broad objective of the UN's SDGs is the basic necessity on the part of engineers to play effective roles in the achievement of the SDGs in which they are involved. The American Society of Civil Engineers (ASCE)[79] defines sustainability as *"a set of economic, environmental and social conditions (The Triple*

Bottom Line) in which all of society has the capacity and opportunity to maintain and improve the quality of life indefinitely without degrading the quantity, quality, or the availability of economic, environmental and social resources." Further, as stated by Prof. Narayan[79], the World Commission on Environment and Development, 1987 noted: *"Humanity has the ability to make development sustainable and ensure that it meets the needs of the present without compromising the ability of the future generations to meet their own needs."* The essence of the approach to sustainable development, as stated above, has to be whole-heartedly felt by all of us (the engineers) for contributing to the achievements of relevant SDGs.

On reaching this stage of this chapter, the necessity of narrowing down the scope of further discussion only to "the role of engineers connected with the construction industry" has been strongly felt in view of the author's limitations of knowledge and experiences. It is, indeed, in this context that the SDGs, namely G6, G7, G9 and G11, have been finally chosen for a detailed discussion.

4.3. SDG 6

Clean Water and Sanitation (Ensure Availability and Sustainable Management of Water and Sanitation for All).

4.3.1. Targets

Under this goal, eight targets have been set for achievement by 2030. These targets[11] are as given below:

- Achieve universal and equitable access to safe and affordable drinking water for all.
- Achieve access to adequate and equitable sanitation and hygiene for all and end open defecation, paying special attention to the needs of women and girls and those in vulnerable situations.
- Improve water quality by reducing pollution, eliminating dumping, minimizing the release of hazardous chemicals and materials, halving the proportion of untreated wastewater, and substantially increasing recycling and safe reuse globally.
- Substantially increase water-use efficiency across all sectors

and ensure sustainable withdrawals and supply of fresh water to address water scarcity and substantially reduce the number of people suffering from water scarcity.

- Implement integrated water resources management at all levels, including through transboundary cooperation, as appropriate.
- Protect and restore water-related ecosystems, including mountains, forests, wetlands, rivers, aquifers and lakes.
  - o 6a. Expand international cooperation and capacity-building support to developing countries in water and sanitation-related activities and programmes, including water harvesting, water efficiency, wastewater treatment, recycling and reuse technologies.
  - o 6b. Support and strengthen the participation of local communities in improving water and sanitation management.

4.3.2. Global Position of Drinking Water, Sanitation and Hygiene

The Sustainable Development Goals Report 2023 of the United Nations[76] observed from a global perspective (In its Visual Summary) the following with respect to the achievement of the targets of SDG 6, mentioned above, till 2022.

- **Observation 1:** 2.2 billion people today lack safely managed drinking water, 3.5 billion people lack safely managed sanitation, and 2.0 billion people lack basic hand washing facilities.
- **Observation 2:** To meet the targets set for this SDG 6, the global rates of progress achieved so far have to be accelerated manifold -six times for drinking water, five times for sanitation and three times for hygiene.

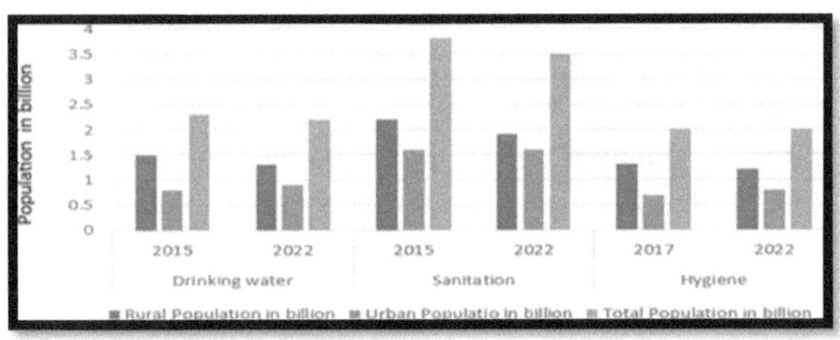

Figure 4.2: Chart Showing the Global Population (Rural & Urban) Without Safely Managed Drinking Water, Sanitation and Hygiene as of 2022 (prepared by author based on data of UN's report[76])

The chart shown in figure 4.2 shows the break-up of the total global population (rural and urban) having no safely managed drinking water, sanitation and hygiene till 2022.

The report[11] states that the demand for water is rising due to rapid population growth, urbanization and increasing pressure from agriculture and energy sectors. Additionally, decades of misuse, poor management and the over-extraction and contamination of freshwater and groundwater supplies have exacerbated water stress and deteriorated water-related ecosystems.

The report[11] has stated that the water stress occurs when the ratio of freshwater to total renewable freshwater resources is above 25 Percent. Based on this parameter, a water-stress map was prepared by marking different regions of the world as the region of critical water-stress (>100), the region of high water-stress (75 to 100), the region of medium water-stress (50-75) and the region of low water-stress (25-50). As shown in the map, India falls in the region of high water stress (as indicated by the colour in the map). In view of this situation, India needs to implement appropriate measures for 'promoting and improving water use efficiency', as conceived in the targets under this Goal.

Having seen the horrifying world scenario with respect to drinking water, sanitation and hygiene, as reflected by the UN's observations noted above, the necessity of making an attempt to critically look into the position of India in general and the north-eastern region in particular, has been strongly felt.

4.3.3. India's Position of SDG 6 in Respect of Global Perspective

The indicators for SDG 6 included in SDR—2023[80] are shown in table 4.1. These indicators are common to all countries covered by the report for the SDG concerned. The SDG 6 Index Score for India (*SDR2023 (Data 1)—Protected View)* is 58.1 as of 2022, against its composite score of 63.4 (Figure 4.1). As stated earlier (with reference to figure 4.1), the performance in SDG 6 for India falls in the category of facing challenges. The seven indicators (Table 4.1) relate to drinking water services, sanitation services and hygiene. The value, rating and the trend for the indicators, as reported[80] for India, are symbolically indicated in the last three columns of table 4.1. As evidenced by the table, only one indicator (6.4) has been achieved, and only one indicator (6.1.1—first row of the table) is moderately improving. The ratings for two indicators (6.2.1 and 6.3.1) have indicated major challenges, though the trend shown for indicator 6.2.1 has been on track.

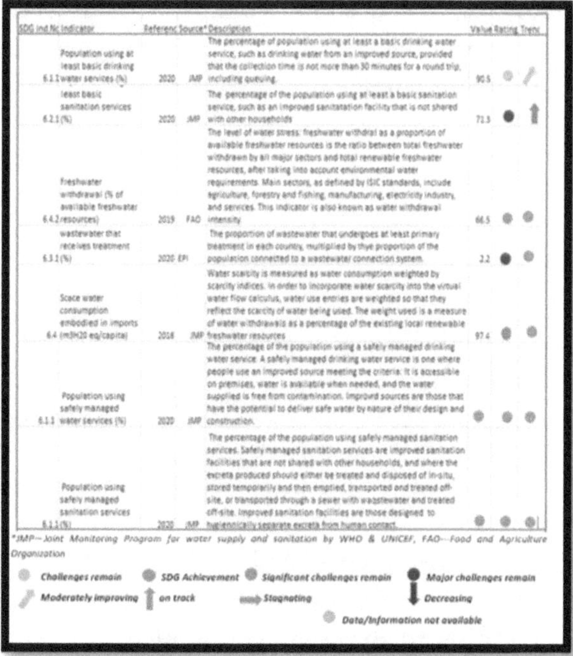

SDG Ind Nc	Indicator	Reference	Source*	Description	Value	Rating	Trend
6.1.1	Population using at least basic drinking water services (%)	2020	JMP	The percentage of population using at least a basic drinking water service, such as drinking water from an improved source, provided that the collection time is not more than 30 minutes for a round trip, including queuing.	90.5		
6.2.1	least basic sanitation services (%)	2020	JMP	The percentage of the population using at least a basic sanitation service, such as an improved sanitation facility that is not shared with other households	71.3		
6.4.2	freshwater withdrawal (% of available freshwater resources)	2019	FAO	The level of water stress: freshwater withdral as a proportion of available freshwater resources is the ratio between total freshwater withdrawn by all major sectors and total renewable freshwater resources, after taking into account environmental water requirements. Main sectors, as defined by ISIC standards, include agriculture, forestry and fishing, manufacturing, electricity industry, and services. This indicator is also known as water withdrawal intensity.	66.5		
6.3.1	wastewater that receives treatment (%)	2020	EPI	The proportion of wastewater that undergoes at least primary treatment in each country, multiplied by thye proportion of the population connected to a wastewater connection system.	2.2		
6.4	Scace water consumption embodied in imports (m3H20 eq/capita)	2016	JMP	Water scarcity is measured as water consumption weighted by scarcity indices. In order to incorporate water scarcity into the virtual water flow calculus, water use entries are weighted so that they reflect the scarcity of water being used. The weight used is a measure of water withdrawals as a percentage of the existing local renewable freshwater resources	97.4		
6.1.1	Population using safely managed water services (%)	2020	JMP	The percentage of the population using a safely managed drinking water service. A safely managed drinking water service is one where people use an improved source meeting the criteria: It is accessible on premises, water is available when needed, and the water supplied is free from contamination. Improved sources are those that have the potential to deliver safe water by nature of their design and construction.			
6.1.1	Population using safely managed sanitation services (%)	2020	JMP	The percentage of the population using safely managed sanitation services. Safely managed sanitation services are improved sanitation facilities that are not shared with other households, and where the excreta produced should either be treated and disposed of in-situ, stored temporarily and then emptied, transported and treated off-site, or transported through a sewer with wastewater and treated off-site. Improved sanitation facilities are those designed to hygienically separate excreta from human contact.			

*JMP—Joint Monitoring Program for water supply and sanitation by WHO & UNICEF, FAO—Food and Agriculture Organization

Table 4.1: Indicators of SDG6 Included for SDR-2023 with Achievements and Trends

(Table prepared by author on the basis of information furnished in the report[80])

The rating given for indicator 6.4.2 shows significant challenges with the trend being unavailable. No data/information has been available for the last two indicators of the table. The analysis of the values, ratings and trends for the indicators is indicative of the necessity of a major thrust to be laid on the implementation of measures of SDG6 in India.

For a better appreciation of the performance of India, the SDG 6 Index Scores of the top-ranking five countries may be viewed in light of that of India, as given in table 4.2. A comparison of India's SDG 6 Index Score of only 58.1 with the corresponding scores of the five top-ranking countries (Fourth column of the table) clearly reflects the poor performance, thereby warranting strong actions on the part of all the stakeholders in our country on general and the NITI Aayog in particular. The reasons for such a poor SDG 6 index score of only 58.1 against the corresponding score of as high as 95.1 (Table 4,2—fourth column)) may possibly be attributed to the non-availability of data/information for the last two indicators, as given in table 4.1. The specific reason(s) for this situation could not be ascertained at this end. A deeper look into this situation obviously suggests an aspect for study on the parts of engineers and administrators involved or concerned.

Rank	Country	Comp. Score	SDG6 Ind. Sc.	SDG7 Ind. Sc.	SDG9 Ind. Sc.	SDG11 Ind. Sc.
1	Finland	86.8	94.3	93	96	91.2
2	Sweden	86	95.1	98	97.6	90.4
3	Denmark	85.7	90.7	87.7	97	93
4	Germany	83.4	88.4	77.2	95.8	90.1
5	Austria	82.3	92.2	86	97	92.5
112	India	63.4	58.1	66.2	51	50

Table 4.2: SDG COMP. Index Score, Individual Index Score for SDG6, SDG7, SDG9 and SDG11 for the Top Ranking Five Countries and India
(Prepared by Author on the Basis of Data given in the report[80])

<u>4.3.4. Achievement of the States of NER in SDG 6 in Indian Perspective</u>

At this stage, an attempt has been made to critically look into the achievement of SDG 6 in different states of North Eastern Region (NER). The Baseline Report of NITI Aayog[81] gives a clear picture in this respect. The NER having 8 percent of India's land, 3.77 percent of its population and 5300 km of international border is the gateway to South-East Asia. Therefore, the development of this region is strategically important in general and with respect to the achievement of the targets of SDGs in particular. The first edition of NER Districts SDG Index Report and Dashboard[82] was published by NITI Aayog and the Ministry of Development of North Eastern Region (M/DoNER) in August 2021. While launching this Report, the Vice Chairman of NITI Aayog stated – *"The North Eastern Region District SDG Index is an important milestone in our SDG journey aimed at leaving no one behind and will strengthen SDG localization by putting the districts, especially in our 8 Northern States, at the forefront of SDG adoption, implementation and monitoring."* The development of the District SDG Index involved six steps[81], which are:

- *Step 1* – NER SDG Conclave 2020 and conceptualization,
- *Step 2* – Draft NER SDG Indicators and district-wise data availability,
- *Step 3* – NER consultation on indicators, methodology and computation,
- *Step 4* – Inputs from States and Districts,
- *Step 5* – Computation of index results and Dashboard development and
- *Step 6* – Launch the Dashboard and results.

The engineers have a specific role to play in step 3 and step 4 (to be discussed at a later stage).

The meaning of "SDG localization" has to be ethically and technically understood in the truest sense of the term. It is the engineer who is expected to play an effective role in the creation of 'vision/strategy documents', which, in fact, forms the first step in the process of developing a region that includes all its states and is comprised of different districts. It is in this context that the creation of the NER Dashboard for the SDG Index has truly been a 'milestone'. As stated in the report[81], *"The index offers insights into the social, economic, and environmental status of the region and the districts in their march towards achieving the SDGs."*

The data on the specified indicators on each target district-wise were collected for 120 districts of the region, and then the composite score in the range of 0 to 100 was computed on the basis of the methodology, as defined in the report [81] for each district state-wise. The districts have been categorized as: (a) Achiever (score–100), (b) Front Runner (score 65–99), (c) Performer (score 50–64) and (d) Aspirant (0–49). Table 4.3, given below, shows the performance of the districts stage-wise on SDG 6, including SDG 6 Index scores of the NER states.

NER States	SDG 6 Index Score*	Total Districts	Dist. covered	Aspirant Dist.	Performer Dist.	Front Runner Dist.	Achiever Dist.	Remarks
Arunachal Pradesh	67	25	all covered	Nil	12	13	Nil	all dist. covered
Assam	64	33	27	Nil	4	23	Nil	6 dist. to be covered
Manipur	87	16	9	Nil	1	8	Nil	7 dist. To be covered
Meghalaya	75	11	11	Nil	10	1	Nil	all dist. covered
Mizoram	85	11	8	Nil	1	7	Nil	3 dist. to be covered
Nagaland	87	12	11	Nil	11	Nil	Nil	1 dist. to be covered
Sikkim	89	4	all covered	Nil	Nil	4	Nil	all dist. covered
Tripura	82	8	all covered	Nil	Nil	8	Nil	all dist. covered

**Based on NITI Aayog's Report[78]; Other data of districts are based on NITI Aayog's Report[81].*

Table 4.3: *SDG 6 Index Scores of NER States and Districts' Performance State-Wise Prepared by Author on the Basis of Data of NITI Aayog[78, 81]*

As per report[78], India's SDG 6 Index Score is 83, which is appreciable. Against this position of India, the performance of Sikkim, Nagaland, Manipur, Mizoram and Tripura on this goal has also been appreciable, as evidenced by the 2nd column of the table. However, the performance of the other three states (Arunachal Pradesh, Assam and Meghalaya) has been below the composite performance of India on the SDGs, with the index score of Assam being the lowest at 64. A deeper look at table 4.3 reflects the fact that all the districts are fully covered in four states: Arunachal Pradesh, Meghalaya, Sikkim, and Tripura. On the other hand, the number of districts yet to be covered in the computation of SDG 6 index scores is shown in the last column of table 4.3. This is an area warranting the attention of those involved in the implementation of SDG 6 in these districts. The development scenario with respect to the implementation of SDG 6 targets district-wise, as indicated by the table, is not uniform in all the states of the region. Only in the case of two states (Sikkim and Tripura), the performance is uniform, and the achievement is in the Front Runner category (65–99). Arunachal Pradesh and Meghalaya have covered all the districts (100%), with the performance being non-uniform. In the case of Arunachal Pradesh, 52% of the districts come under the front-runner category (65–99), and the remaining 48% come under the performer category (50–64). On the other hand, in the case of Meghalaya, only 9.09% of districts come under the front-runner category, and the remaining 90.91% come under the performer category. All the other four states have not covered all the districts, and at the same time, the performance has also been non-uniform in the covered districts. The percentage of uncovered districts has been: 43.75% in Manipur, 27.27% in Mizoram, 18.18% in Assam and 8.35% in Nagaland. This situation is likely to change with the release of the next edition of the SDG Index Report by NITI Aayog. This is an important area requiring immediate attention from the implementing agencies (mostly engineers) of the states concerned.

4.3.5. Performance of the Capital Cities of NER

At this stage, an attempt has been made to look into the present position of the performance of NER in SDG 6 in the urban areas. The NITI Aayog developed the SDG Urban Index and Dashboard[83] with the objective of making a brief analysis of the extent of SDG performance for the urban areas of India. This has been the latest addition, following the monitoring of the progress of SDGs at national, state, and district levels. This dashboard has considered 56 urban units (under ULBs) of India, including all the capital cities of the NER. The Index Framework for these urban units consists of 77 indicators covering 15 SDGs, excluding SDG 14 and SDG 17. Table 4.4 gives the general view of the performance of all the capital cities of NER.

Capital cities of NER (Col.1)	SDG Urban Index Score (Col. 2)	Rank in India (Col.3)	Performance Category* (Col.4)	Eight top-ranking cities of India with rank and SDG Index Score** (Col.5)
Aizwal (Mizoram)	69.07	13	Front Runner	Shimla (1, 75.50)
Shillong (Meghalaya)	68.29	17	Front Runner	Coimbatore (2, 73.29
Gangtok (Sikkim)	65	31	Front Runner	Chandigarh (3, 72.36)
Agartala (Tripura)	64.79	32	Performer	Tiruvanantapuram 3, 72.36)
Imphal (Manipur)	59.93	43	Performer	Kochi (5, 72.29)
Kohima (Nagaland)	58.07	50	Performer	Panaji (6, 71.86)
Guwahati (Assam)	55.79	53	Performer	Pune (7, 71.21)
Itanagar (Ar. Pradesh)	55.29	54	Performer	Tiruchirapalli (8, 70.00)

*Front Runner (65—99), Performer (50—64) and Aspirant (0—49). **The first figure within bracket indicates the all-India rank and the second one represents the SDG Urban Index Score.

Table 4.4: SDG Index Scores, All India Rank & Performance Category for the Capital Cities of NER (Prepared by Author Based on Data of Dashboard[83])

As indicated by table 4.4, the SDG urban index for each of the capital cities of the states of NER is not encouraging. Only for Aizawl (MZ) and Shillong (ML), the urban SDG Indices *(Aizawl – 69.07 and Shillong – 68.29, as in Column 2)* are more than the corresponding state's SDG Index (MZ – 68 and ML – 60), as stated earlier. For all the remaining capital cities of NER, the urban SDG Indices are less than the corresponding state's SDG Index (as suggested by a comparison of column 2 of table 4.4 and column 2 of table 4.5). As indicated by column 3 of table 4.4, Aizawl and Shillong have performed well with respect to the SDG Urban Index, holding all India ranks of 13 and 17, respectively. However, the performance of the other six cities has not been good, as evidenced by the all-India ranks held by them in all the SDGs, with the lowest ranks in NER being held by Guwahati (53) and Itanagar (54). It is disappointing to note that Guwahati and Itanagar are two of the five worst-performing cities among the 56 capital cities of India with respect to the Urban SDG Index. Since the aspects of SDG 6 are of primary concern at this stage of the discussion, an attempt has been made to look into the performance of these urban areas of NER with respect to this goal (SDG 6). Table 4.5 has been prepared on the basis of data given in NITI Aayog's Report[83].

Capital Cities of NER* (Col.1)	State's SDG Index** Col.2)	SDG 6 Urban Index (Col.3)	All India Rank (Col.4)	Performance Category*** (Col.5)
Gangtok (SK)	71	72	32	Front Runner
Imphal (MN)	64	66	42	Front Runner
Kohima (NL)	61	66	42	Front Runner
Itanagar (AR)	60	65	44	Front Runner
Shillong (ML)	60	65	44	Front Runner
Agartola (TR)	65	64	48	Performer
Guwahati (AS)	57	62	49	Performer
Aizwal (MZ)	68	57	52	Performer

*State' name in short-form indicated within bracket, **Data from Report[78]. ***Front Runner (65—99), Performer (50—64).

Table 4.5: SDG 6 Urban Index for the Capital Cities of NER
(Prepared by Author on the basis of Data of Reports[78, 83])

Out of 56 capital cities considered by NITI Aayog[83] for computation of the SDG 6 urban Index in India, the ranks held by the capital cities of NER are those indicated in table 4.5 (column 4). The ranks so held are indicative of the poor performance of NER capital cities, particularly in view of the SDG 6 India Index of 83 (as stated earlier). For all the capital cities of NER, the performance with respect to SDG 6 has been below the SDG 6 India Index of 83, suggesting thereby a tremendous scope for contribution by the engineers of NER associated with the formulation, monitoring and evaluation of different schemes covering the targets of SDG 6. The main objective of the development of the urban SDG index has been to localize the strengths and gaps of Urban Local Bodies (ULBs) in the implementation of different projects relating to the sustainable development of urban areas. Therefore, the urban indices (both the composite SDG Indices and SDG 6 Indices) of capital cities of NER point to the urgent need for a critical review of the present position by the engineers engaged in different ULBs of NER for increasing the pace of progress towards achieving the SDG targets. The major issues relate to salient aspects of project management, which broadly include formulation and implementation of different projects with due control of quality and timely completion (thereby avoiding cost-over-run). There are many examples of poor quality in implementation and cost overruns that are accountable for the excessive time unduly taken for completion. In these activities, the major role is obviously played by our engineers. It is truly in this context that the engineers, in general, and engineers of NER, in particular, are expected to rise to the occasion and play an effective role in raising the present level of performance with respect to SDGs in general and SDG 6 in particular. In this context, the recent bursting of a water distribution pipeline in Guwahati City, as shown in figure 4.3, may be referred to. This type of failure is avoidable in view of modern-day technology. It is now a recognized fact that engineers have to play their role under different pressures and be accountable for the degradation of ethical values in society in general.

Image 4.1: Photo [159] Showing the Recent Bursting of Water Distribution- Pipe-Line in Guwahati City
Source:
https://www.google.com/search?vsrid=CLKRga2B3Jz6OBACGAEiJDc1ZDUzMzA0LTljN WUtNGVmMi05NjA3LTVhNmIwMDZhZWIyYw&gsessionid=56JVeGGvmM0ttFpJfxwrbJF HMHC0dMeDzGr081JiTxs556Kq

The excerpt taken from UN's Report[11], which appears in image 1.2 (of chapter 1), corroborates the contention of lack of ethical values in developmental activities.

The water crisis in cities like Guwahati has been a known one despite the fact that the sources of surface water are abundantly available. Against this situation, many households in this city (Guwahati) are dependent on groundwater drawn through deep tube wells installed at their own cost, leading to very high unit costs. This is, indeed, an area in which the policy-makers and engineers associated with the ULBs have to do a lot in light of the absolute necessity of speeding up the progress of the projects of SDG 6 in urban areas, as reflected by the analysis presented above. The indicators for SDG 6 in urban areas, adopted by NITI Aayog[83] for computation of urban index are:

- Indicator 1: Percentage of sewage treatment plant capacity utilized out of installed capacity/ percent,
- Indicator 2: Coverage of stormwater coverage network/(km x100),
- Indicator 3: Percentage of urban households with excess to improved sanitation facilities/percent,
- Indicator 4: Average quantity of water supplied in the city/ 1pcd,
- Indicator 5: Percentage of schools with separate toilets for girls/percent and
- Indicator 6: Percentage of the population with an improved source of drinking water/percent.

The scores obtained by the eight capital cities on these indicators are given in table 4.6 below.

Capital; Cities of NER (Col. 1)	Indicator 1 (100)* (Col. 2)	Indicator 2 (50.79)* (Col. 3)	Indicator 3 (100)* (Col. 4)	Indicator 4 (135)* (Col. 5)	Indicator 5 (100)* (Col. 6)	Indicator 6 (100)* (Col.7)
Agartola (TR)	18.75	0.5	95.67	135	92.41	98.22
Aizwal(MZ)	0	0	99.36	78	98.88	
Gangtok(SK)	78.89	0	99.01	80	100	
Guwahati(AS)			96.66	20.36	90.99	82.57
Imphal(MN)			93.59	116.72	93.41	50
Itanagar(AR)			92.59	2.5	95.9	9
Kohima(NL)			98.15	15.87	100	81
Shillong(ML)		0	97.41	90	95.92	87.44

*Set targets for individual indicator

Table 4.6:   *Index Scores Obtained by Cities of NER on Indicators of SDG 6 for Urban Area (Prepared by Author on the basis of Data of the Report[83])*

An indicator-wise analysis of this table (as presented below) leads to the volume of scopes for immediate actions to be pursued by planners, engineers and policy-makers of ULBs of urban areas and also by researchers of different technical institutes (the budding engineers at the levels of different degrees (under-graduate and post-graduate including PhD)).

As reflected in table 4.6, there is no sewage treatment plant (Indicator 1) installed in six cities (including Guwahati) of NER. There are some in Agartala (TR) with a score of 18.75 and Gangtok (SK) with a score of 78.89 (column 2). Guwahati is the largest of all the cities in NER, and it has no data on Indicator 1 (Table 4.6—Column 2). For a city like Guwahati, the time has been overdue for *'hybrid and Off-site Systems'*, which *'require provisions for transporting wastewater from the toilet via a system of sewers to the treatment facility'*, as recommended in the Guide84 of Government of India. On the other hand, even in the case of Indicator 2, the performance of all the cities of NER is almost nil. However, the performance of all the cities in the case of Indicator 3 (column 4) is very good. The performance of two cities, namely Guwahati and Itanagar, with respect to Indicator 4 (the most important indicator of supply of drinking water), is extremely poor, with the average supply achieved till 2020-21 being 20.36 and 2.5, respectively, against the average target of 135 pcd. Against this situation, the achievement with respect to Indicators 5 and 6 has been highly appreciable for all the cities (the last two columns of table 4.6). In all the cities of NER, as clearly indicated by Indicators 1 and 2 (second and third columns of table 4.6), the problems of sewage disposal, drainage, etc., are apparent. This is an area requiring the attention of our engineers associated with the ULBs with due regard to the broad guidelines given by the Government of India[84] of Government of India. On the other hand, even in the case of Indicator 2, the performance of all the cities of NER is almost nil. However, the performance of all the cities in the case of Indicator 3 (column 4) is very good. The performance of two cities, namely Guwahati and Itanagar, with respect to Indicator 4 (the most important indicator of supply of drinking water), is extremely poor, with the average supply achieved till 2020-21 being 20.36 and 2.5, respectively, against the average target of 135 pcd. Against this situation, the achievement with respect to Indicators 5 and 6 has been highly appreciable for all the cities (the last two columns of table 4.6). In all the cities of NER, as clearly indicated by Indicators 1 and 2 (second and third columns of table 4.6), the problems of sewage disposal, drainage, etc., are apparent. This is an area requiring the attention of our engineers associated with the ULBs with due regard to the broad guidelines given by the Government of India[84]. The guidelines given do cover a wide area related to sanitation and hygiene aspects. The problems faced today in our urban areas (particularly those of NER) are the creation of a combination of many factors, the salient of which are the non-enforcement of the existing laws of ULBs and the lack of the adoption of the appropriate technology under variable situations. It is in this context that the engineers and policy-makers concerned have to play their expected role in the formulation and implementation of sanitation projects by giving due respect to the appropriate technology, as set by the Government of India[84].

*Image 4.2: A Photo Showing the Dumping of Solid Wastes in a
Particular Location of Guwahati City*
Source: Photo taken by the author in June 2024

4.3.6. Overall Scenario of NER in SDG 6

Coming to the end of the discussion on the present status of SDG 6 in NER, let us view the overall scenario of SDG 6, as indicated by the coloured map *(Taken from the Baseline Report[81])* of NER, given in figure 4.6 below:

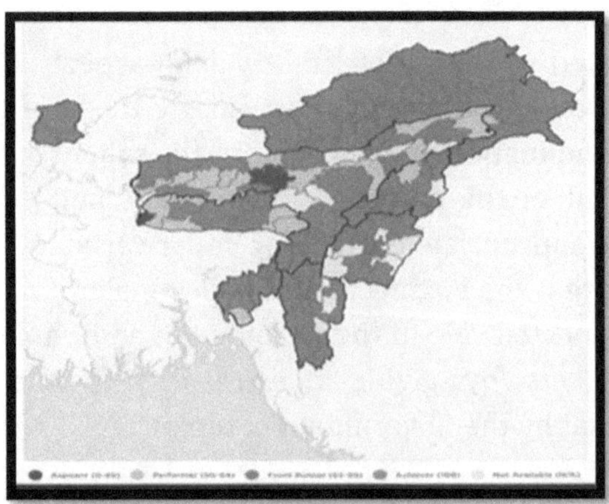

Image 4.3: MAP[81] of NER Showing Performance of the States of NER on SDG 6

The map of figure 4.6 clearly localises the thrust area to increase the pace of progress (the areas marked as yellow and red). This aspect may be better appreciated on a critical look at table 4.7, given below. This table shows the state-wise performance of each of the eight indicators adopted for the computation of the SDG 6 index. The eight indicators are:

- Indicator 6.1(a): The percentage of the rural population getting safe and adequate drinking water within premises through Pipe Water Supply (PWS),
- Indicator 6.1(b): The percentage of the rural population having improved sources of drinking water,
- Indicator 6.2(a): The percentage of individual household toilets constructed against target (SBM(G)),
- Indicator 6.2(b): The percentage of districts verified to be ODF (SBM(G)),
- Indicator 6.2(c): The percentage of schools with separate toilets for girls,
- Indicator 6.3: The percentage of industries (17 categories of highly polluting industries/grossly polluting industries/red category of industries) complying with wastewater treatment as per CPCB norms,
- Indicator 6.4: The percentage of groundwater withdrawal against availability and

- Indicator 6.6: The percentage of blocks/*mandals*/*talukas* over-exploited.

The data given in this table have been taken from the relevant tables for all states/UTs of India in the Dashboard of NITI Aayog[84].

States of NER* Col. 1	Ind. 6.1(a) Col. 2	Ind. 6.1(b) Col. 3	Ind. 6.2(a) Col. 4	Ind. 6.2(b) Col. 5	Ind. 6.2(c) Col. 6	Ind. 6.3 Col. 7	Ind. 6.4 Col. 8	Ind. 6.5 Col. 9
Arunachal Prad.(67)	34.13	92.64	100	100	70.12	70.89	0.37	0
Assam(64)	25.7	74.72	100	100	75.3	90.02	11.25	0
Manipur(87)	69.55	100	100	100	77.84	100	2.56	0
Meghalaya(75)	23.49	100	100	100	67.98	99.38	2.44	0
Mizoram(85)	46.17	100	100	100	85.48	97.14	5.26	0
Nagaland(87)	0.14	100	100	100	90.33	100	1.01	0
Sikkim(89)	37.42	100	100	100	99.34	96.77	0.06	0
Tripura(82)	63.05	84.84	100	100	88.18	100	8.06	0

The figures within bracket indicate the states' index on SDG 6

Table 4.7: Performance of the States of NER on the Indicators of SDG6 (Prepared by author on the basis of data given in the Dashboard[84])

As indicated by table 4.7 (column 2), all the states of NER have got to speed up the pace of progress on indicator 6.1 (a). Secondly, the state of Assam has to pay more attention to indicator 6.1(b) as well (as reflected by Column 3 of the table). The most appreciable aspect is the performance of all the states of NER on indicators 6.2(a) and 6.2(b) (the performance being 100 for all), as reflected by columns 4 and 5 of the table. On the other hand, the first four states of column 1 of the table have to increase the pace of progress with respect to indicator 6.2(c). Similarly, Arunachal Pradesh has to increase the pace of progress on indicator 6.3. The district-wise performance on each of the indicators of SDG-6 for each state of NER is available in the Dashboard[81]. A look at those data enables one to derive a localised view of the districts requiring immediate attention.

A lot of work has been done in pursuit of achieving the targets set for SDG 6, as evident from the discussion presented above. Our engineers involved in these works would possibly be in a position to identify strengths and gaps reflected through this discussion. This discussion, however, does not cover a very important aspect, nor has it been covered in the reports and other literature referred to herein. This aspect is the quality of the works already executed under SDG 6. This aspect is very important in the sense that it is the quality of execution and maintenance that eventually ensures the true spirit of sustainability in terms of serviceability and durability. It is truly in this context that there is a tremendous scope for research and studies to be directed towards the evaluation of the quality of the work (both execution and maintenance) completed. For example, the case of the construction of toilets constructed with the objective of making all areas 'Open Defecation Free (ODF)' may be taken. All these toilets have to be serviceable and durable with respect to sanitation and hygiene, and the basic requirement for this is obviously the availability of adequate water. These aspects need to be studied in the form of projects to be undertaken by our engineers particularly the budding and the fresh ones *(as stated earlier).*

4.4. SDG 7

Affordable and Clean Energy (Ensure access to affordable, reliable, sustainable and modern energy for all).

<u>4.4.1. Targets</u>

The following are the targets set for this SDG:

- By 2030, universal access to affordable, reliable and modern energy services has to be ensured.
- By 2030, make sure the share of renewable energy in the global energy mix increases substantially.
- By 2030, make sure the global rate of improvement in energy efficiency doubles.
- 7.a – By 2030, international cooperation should be enhanced to facilitate energy research and technology, including renewable energy, energy efficiency, and advanced and cleaner fossil-fuel technology, and investment in energy infrastructure and clean energy technology should be promoted.
- 7.b – By 2030, infrastructure should be expanded, and there should be an upgrade in technology for supplying modern and sustainable energy services for all in developing countries, in particular, least developed countries, small island developing states, and landlocked developing countries, in accordance with their respective support programs.

4.4.2. Global Position of Affordable and Clean Energy (SDG 7)

The Sustainable Development Goals Report 2023 of the United Nations[76] observed in a global perspective (In its Visual Summary) the following with respect to the achievement of the targets of SDG 7, mentioned above till 2022.

- **Observation 1**: 675 million people in the world still live in the dark (as of 2021). 4 in 5 of them are in Sub-Saharan Africa.

- **Observation 2:** If the current trends continue, 1 in 4 people in the world will still use unsafe and inefficient cooking systems by 2030.

- **Observation 3:** Modern renewables power is 28.2% of electricity but remains low in heating (only 10.4%) and transport (only 4%) (as of 2020).

- **Observation 4:** The energy efficiency improvement rate has been 1.4% during 2015—2020 against the required rate of 3.4% during 2020—2030. The rate needs to be doubled to meet the target.

- **Observation 5:** International public finance for clean energy for developing countries continues to decline from $26.4 billion in 2017 to $10.8 billion in 2021.

Having seen the world scenario with respect to SDG 7, as reflected by the UN's observations noted above, the necessity of making an attempt to critically look into the position of India, in general, and the north-eastern region, in particular, has been strongly felt.

4.4.3. India's Position of SDG 7 with Respect to Global Perspective

India's SDG 7 Index[77] has been 66.2, as well-reflected in figure 4.1. It may be noted that the SDG 7 India index (66.2) has been higher than its composite SDG Index of 63.4 as of 2022[77]. The 2023 Dashboards[77,80] show *Levels and Trends* of SDG 7 under different indicators. The performance of India in each of the indicators of this SDG is shown in table 4.8.

SDG Ind.No.	Indicator	Reference	Source*	Description	Value	Rating	Trend
7.1.1	Population with access to electricity (%)	2020	,IEA, IRENA, UNSD, WB, WHO	The percentage of the population who has access to electricity	99	●	↑
7.1.2 (7a)	Population with access to clean fuels and technology for cooking (%)	2020	WHO	The percentage of population primarily using clean fuels and technologies for cooking (%). Under WHO guidelines, kerosene is excluded from clean cooking fuels.	67.9	◔	↑
7.2	CO_2 emmissions from fuel combustion per total electricity output (MtCO$_2$/Twh)	2019	IEA	A measure of the carbon intensity of energy production, calculated by dividing CO_2 emmissions from the combustion of fuel by electricity output. The data are reported in Megatonnes per billion kilowatt hours.	1.5	●	◢
7.2.1	Renewable energy share in total final energy consumption (%)	2019	IEA, IRENA, UNSD, WB, WHO	The share of renewable energy in the total final energy consumption. Renewable energy includes hydro, solid biofuels, liquid biofuels, biomass, modern biomass, wind, solar, geothermal, tide/wave/oceans and renewable municipal waste. It does not include traditional biomass-----local solid biomass resources (e.g. wood, charcoal, dung, agricultural residues) used in low-income households that do not have access to modern cooking fuels or technologies.	15.9	●	→

*IEA---International Energy Agency, IRENA---International Renewable Energy Agency, UNSD—United States Statistics Division, WB---World Bank, WHO---World Health Organization

● SDG Achievement   ● Major challenges remain   ● Significant challenges remain   ◔ Challenges remain

↑ On track | Decreasing   → Stagnating   ◢ Moderately improving

Table 4.8: Performance of India on Indicators of SDG 7
(Prepared by Author on the Basis of Data Given In Dashboard[77, 80])

As reflected by the SDG Indicator No. 7.1.1 (first row of table 4.8), the achievement on *'access to electricity'* has been excellent with 99% (Column under Value)—rating and trend being *'SDG Achievement'* and *'on track,'* respectively. However, in all other indicators, there exist challenges of the order, as indicated symbolically in the table (including trends). A comparison of India's SDG 7 Index Score of 66.2 with the corresponding scores of the five top-ranking countries[80] (Fifth column of table 4.2) clearly reflects the poor performance, thereby warranting strong actions on the part of all the stakeholders in our country on the general and the NITI Aayog in particular.

<u>4.4.4. Achievement of the States of NER in SDG 7 in Indian Perspective</u>
The position of the states of NER with respect to the achievement of SDG 7 is given in table 4.9 (prepared on the basis of data given in NITI

Aayog's reports[78, 81]. As per report[78], India's SDG 7 Index Score is 92.02 (as of 2020), which is an appreciable one. However, as per UN's Report[80], India's SDG 7 Index Score as of 2022 is 66.2 (Table 4.2— Fifth Column). The reasons for this huge difference may possibly be attributed to the fact that NITI Aayog has computed the Index Score for SDG 7 on the basis of only two indicators *(as stated below for 2020)* against four indicators (table 4.8) considered by the UN in 2022[80]. For a reasonable analysis, the performance of the states of NER for SDG 7, the data of 2020, as given by NITI Aayog[78, 81] have been taken into account.

The two indicators of SDG 7, as considered by NITI Aayog[81] are:

- Indicator 1: *Percentage of LPG + PNG connections against the number of households* and

- Indicator 2: *Percentage of households electrified.*

A comparison of these two indicators with those considered by the UN, as given in table 4.8, reflects the fact that NITI Aayog[81] has excluded the last two indicators (7.2 & 7.2.1, first column of table 4.8) for reasons not understood by the author. Against this position of India, the performance of NER states has been analyzed. Sikkim and Mizoram, each having an index score of 100 on this goal, have been highly appreciable, as evidenced by the 2nd column of the table. However, the two states, namely Meghalaya, with a score of 50 and Nagaland, with a score of 69 (column 2 of the table), have been the lowest performers, far below India's index score of 92.02, thereby warranting immediate improvement measures on the parts of the stakeholders. The other four states of NER have shown appreciable progress.

A deeper look at table 4.9 reflects the fact that all the districts have been fully covered in four states: Arunachal Pradesh, Meghalaya, Sikkim, and Tripura. On the other hand, the number of districts yet to be covered in the computation of SDG 7 index score is shown in the last column of table 4.9. This is an area warranting the attention of those involved in the implementation of SDG 7 in these districts. The development scenario with respect to the implementation of SDG 7 targets district-wise, as indicated by the table, is not uniform in all the states of the region. Only in the case of Sikkim, all the districts have been covered, the performance is uniform, and the achievement is in the front-runner category (65–99). Arunachal Pradesh, Tripura, and Meghalaya have covered all the districts (100%), with the performance being non-uniform. In the case of Arunachal Pradesh, 28% of the districts are in the achiever category (100%), 52% of the districts come under the front-runner category (65-99), and the remaining districts are in the performer category (50-64) and the aspirant category (0-49), respectively. On the other hand, in the case of Meghalaya, only 27% of districts come under the front-runner category, and the remaining are either in the performer category or in the aspirant category. In the case of Tripura, 62.5% of the districts are in the front-runner category, and the remaining is in the performer category. All the other four states have not covered all the districts, and at the same time, the performance has also been non-uniform in the covered districts. The percentages of uncovered districts have been: 43.75% in Manipur, 27.27% in Mizoram, 18.18% in Assam and 8.33% in Nagaland. This situation is likely to change with the release of the next edition of the SDG Index Report by NITI Aayog. This is an important area requiring immediate attention from the implementing agencies (mostly engineers) of the states concerned.

NER States	SDG 7 Index Score*	Total Districts	Dist. covered	Aspirant Dist.	Performer Dist.	Front Runner Dist.	Achiever Dist.	Remarks
Arunachal Pradesh	85	25	all covered	4	1	13	7	all dist. covered
Assam	98	33	27	Nil	5	22	Nil	6 dist. to be covered
Manipur	96	16	9	Nil	2	7	Nil	7 dist. To be covered
Meghalaya	50	11	11	1	7	3	Nil	all dist. covered
Mizoram	100	11	8	Nil	0	8	Nil	3 dist. to be covered
Nagaland	69	12	11	3	5	3	Nil	1 dist. to be covered
Sikkim	100	4	all covered	Nil	Nil	4	Nil	all dist. covered
Tripura	83	8	all covered	Nil	3	5	Nil	all dist. covered

*Based on NITI Aayog's Report[78]. Other data of Districts
Are Based on NITI Aayog's Report[81]
Table 4.9: SDG 7 Index Scores of NER States and Districts' Performance State-Wise
(Prepared by author on the basis of data of NITI Aayog[78 & 81])

As stated earlier, the objective of launching SDG Index and Dashboard[81] for NER has been to facilitate the localizing of districts for paying more attention to speed up the pace of progress in a particular SDG. Therefore, the district-wise achievements of the

states need to be analyzed to find the districts of a state for taking
necessary measures to increase the pace of progress.

4.4.5. Performance of the Capital Cities of NER on SDG 7

The performance in all SDGs for the capital cities of NER has already
been analyzed under article 4.3.5 with reference to table 4.4. Now, the
performance of these cities with respect to SDG 7 is analyzed with
reference to table 4.10. The performance of Itanagar (AR) and Aizawl
(MZ) has been very good, with all-India Rank of 2 and 4 *(among 56
cities of India),* the SDG 7 Index Scores being 98 and 97 (column 3)
respectively. The scores for SDG 7 for these two cities have been
much higher than the corresponding state's scores (column 2 of the
table). On the other hand, the poorest performance has been achieved
by Imphal (MN) with the all-India Rank of 49 (column 4), the SDG 7
index score being only 53 (column 3), appreciably less than its state-
SDG 7 index score of 64 (column 2). For three cities: Shillong, Kohima
and Gangtok, the performances have been good—all falling in the
front-runner category, the all-India ranks being 17, 27 and 35
respectively. The remaining three states (Agartala, Guwahati and
Imphal) with lower all-India ranks (column 4 of the table) have got to
take measures to speed up the pace of progress. It is in this context
that those involved in the tasks of formulating, implementing, and
monitoring SDG7-aligned projects under ULBs have to look into the
reasons leading to the poor pace of progress. The possible reasons for
this situation (as could be conceived at this end with limited data)
may be possibly attributed to one or more of:

- The poorer section of citizens residing in congested locations
  such as slum areas being unreached by the benefits of the
  targets of SDG 7,
- The high density of urban population having reflection on the
  computation of percentages of target-achievements,
- Errors in data inputs, etc.

The ascertaining of the proper reasons thereof to be followed
by necessary improvement measures appears to be of absolute
necessity.

As in the case of states (as mentioned under article 4.4.4), only two SDG 7 indicators have been accounted for by NITI Aayog[83] against the four indicators considered by the UN (Table 4.8). The two indicators considered for the cities are the same as those mentioned earlier (under article 4.4.4). The inclusion of the last two indicators of table 4.8 in the computation of SDG 7 index scores for the cities will possibly substantially impact the urban indices shown in table 4.10.

Capital Cities of NER* (Col.1)	State's SDG Index**(col.2)	SDG 7 Urban Index (Col.3)	All India Rank Col.4)	Performance Category***(Col.5)
Itanagar (AR)	60	98	2	Front Runner
Aizwal (MZ)	68	97	4	Front Runner
Shillong (ML)	60	89	17	Front Runner
Kohima (NL)	61	83	27	Front Runner
Gangtok (SK)	71	79	35	Front Runner
Agartala (TR)	65	69	40	Front Runner
Guwahati (AS)	57	68	41	Front Runner
Imphal (MN)	64	53	49	Performer

*State' name in short-form indicated within bracket, **Data from Report[78]./***Front Runner (65— 99), Performer (50—64).

Table 4.10: SDG 7 Urban Index for the Capital Cities of NER (Prepared by the Author on the basis of Data of Reports[78, 83])

The other aspects, such as affordability, efficiency, etc., with respect to the use of energy in households and industries, as conceived in setting the targets of SDG 7, are not reflected well in the data provided through different reports. In addition, aspects such as the adoption of renewable energy, reduction of losses of energy in transmission and distribution, and reduction of losses in terms of theft of energy (to be duly assessed through energy auditing, etc.) need to be given due consideration by the engineers involved. There was a stage in which the transmission and distribution losses, including theft of power, went up to 24 percent of the power generated (in the case of some states).

While concluding the discussion on SDG 7, it may be stated that substantial progress has been made in the targets set for this goal (limited to G 7.1), as reflected by different SDG 7 Indices mentioned herein. However, the aspects of sustainability have to be weighed by looking into parameters such as the availability of power in terms of hours per day on an average over a month or a year in a particular village or a city or a district/ state, the affordability in terms of the unit cost of energy born by consumers, etc. It is in this context that the research or detailed study on these aspects needs to be taken up at different levels, as mentioned earlier.

4.4.6. Overall Scenario of NER in SDG 7

Coming to the end of the discussion on the present status of SDG 7 in NER, let us view the overall scenario of SDG 7, as indicated in table 4.9, given earlier. The total no. of districts[81] in the whole reason is 120, out of which 17 districts (last column of table 4.9) are yet to be covered in the computation of the SDG 7 index (as of 2020). The reason for non-inclusion is apparently the non-availability of the necessary data. The stakeholders concerned need to seriously look for the necessary corrective (or inclusive) measures. On the other hand, only 7 districts (column 8) have so far achieved the target, all these districts being in Arunachal Pradesh. The total no. of districts falling in the front-runner category is 65 (column 7 of the table), which is 54.2% of total districts, an obvious indication of an overall good performance. The remaining districts (8 in the aspirant category and 23 in the performer category) do require measures for increasing the pace of progress.

4.5. SDG 9

Industry, Innovation and Infrastructure (Build resilient infrastructure, promote inclusive and sustainable industrialization and foster innovation).

4.5.1. Targets

This goal has set eight targets as:
- (9.1) Develop quality, reliable, sustainable and resilient infrastructure, including regional and trans-border infrastructure, to support economic development and human well-being, with a focus on affordable and equitable access for all,
- (9.2) Promote inclusive and sustainable industrialization and, by 2030, significantly raise the industry's share of

employment and gross domestic product in line with national circumstances and double its share in the least developed countries,

- (9.3) Increase the access of small-scale industrial and other enterprises, particularly in developing countries, to financial services, including affordable credit and their integration into value chains and markets,
- (9.4) By 2030, upgrade infrastructure and retrofit infrastructures to make them sustainable, with increased resource-use efficiency and greater adoption of clean and environmentally sound technologies and industrial processes, with all countries taking action in accordance with their respective capabilities,
- (9.5) Enhance scientific research, and upgrade the technological capabilities of industrial sectors in all countries, particularly developing countries, including, by 2030, encouraging innovation and substantially increasing the number of research and development workers per 1 million people and public and private research development funding,
- (9a) Facilitate sustainable and resilient infrastructure development in developing countries through enhanced financial, technological and technical support to African countries, least developed countries, landlocked developing countries and small island developing states,
- (9b) Support domestic technology development, research and innovation in developing countries, including by ensuring a conducive policy environment for, inter alia, industrial diversification and value addition to commodities and
- (9c) Significantly increase access to information and communications technology and strive to provide universal and affordable access to the internet in the least developed countries by 2030.

<u>4.5.2. Global Position of Industry, Innovation and Infrastructure (SDG 9)</u>

The UN's Report[76], 2023 observed from a global perspective (In its

Visual Summary) the following with respect to the achievement of the targets of SDG 9, mentioned above, till 2022.

- *Observation 1:* Global manufacturing growth slowed down to the level of 3.3% in 2022 from that of 7.4% in 2021. The reasons identified for this slow-down are inflation, energy price shocks, supply disruption and global economic deceleration. The progress in the least developed countries *(LDCs: Africa—33, Asia—8, Caribbean—1 & Pacific—3, as of December 2023)* has been far from reaching the set target. However, medium-high and high-technology industries demonstrated strong growth in 2022 but with significant regional variations.

- *Observation 2:* The global carbon dioxide (CO_2) emissions from energy consumption and industrial processes grew to a record high of 36.8 billion metric tons.

- *Observation 3:* 95 percent of the world's population has access to mobile broadband. However, some areas are underserved.

Having seen the world scenario with respect to SDG 9, as reflected by the UN's observations noted above, the necessity of making an attempt to critically look into the position of India, in general, and the north-eastern region, in particular, has been strongly felt.

4.5.3. India's Position of SDG 9 with Respect to Global Perspective

India's SDG 9 Index[77] has been 51.0, as well-reflected in figure 4.1. It may be noted that the SDG 9 India index (51.0) has been lower than its composite SDG Index[77] of 63.4 as of 2022. The 2023 Dashboards[80] show *Ratings and Trends* of SDG 9 under different indicators. The performance of India in each of the 7 indicators of this SDG is shown in table 4.11. However, the UN's report[80] considered a total number of 11 indicators. Four indicators for which no data has been available for India are:

- Indicator 9.5.2: Researchers (per 1,000 population),
- Indicator 9.5: Triadic patent families filed (per million people),

- Indicator 9.5: Income (percentage points) and
- Indicator 4.3: Female share of graduates from STEM fields at the tertiary.

The reasons for the non-availability of data for these four indicators for India could not be ascertained from the author's end. In fact, the data for all the eleven indicators for the top-ranking countries, such as Finland, Denmark, etc., do exist in the report[80]. This situation indicates a lapse on the part of India's SDG management regarding the data compilation or data-furnishing *(relating to the above-stated four indicators).*

An analysis of table 4.11 indicates that only two indicators, appearing in the 5th and the 7th rows, have achieved good ratings (SDG achievement). However, the trends could not be ascertained at the UN's end due to the non-availability of information. On the other hand, challenges in variable measures (major challenges, significant changes and challenges—rating column) remain for all the remaining five indicators. However, the trends are on track for the indicators appearing in the 2nd and the 3rd rows of the table. The trend for the indicator in the 4th row shows the status of moderately improving, while that for indicator 9.5 (6th row) indicates stagnation. The trend for indicator 9.1.1 (1st row) has also not been assessed for want of information.

Indicator	Indicator No.	Reference	Source*	Descriptio	Value	Rating	Trend
Rural population with access to all-season roads (%)	9.1.1	2022	SDSN(2023), based on Workman, R & McPherson, K., TRL (2019)	Proportion of the rural population that lives within 2 km of an all-season road. An all-season road is one that is motorable throughout the year but may be temporarily unavailable during inclement weather	84.2	⦾	⦾
Population using the internet (%)	17.8.1	2021	ITU	The percentage of population who used the internet from any location in the last three months. Access could be via a fixed or mobile network	46.3	●	↑
Mobile broadband subscriptions (per 100 population)	9c.1 & 17.6.1	2021	ITU	The number of mobile broadband subscriptions per 100 population. Mobile broadband subscriptions refer to subscriptions to mobile cellular networks with access to data communications (e.g. the internet) at broadband speed, irrespective of device used to access the internet.	54.4	●	↑
Logistics Performance Index: Quality of trade and transport-related infrastructure (worst 1-5 best)	9	2018	World Bank	Survey-based assessment of the quality of trade and transport related infrastructure, e.g. ports, roads, railroads and information technology, on a scale from 1 (worst) to 5 (best)	2.9	⦾	╱
The Times Higher Education Universities Ranking: Average score of top 3 universitie (worst 0-100 best)		2022	Times Higher Education	The average of the top three universities in each country that are listed in the global top 1,000 universities in the world. For countries with at least one university on the list, only the score of the ranked university was taken into account. When a university score was missing in the Times Higher Education World University Ranking, an indicator from the Global Innovation Index on the top 3 universities in Quacquarelli Symonds (QS) University Ranking was used as a source as available.	45.7	●	⦾
Articles published in academic journals (per 1,000 population)	9.5	2021	Scimago Journal Rank	Number of citable documents published by a journal in the three previous years (selected year documents are excluded). Exclusively articles, reviews and conference papers are considered.	0.2	●	⟹
Expenditure on research and development (% of GDP)	9.5.1	2018	UNESCO	Gross domestic expenditure on scientific research and experimental development (R&D) expressed as a percentage of Gross Domestic Product (GDP). We assumed zero R&D expenditure for low-income countries that do not report any data.	0.7	●	⦾

*SDSN—Sustainable Development Solutions Network, ITU--- International Telecommunication Union, UNESCO--- United Nations Educational, Scientific and Cultural Organization.

Rating: ⦾ SDG Achievement ● Major Challenges ● Significant Challenges ⦾ Challenge remain

Trend: ↑ On track ⦾ Information unavailable ⟹ Stagnating ╱ Moderately improving

Table 4.11: *Performance of India on Indicators of SDG 9 (Prepared by Author on The Basis of Data Given in Dashboard[80])*

India's overall performance on SDG 9 may be better understood by a comparison of its index score with those of the corresponding scores of the five top-ranking countries[80] (6th column of table 4.2). The index score of only 51.0 for India on this goal has been appreciably less than those of the top-ranking countries, thereby showing the tremendous gap[80] existing as of 2022 in the formulation, implementation, monitoring and evaluation of the measures necessary for increasing the pace of progress (on SDG 9). It is in this context that the stakeholders, including the engineers involved have to contribute a lot towards the improvement of the situation.

4.5.4. Achievement of the States of NER in SDG 9 from Indian Perspective

The position of the states of NER on the achievement of SDG 9 is shown in table 4.12 (prepared on the basis of data given in NITI Aayog's reports[78, 81]. As per report[78], India's SDG 9 Index Score is 55 (as of 2020). The position of performance of the states of NER on SDG 9 is indicated by the Index scores[84], which are (in order of highest to lowest scores): Sikkim (52), Assam (39), Manipur (35), Tripura (35), Mizoram (32), Arunachal Pradesh (31), Nagaland (30) and Meghalaya (25). As evident from the scores (shown within the bracket in the 1st column of table 4.12), only Sikkim is in the performer category, and all the remaining seven states are in the aspirant category. Seven national-level indicators (covering four out of eight targets of this goal) were taken into account while computing the SDG 9 Index scores. These indicators are:

- Indicator A (G9.1): The percentage of the targeted habitations connected by all-weather roads under Pradhan Mantri Gram Sadak Yojana (PMGSY),
- Indicator B (G 9.1): Score as per Logistics Ease Across Different States (LEADS) report,
- Indicator C (G 9.2): The percentage share of GVA in manufacturing to total GVA (current prices),
- Indicator D (G 9.2): Manufacturing employment as a percentage of total employment,
- Indicator E (G 9.5): Innovation Score as per the India Innovation Index,
- Indicator F (G 9c): Number of mobile connections per 100 persons (mobile density) and
- Indicator G (G 9c): Number of internet connections per 100 population.

The performance of different states of NER on each of the above-noted indicators of SDG 9 is shown in table 4.12.

States*	Ind. A	Ind. B	Ind. C	Ind. D	Ind. E	Ind. F	Ind. G
Sikkim (52)	93.71	2.9	45.43	3.31	20.28	99.44	51.74
Assam (39)	94.38	3	12.25	10.55	16.38	67.51	41.57
Manipur (35)	89.26	2.42	2.42	12.11	22.78	72.97	52.34
Tripura (35)	95.87	2.95	3.31	6.38	12.84	75.78	52.34
Mizoram (32)	67.24	2.31	0.64	5.34	16.93	109.73	52.34
Arunachal Prad. (31)	81.75	2.77	3.2	2.05	14.9	84	57.34
Nagaland (30)	87.16	2.28	1.37	8.11	14.11	74.27	52.34
Meghalaya (25)	63.18	2.56	8.88	1.27	12.15	70.23	52.34
India (55)**	**97.65**	**3.18**	**16.1**	**12.07**	**85.39**	**84.38**	**55.41**
Targets set	*100*	*5*	*25*	*20*	*100*	*100*	*100*

**Figures within bracket indicate SDG 9 Index Scores for the individual states, **India's SDG 9 Index Scores are given for a direct comparison of the corresponding values of the states.*

Table 4.12: Performance of the States of NER on Indicators of SDG 9 (Prepared by Author on the basis of data given in the report[78, 81])

The performance of all the states except Meghalaya *(with a score of 63.18*, as shown in the *2nd column)* has been in the front-runner category (65-99) on Indicator A. However, India's index score (97.65) for the same indicator has been higher than those of all the states of NER. All the states' achievements on Indicator B (3rd column) have been around 50% of the set target of 5 (last row), with achievement being less than that of India. Similarly, the performance of all the states on Indicator C has been poor except for Sikkim, which has achieved an index score of 45.43 (column 4), appreciably more than the set target of 25. On the other hand, there exist significant gaps in the performance of Indicators D & E for all the states, as borne out by the scores shown in columns 5 and 6 of the table. The performance of all the states on Indicators F & G has been comparable to the corresponding India's scores, as evident from the data of the last two columns of the table. The impact of this goal on the country's GDP and employment scenario (particularly in the manufacturing sector) is understandable. The index score of only 55 as of 2020 (51.0 as of 2022[77]) indicates the urgency of measures to speed up the pace of progress at the national level. Against this situation in our country, a critical look at table 4.12 still reflects a poorer status with respect to indicator-wise performance on this goal by different states of NER, as briefly discussed above.

NER States*	Total Districts	Asp. Dist.**	Perf. Dist.**	FR Dist.**	Achr. Dist.**	Dist. Not Covered
Arunachal Prad. (23)	25	17	7	1	0	0
Assam (39)	33	0	0	27	0	6
Manipur (35)	16	0	2	7	0	7
Meghalaya (25)	11	5	4	2	0	0
Mizoram (32)	11	0	2	6	0	3
Nagaland (30)	12	6	5	0	0	1
Sikkim (52)	4	0	0	4	0	0
Tripura (35)	8	0	0	8	0	0

*The figures within bracket indicaet the SDG 9 Index Scores for the respective states[78, 41]. **Asp.-------Aspirant (0—49), Perf. ---Performer (50 ---64), FR---Front Runner (65—99) and Achr.---Achiever (100)

Table 4.13: SDG 9 Index Scores of NER Stares & Districts' Performance State-Wise (Prepared by author on the Basis of data of NITI Aayog[78, 81])

The index scores on SDG 9 for the districts shown in table 4.13 have been based on only four indicators (Index A, B, F & G). All the districts for these indicators have been covered in four states (AR, ML, SK, and TR), while some districts (as appearing in the last column of the table) are yet to be covered. However, the specific reasons for not covering them are not known. On the other hand, the performance of the states on this goal, as indicated by the figures within the bracket in the 1st column, has been poor for all the states except Sikkim, with a score of 52. The policy-makers and engineers involved need to identify the gaps, and thereafter, the appropriate measures need to be taken to improve the pace of progress at the district levels.

4.5.5. Performance of the Capital Cities of NER

At this stage, an attempt has been made to look into the status of performance on SDG 9 in the capital cities of NER on the basis of the data available in SDG Urban Index and Dashboard[84], NITI Aayog, 2021—22. As stated earlier, 56 urban cities in the country have been covered for the computation of the urban index. The position of the performance on SDG 9 in the capital cities of NER is shown in table 4.14.

Capital City*	Ind. 1**	Ind. 2**	Ind. 3**	Ind. 4**	Ind. 5**
Shillong (70, 4)	11	0.56	5.9	1.13	NA
Kohima (66, 9)	60	1.01	0	3.03	56.31
Imphal (60, 20)	8	1.93	0	8.69	100
Aizawl (58, 24)	23	0.34	0	2.73	100
Guwahati (48, 37)	21	0.83	0.29	1.45	4.65
Gaangtok (45, 41)	20	2.99	0	2.99	7.32
Agartala (40, 43)	39	0	0.23	1.5	46.38
Itanagar (34, 49)	35	0	0	1.68	NA
Targets	*80*	*0.5*	*1.93*	*1.44*	*100*

*The first figure within bracket indicates the SDG 9 Index Score for the respective state and the second one indicates its rank among the 56 cities of India, ** Index Score on Individual Indicator of SDG 9.*

Table 4.14: Performance of Capital Cities of NER on SDG 9
(Prepared by Author on the Basis of Data Given By NITI Aayog[83])

As clearly shown in table 4.14, the performance of all the capital cities of NER, except for Shillong and Kohima, is far behind that of Surat (Gujarat), which holds rank 1 with an SDG9 Index of 78. For further localization of gaps, the performance of each city on each of the 5 indicators considered for computation of the SDG9 index needs to be critically analyzed. The indicators considered are:

- Indicator 1: Data Maturity Assessment Framework Score,
- Indicator 2: Number of Start-ups promoted under Atal Innovation Mission per 1,00,000 population,
- Indicator 3: Number of Incubation Centre/Skill Development Centre per 1,00,000 population,
- Indicator 4: Number of Atal Tinkering Labs per 1,00,000 population and
- Indicator 5: Percentage value of smart city projects completed against tendered.

The scores on these indicators are given in table 4.14.

The strengths and gaps are well-indicated by the scores appearing under each indicator against the set targets (the last row of the table). The policy-makers and the engineers concerned need to pay attention to the areas warranting measures for improving the scores. The city of Guwahati, being the gateway to NER, in particular, and to South-East Asia, in general, has to be critically attended to — as an example, the case of Indicator 5 (which is apparently a measure of the progress of different projects under smart city mission) may be taken. As indicated by the last column of table 4.14, the performance appears to be extremely poor, the achievement being only 4.65 against the set target of 100. The PMU (Project Management Unit) concerned needs to take immediate measures for appreciable improvement. In fact, all cities need to identify the gaps, as reflected by the table, and take appropriate follow-up actions to increase the pace of progress. It may be recalled that the very purpose of the publication[82] has been to facilitate the localization of strengths and gaps in the implementation of SDG-aligned projects for achieving the targets. On the other hand, the performance of all the cities of NER on indicator 1, except for Kohima (60), has been extremely poor, the scores being less than 50% of the set target of 80 (column 2 of the table). Indicator 1 is very important in today's context of technological development. It is Data Maturity Assessment Framework (DMAF) and has been designed by Ministry of Housing and Urban Affairs[85] with the basic objective of helping the cities for self-evaluation. The poor performance of the cities on this indicator is obviously indicative of a significant gap with respect to the design of the framework for the respective cities in conformity with the guidelines[85] of MoHUA. Engineers have a tremendous role to play in this respect because we know the utility of data in today's context of sustainable development, and that too in developing a smart city in the true sense. This is an area in which research, study and discussion among policy-makers, citizens and engineers are of vital importance.

4.5.6. Overall Scenario of NER in SDG 9

Coming to the end of the discussion on the present status of SDG 9 in NER, the overall scenario of SDG 9, as indicated in table 4.13 given above, has not been appreciable. A comparison of this table with table 4.9 reflects the fact that the performance of the districts of all the states of NER on SDG 9 has been poorer than that in SDG 7. On the other hand, the number of districts yet to be covered (or included) is the same (17 nos.) for both SDG 7 and SDG 9 (as of 2020[81]). The reason for non-inclusion is apparently the non-availability of the necessary data. The stakeholders concerned need to seriously look for the necessary corrective (or inclusive) measures.

4.6. SDG 11

Sustainable Cities and Communities. (Make cities human settlements inclusive, safe and resilient).

<u>4.6.1. Targets</u>

The basic objective of this goal (SDG 11) has been to promote inclusive and sustainable urbanization. The broad meaning of making a city sustainable is the creation of career and business opportunities, safe and affordable housing and building resilient societies and economics. To achieve this objective, ten targets, as given below, have been set. These are:

- (11.1): By 2030, ensure access for all to adequate, safe and affordable housing and basic services and upgrade slumps,
- (11.2): By 2030, provide access to safe, affordable, accessible and sustainable transport systems for all, improving road safety, notably by expanding public transport, with special attention to the needs of those in vulnerable situations, women, children, persons with disabilities and older persons,
- (11.3): By 2030, enhance inclusive and sustainable urbanization and capacity for participatory, integrated and sustainable human settlement planning and management in all countries,
- (11.4): Strengthen efforts to protect and safeguard the world's cultural and natural heritage,
- (11.5): By 2030, significantly reduce the number of deaths and number of people affected and substantially decrease the direct economic losses relative to the global gross domestic product caused by disasters, including water-related disasters, with a focus on protecting the poor and people in vulnerable situations,
- (11.6): By 2030, reduce the adverse per capita environmental impact of cities by paying special attention to the quality and municipality and other waste management,
- (11.7): By 2030, provide universal access to safe, inclusive and accessible green and public spaces, in particular for

women and children, older persons and persons with disabilities,

- (11.a): Support positive economic, social and environmental links between urban, peri-urban and rural areas by strengthening national and regional development planning,
- (11.b): By 2030, substantially increase the number of cities and human settlements adopting and implementing integrated policies and plans towards inclusion, resource efficiency, mitigation and adaptation to climate change, resilience to disasters, and develop and implement, in line with the Sendai Framework for Disaster Risk Reduction 2015—2030, holistic disaster risk management at all levels,
- (11.c): Support least developed countries through financial and technical assistance in building sustainable and resilient buildings utilizing local materials.

4.6.2. Global Position of Sustainable Cities and Communities (SDG 11)

The UN's Report[76], 2023 observed from a global perspective (In its Visual Summary) the following with respect to the achievement of the targets of SDG 11:

Observations as of 2020 are:

- 1.1 billion people live in slums, and 2 billion more are expected in the next 30 years,
- One out of two urban residents has convenient access to public transport,
- Three out of four cities have less than 20% of their area dedicated to public spaces and streets *(much lower than the target of 45-59%).*
- Towns experience poorer air quality than cities in eastern and south-eastern Asia and
- In developing countries, one billion people lack access to all-weather roads.

Having seen the broad world scenario on SDG 11, an attempt has been made to analyze India's position on this goal.

4.6.3. India's Position of SDG 11 with Respect to Global Perspective

India's SDG 11 Index[77] has been 50.0, as well-reflected in figure 4.1. It has been less than its composite SDG Index of 63.4 as of 2022[77]. The 2023 Dashboards[80] show *Ratings and trends* of SDG 11 under different indicators. The performance of India in each of the 4 indicators is shown in table 4.15. However, the UN's report[80] considered a total of 6 indicators (all being shown in the table). The two indicators for which no data have been available for India are those appearing at the end of the table. Against this situation in India, all the values, ratings and trends do exist in the report[80] for the top-ranking countries like Finland, Denmark, etc. The reasons for the non-availability of data for these two indicators for India could not be ascertained from the author's end. This situation indicates a lapse on the part of India's SDG management with respect to data compilation or data furnishing *(relating to the above-stated 2 indicators)*. An analysis of table 4.15 indicates that only one indicator *(11.2.1—4th one in the table)* has achieved good ratings *(SDG achievement)*, the trend being on track (last column). On the other hand, major challenges *(rating column of the table)* do exist for all the remaining 3 indicators. The trends, as indicated in the table *(last column)*, are 'stagnating' for the 1st indicator (11.1.1) and 'decreasing' for both the 2nd and the 3rd indicators, as shown in the table.

India's overall performance on SDG 11 may be better understood by comparing its index score with those of the corresponding scores of the five top-ranking countries[80] (7th column of table 4.2). The index score of only 50.0 for India on this goal has been appreciably less than those of the top-ranking countries, thereby showing the tremendous gap existing as of 2022 in the formulation, implementation, monitoring and evaluation of the measures necessary for increasing the pace of progress (on SDG 11). It is in this context that the stakeholders, including the engineers involved, have to contribute a lot towards improving the situation.

Indicator	Ind. No	Reference	Source*	Descriptio	Value	Rating**	Trend**
Proportion of urban population living in slumps (%)	11.1.1	2020	UN Habitat	Population living in the slums is the proportion of the urban population living in slum households. A slum household is defined as a group of individuals living under the same roof lacking one or more of the following conditions: access to improved water, access to improved sanitation, sufficient living area, housing durability and security of tenure.	49	●	➡
concentration of particulate matter of less than 2.5 microns in diameter (PM 2.5) ((mg/m3)	11.6.2	2019	IHME	Air pollution measured as the population-weighted mean annual concentration of PM2.5 for the urban population in a country. PM2.5 is suspended particles measuring less than 2.5 micons in acrodynamic diameter, which are capable of penetrating deep into the respiratory tract and can cause severe health damage.	90.6	●	⬇
Access to improved water source, piped (% of urban population)	11.1	2020	WHO and UNICEF	The percentage of the urban population with access to drinking water piped on premises. An improved drinking water source is one that, by the source of its construction and when properly used, adequately protects the source from outside contamination, particlarly fecal matter.	65.9	●	⬇
Sanitation and public transport (%)	11.2.1	2022	Gallup	The percentage of the surveyed population that responded satisfied to the question in the city or area where you live, *Are you satisfied or dissatisfied with the public transportation system ?*	77	●	⬆
Population with rent overburden (%)	11.1	2019	OECD	Percentage of the population living in householdes where the total housing costs represent more than 40% of the disposable income	....	....	...
Proportion of population with access to points of internet within a 15 min walk (%)		2022	SDSN(2023) based on Nicolett i,L. et al	The percentage of the population in urban areas living within 15-minute walking distance from a point of interest (i.e. hospitals, schools, supermarkets, restaurants, etc.). Distance is established through pedestrian street network data and the percentage of population in the radius is estimated using guided population density.	.....	....	.....

*IHME---Institute of Health Metrics and Evaluation, OECD---Organisation for Economic Co-operation and Development (other terms are as defined earlier. **Symbols adopted for Ratings and Trends are as defined in Table 4.11*

Table 4.15: Performance of India on Indicators of SDG 11 (Prepared by author on the basis of data given in Dashboards[80])

4.6.4. Achievement of the States of NER in SDG 11 from Indian Perspective

The position of the states of NER on the achievement of SDG 11 is given in table 4.16 (prepared on the basis of data given in NITI Aayog's reports[78, 81]). As per report[78], India's SDG 11 Index Score is 79 (as of 2020). The position of the performance of the states of NER on SDG 11 is indicated by the Index scores[84], which are (in order of highest to lowest scores): Sikkim (85), Tripura (67), Manipur (65), Mizoram (61), Assam (55), Meghalaya (51), Nagaland (48) and Arunachal Pradesh (39). As evident from the scores (shown within the bracket in the 1st column of table 4.16), only Sikkim, Tripura and Manipur are in the front-runner category (65—99). Mizoram, Assam and Meghalaya are in the performer category (50—64). The remaining two states (Nagaland and Arunachal Pradesh) are in the aspirant category (0—49). Eight national-level indicators were taken into account while computing the SDG 11 Index scores. These indicators are:

- Indicator A (Target 11.6): The percentage of wards with 100% door-to-door waste collection (SBM(U)),
- Indicator B (Target 11.1): The percentage of individual household toilets constructed against target (SBM(U)),
- Indicator C (Target 11.6): The percentage of wards with 100% source segregation (SBM(U)),
- Indicator D (Target 11.1): The percentage of urban households living in *Katcha* houses,
- Indicator E (Target 11.6): Installed sewage treatment capacity as a percentage of sewage generated in urban areas,
- Indicator F (Target 11.1): The percentage of urban households with drainage facilities,
- Indicator G (Target 11.6): The percentage of MSW processed to the total MSW generated (SBM(U)) and
- Indicator H (Target 11.2): Deaths due to road accidents in urban areas *(per 1,00,000 population).*

These indicators cover only three targets out of ten targets set by the United Nations. The reasons thereof have been stated[80] as– *"These indicators have been selected based on the availability of data at the sub-national level and to ensure compatibility across States and UTs."* This position obviously implies that seven out of ten set targets have yet to be implemented in many of the states/UTs of the country. This situation is apparently a pointer to the possibility of the failure of many states/UTs to achieve all the set targets by 2030, warranting strong measures for increasing efforts manifold on the part of all those involved in the implementation of SDGs. The performance of different states of NER on each of the eight indicators of SDG 11 has been shown in table 4.16.

States*	Ind. A	Ind. B	Ind. C	Ind. D	Ind. E	Ind. F	Ind. G	Ind. H
Sikkim (85)	100	67	94.34	1.2	92.68	89.3	70.67	8.7
Tripura (67)	96.13	101	88.71	2.2	4.57	44.4	62.81	5.69
Manipur (65)	100	86	67.65	0.7	18	33.3	69.73	3.98
Mizoram (61)	100	18	87.12	1.3	9.8	52	80.08	5.09
Assam (55)	87.91	97	42.74	0.4	0.11	58.7	63.24	24.7
Meghalaya (51)	61.4	30	70.18	0	0	75.8	65.12	5.58
Nagaland (48)	63.25	68	32.48	0.7	0	59.5	67.87	1.14
Arunachal Prad. (39)	82.43	80	48.65	8.9	0	59.4	23.97	11.76
India (79)**	**96.17**	**105**	**78.08**	**0.8**	**38.86**	**87.6**	**68.05**	**12.2**
Targets set	*100*	*100*	*100*	*0*	*100*	*100*	*100*	*7.05*

**Figures within brackets indicate the SDG 11 Index Scores of the states of NER, **India's SDG 11 Index Scores are given for a direct comparison with the corresponding values of the individual states.*

Table 4.16: Performance of the States of NER on Indicators of SDG 11 (Prepared by author on the basis of data given in the report[78, 81])

The best performance among the states of NER has been shown by Sikkim on each of the indicators of this goal, as borne out by the index scores appearing in table 4.16 (1st row), the scores being appreciably close to the targets set (last row). Other seven states have performed non-uniformly on all the indicators. Tripura's performance on Indicator E has been very poor, with an index score of only 4.57, which is against India's score of 38.86. The same is the performance for the remaining six states on this indicator (Indicator E, 6th column). All the states have performed well on Indicators A & B, though the performance of Mizoram on Indicator B has been only 16 (3rd column). On the other hand, Assam, Nagaland and Arunachal Pradesh have been far behind with scores of 42.74, 32.48 and 48.65, respectively, on Indicator C (4th column), compared to India's score (78.08). All the states except Arunachal Pradesh have performed reasonably well on Indicator D. The performance of Arunachal Pradesh on this indicator has been 8.9 against the set target of zero (5th column). The performance on Indicator F of this goal has also not been satisfactory for all the states, excluding Sikkim and Meghalaya, having appreciable scores of 89.3 and 75.8, respectively, against India's achievement of 87.6 (7th column of the table). On the other hand, all the states, except for Arunachal Pradesh, have performed reasonably well on Indicator G against India's score of 68.05 (8th column). Arunachal Pradesh, with a poor score of only 23.97, needs to pay special attention to this indicator. The performance of Assam on

Indicator H *(deaths due to road accidents)* has been the poorest among the states of NER, with a high percent of deaths *(24.7 per 1,00,000 population, the last column of the table)* against India's average of 12.20. The best performance has been for Nagaland (only 1.14). The achievement of the other six states of the region has been appreciable, with death percentages being less than the set target of 7.05, except for Sikkim, with an index of 8.7, which is slightly in excess of the said target.

The analysis presented above clearly indicates the indicator-wise gaps requiring attention for appreciable improvement in the present level of performance of respective indicators. At this stage, an attempt is made to analyze the performance of SDG 11 in the capital cities of NER, particularly in view of the impact of the Goal (SDG 11) on the growth of GDP and employment.

4.6.5. Performance of the Capital Cities of NER on SDG 11

A gloomy picture with respect to the performance of the capital cities of NER on SDG 11 is evident in table 4.17 appearing below:

Capital Cities* (Col.1)	Rank** (Col.2)	Cities' Index Score (Col.3)	Ind. 1*** (Col.4)	Ind. 2*** (Col.5)	Ind. 3*** (Col.6)	Ind. 4*** (Col.7)
Agartola (67)	41	56	1430.27	8.25	44.02	74.7
Shillong (51)	47	50	1036.12	4.52	146.92	0
Aizawl (61)	49	49	1560.76	6.18	16.76	72.91
Gangtok (85)	51	47	1650.31	11.97	88.17	0
Guwahati (55)	52	43	1329	---	57.87	67.19
Itanagar (39)	54	39	1071.06	25.21	83.79	20
Kohima (48)	55	29	1591.89	---	26.69	49.94
Imphal (65)	56	26	1500.83	8.21	4.57	0
Targets set			*5360*	*6*	*100*	*100*

*Figures within bracket indicate SDG 11 Index for the corresponding state, **Ranks among the 56 cities considered for index computation, ***Scores computed on indicators, stated below*

Table 4.17: Performance of the Cities of NER on SDG 11
Including Scores on Each Indicator
(Prepared by Author on the basis of data given in the reports[78, 83])

The deplorable condition of the capital cities of NER on SDG 11 is clearly evidenced by the ranks held (column 2 of table 4.17). The composite scores of the states on this goal are indicated within the bracket in the first column of the table for a direct comparison of the index scores of the capital cities (column 3 of the table) on SDG 11. This comparison reveals the fact that the index scores (column 3) of all the capital cities, except for Itanagar, have been lower than those of the corresponding states on SDG 11. Only in the case of Itanagar, the level of achievement *(only 39, though poor in both the states and capital cities)* has been the same. Only two cities, Agartala and Shillong, are in the performer category (50—64), and all the remaining six cities are in the aspirant category (0—49). Positive measures are the utmost need of the hour. There are a number of reasons for this situation in NER. *(A detailed discussion on different aspects bearing on urbanization with specific reference to NER appears in Chapter 3).* A special reference to the City of Guwahati may be made at this stage since it is the major city in NER. Its rank is one of the lowest in the country (fourth lowest in the country) and 52nd among the 56 cities considered for computation of the SDG 11 Index score (as mentioned in Chapter 3). This position ought to be a matter of great concern for policy-makers, urban planners, engineers, builders, ULBs, etc. For a better appreciation of the situation of NER cities, the performance of the top-ranking five cities[83] on SDG 11 may be stated as Nashik (92.00), Surat (92.00), Chandigarh (90.00), Vadodara (89.00) and Ahmedabad (87.00).

The indicators[83] considered in computing the SDG 11 index score for the 56 cities of the country are:

- Indicator 1: Swachh Survekshan Score (Target 5360),
- Indicator 2: Death rate due to road traffic accidents per 1,00,000 population (Target 6),
- Indicator 3: The percentage of houses completed against sanctioned under PMAY (urban) (Target 100%) and
- Indicator 4: The percentage of Municipal Solid Waste (MSW) treated against MSW treated (Target 100%).

The indicator-wise performance of all the capital cities of NER on SDG 11 is given in table 4.17.

A critical look at table 4.17 leads to a number of gaps:

- All the capital cities of NER are far behind the target set for Indicator 1;

- In the case of Guwahati and Kohima, no score for Indicator 2 *(the important parameter relating to death rate due to road accidents)* is available. Although Shillong and Aizawl have an appreciable performance on this indicator, the remaining cities need to improve their performance on this indicator;

- Indicator 3 relates to the housing sector. The score has been computed by taking the sanctioned projects under PMAY (urban), implying that the funds required are available. Shillong has performed extremely well, with a score of 146.92, which is appreciably more than the set target of 100%. Gangtok and Itanagar have also performed well, with scores of 88.17 and 83.79, respectively. However, the performance on this indicator for all the remaining cities has been poor, with the city of Imphal being the poorest performer, with a score of only 4.57;

- Indicator 4 relates to solid waste management. As reflected by the last column of table 4.17, three cities, namely Gangtok, Imphal and Shillong, have a score of zero. This aspect needs to be taken up by the respective governments. The performance of Itanagar has also been very poor, with a score of only 20 against the set target of 100. The remaining five cities have performed well, though there is a need for further improvement.

4.7. Concluding Remarks

While concluding this chapter, two broad points may be briefly dealt with. Firstly, many of the important targets set by the United Nations have not been covered by indicators considered for the computation of corresponding SDG Indices by NITI Aayog. For example, Target 11.b under SDG 11 *(which is a very important target since it relates to many important aspects, including holistic risk management in urban areas, as included in Sendai Framework for Disaster Risk Reduction, 2015—2030)* has not been covered by the indicators considered for computation of urban SDG 11 index. The major reason for this has been, as stated by NITI Aayog, the compulsion to maintain compatibility among all the states in the computation of index scores since sub-national data-input agencies have not provided uniform data for indicators. This situation apparently indicates that many of the set-targets are yet to be taken up for implementation. This aspect needs to be appropriately looked into by policy-makers and implementing agencies in different states.

The second point relates to the 'design, monitoring and evaluation' of the SDG-aligned projects, on which the most important outcomes, such as *'level of achievement of project objectives, development effectiveness, efficiency, impact and sustainability'* depend. Apparently, the Government of India, Ministry of Statistics and Program Implementation, in relation to the SDG-aligned projects, have taken appreciable care by bringing out the Guidance on Monitoring Framework[86] for SDGs at the sub-national level. Apparently, all the states/UTs of the country have developed the said framework at respective sub-national levels. However, in view of gaps in the performance of the four SDGs (6,7,9 and11), as well reflected by the analysis presented in this chapter, it is strongly felt that there is an urgent need for strengthening the Monitoring Framework in many of the states of NER in particular, with due consideration to the gaps at district/block/Taluka levels. There is a tremendous scope of independent studies by researchers, academicians, engineers and the general public with regard to the evaluation of different SDG-aligned projects at different levels with respect to quality, effectiveness, sustainability, etc. Different social organizations, local bodies of engineers, etc., may also study these aspects district-wise or block-wise.

In conclusion, it may be stated that the analysis of the type presented in this chapter needs to be updated as and when the subsequent SDG Index Reports (referred to in this chapter) are released by NITI Aayog.

Chapter 5 | Sustainability and Construction Project Management

5.1. Introduction

Sustainability with respect to both 'human and natural resources' and 'environment' has put tremendous pressure today on the approach to the management of construction projects. The adoption of sustainability principles, as made available through extensive research and development works around the world, in the appropriate stages of construction project management has today become a social responsibility for all the stakeholders of the construction sector. By now, many research works about sustainability principles to be adopted in different stages of construction project management have been done. A review of literature with a critical analysis (identifying gaps for further research) was carried out by M. Ershadi[87] et al. It was noted in this review: *'Traditional construction methods are no longer viable to deal with the increased pressure to comply with environmental standards and commit to social responsibility. Construction organizations are seeking approaches to transition from traditional to sustainable construction methods that help them achieve their business goals without distorting the environment (Oke et al., 2019)'.*

Sustainable CPM basically aims to ensure environmental, economic, and social sustainability. It is in this context that a broad understanding of various aspects of a construction project, which are responsible for causing an adverse impact on these three pillars of sustainability, has been necessary. As given in the Guide to Sustainable Construction[88], the benefits to accrue on the adoption of sustainable construction with respect to these three pillars of sustainability are:

- ❖ *Environmental:*
- *Sustainable construction has a lower environmental impact. It adopts products and processes which are more environmentally friendly.*

- *The whole lifetime of a building/project is taken into account rather than just the construction phase.*
- *Sustainable construction aims to maintain and enhance the natural environment.*

❖ *Economic:*

- *Sustainable construction can also bring cost savings.*
- *Proper consideration of building design, construction and operation can reduce the overall cost of a building throughout its lifetime.*
- *Many sustainable projects are no more expensive than standard options if properly planned at the design stage; this is vital because the efficiency of construction projects is generally measured in terms of cost per square metre.*
- *Sustainable buildings, structures, and infrastructure can help encourage economic prosperity. Better living and working environments help improve productivity.*

❖ *Social:*

- *Sustainable construction creates better environments for people to live and work in.*
- *Sustainable buildings can help improve levels of well-being; this can have knock-on effects in areas such as health and education.*
- *Carefully planned, sustainable buildings and estates promote lower levels of crime and other social problems.*

As evident from the above-noted benefits, the three pillars are interlinked and therefore, a sustainable construction project can be achieved only when due considerations to all three pillars are given. The scenario of construction activities, as seen in India, particularly in urban areas, suggests two areas that need serious attention. These two areas are:

- The lack of adequate awareness about the different aspects of sustainable construction among the stakeholders of the construction industry (excluding some progressive construction organizations and Owners) and

- The lack of adequate awareness among the general public about the adverse impacts of inappropriately managed construction of buildings/infrastructure in light of the three pillars of sustainability.

One of the objectives of the discussion under this chapter has been to throw some light on these two broad areas in full appreciation of the need for a *'balance for environmental, economic and social objectives.'*

5.2. Factors Responsible for Adverse Impact on Sustainability

Buildings and infrastructure make a tremendous contribution to the economic growth of a nation. Against this position, the construction of these facilities is also a major contributor to the adverse impact on the three pillars of sustainability (environmental, social and economic), including the generation of a substantial quantity of greenhouse gas (leading to climate change). On many occasions, these adverse impacts are seen to be overlooked.

A construction project primarily uses three types of resources: materials, manpower and machinery. The construction sector is responsible for generating a huge quantity of solid waste. As reported[87], it accounts for '... *over 30% of the extraction of natural resources, as well as 25% of solid waste in the world'.* According to another assessment[89], about 3% to 5% of the materials are wasted in construction projects during execution. The wastage of materials is very often seen to be caused by a number of reworks, which are mostly accountable for factors such as wrong planning, wrong preliminary investigations like surveys, soil exploration, changes in Owners' requirements, etc. The other two resources (manpower and machinery), if not appropriately managed, contribute substantially to the adverse impacts on sustainability. Therefore, the essence of sustainable construction project management consists of an attempt to optimize the use of these resources, and the process of optimization has to be carried out by the project manager or project consultant (May it be individuals or organizations) at every stage of project management starting from project conception to the commissioning and handing-over to the Owner. The different aspects of optimization will be discussed in greater detail while dealing with the relevant stages of construction project management at a later stage in this chapter. This process of optimization needs to be based on the adoption of sustainable construction practices, which consist of the adoption of alternative construction methods (in preference to traditional ones) and green materials (such as green concrete, sustainable finishing products, etc.). In this context, the words[88] of a former prime minister of Norway (Gro Harlem Brundtland), by which she described sustainable development, may be quoted as: *'Development that meets the needs of the present without compromising the ability of future generations to meet their own needs'.*

A tough question that is very often raised is: *'Who is responsible for sustainable construction?'* A straight-forward answer to this question is apparently: *'The whole society of human beings'* since the construction of all facilities (buildings of any type, infrastructure of any type, structures of any type) is carried out for the sustainable services of mankind. Therefore, in a broader sense of the term 'sustainable construction', each and every member of the society is responsible for variable measures for sustainable construction/development. Therefore, the basic necessity for proceeding with sustainable construction/development consists of the extent of ethical values in society. The technical aspects are to be obviously taken care of by the stakeholders involved in different stages of sustainable construction project management. However, there are many elements bearing on the ethical values of society, which do play significant roles in the activities of the construction industry in countries like India, where it (the construction industry) is treated as an industry of making money. In recent times, enormous cases of corruption in India, which have been talked about in different forums, are clear examples. The ethical values in the society in any country count significantly in the efforts directed towards the implementation of sustainable construction projects. It is truly in this context that creating awareness about the absolute necessity of sustainable construction among all sections of the society has become an important aspect. A detailed discussion on the impact of unethical practices is outside the scope of this chapter. Apart from ethical values, there is a need to create general awareness in society (particularly among the citizens of urban areas) about the fact that there exist different standards, acts, rules and regulations controlling adverse environmental and social impacts likely to be caused by construction projects in general. On the other hand, the technical persons involved in different stages of a construction project need to know these standards, acts, rules and regulations deeply before getting involved in the construction project management. The latest standards and regulations in India are covered in the Draft Building Construction Environment Management Regulations, 2022, notified by Ministry of Environment, Forest and Climate Change[90], Govt. of India. This draft Regulations shall apply to projects involving the construction of buildings covering an area of 5000 sqm or more (including new building projects and expansion/repair of old buildings). Under this draft Regulations, the project management authorities will be under environment management obligations

- *To manage and maintain drainage systems at construction sites,*
- *To implement soil erosion control measures,*
- *To adopt water conservation measures,*
- *To reuse treated wastewater,*
- *To manage solid waste,*
- *To conduct tree planting and*
- *To manage air and noise pollution.*

All these aspects need to be duly accounted for in the sustainable construction project management with due regard to the other laws and regulations, which include[90]:

- Solid Waste Management Rules, 2016,
- Plastic Waste Management Rules, 2016,
- Hazardous & Other Wastes (Management and transboundary Movement) Rules, 2016,
- Bio-Medical Waste Management Rules, 2016,
- Noise Pollution (Regulation and Control) Rules, 2000,

- Construction & Demolition Rules, 2016 and
- Dust Mitigation Measures for Construction and Demolition Activities.

In addition, the National Building Code[91] 2016 has included an additional chapter (Chapter 11) for the sustainability approach to the construction of buildings. The code is a *national instrument providing guidelines for regulating the building construction activities across the country*. In addition, BIS has published a Guide[92] to facilitate the understanding of the provisions of NBC. Similarly, the Central Pollution Control Board, MoEFCC, has Guidelines[93] on the environmental management of C & D Waste (prepared in compliance with Solid Waste Management Rules, 2016).

As briefly discussed above, even in India, there are many rules, regulations, laws, and guidelines that encourage the adoption of sustainable construction project management. What is required today is a sincere incorporation of the available knowledge into the construction projects with due respect to the rules and regulations of the country. For this purpose, obviously, adequate awareness of the parts of stakeholders of the construction industry, in particular, and the public, in general, is a prerequisite. Some of the aspects of the incorporation of sustainable measures into the different stages of construction project management are discussed below *(within the limitations of the author's knowledge and experiences).*

5.3. Different Stages of Sustainable Construction Project Management
The most important player in the whole process of construction project management is the Project Manager (also popularly called Project Consultant in India). The engagement of a Project Consultant for a particular construction project is the first step and has to be judiciously made by the Developer (i.e. the Client or the Owner) of the project. It may be noted that, for some of the construction projects of conventional type, some authorities (Government and semi-government) have their in-house project management units or departments. The Project Consultant (PC) is an organization or a team with adequate knowledge in both legal and technical aspects of the type of project concerned. The selection of a competent PC is of

primary importance since the quality and the effectiveness of the project are fully dependent on its ability (with respect to knowledge, experience and integrity) to provide the desired standard of construction project management, which duly accounts for all legal and technical aspects (*with due regard to standards, rules and regulations, as briefly discussed above under the preceding subhead)* relating to the project. The philosophy of construction project management primarily consists of ensuring 'safety, serviceability and durability' in a traditional project. However, when the 'sustainability approach', as included in NBC[91] and Environment Regulations[90] is adopted, due consideration to Environmental Impact Assessment (EIA) and Social Impact Assessment (SIA), with the adoption of sustainable materials to the possible extent, becomes additionally necessary. On the other hand, the aspect of maintenance also becomes an important factor, since the extent of environmental and social impact is dependent on proper maintenance of the project during its lifecycle.

Two approaches with respect to the engagement of Project Consultants appear to be prevalent - one is the engagement of a single consultant/project manager, while the other one is the engagement of multiple consultants for different modules of a construction project. However, for massive projects, the engagement of a single project consultant seems to be preferred in most of the projects. In the case of a single consultant (a competent organization), it will be the responsibility of the project consultant to hire specialists' services as and when required for different stages of construction project management, depending on the type of the project.

The different stages of construction project management with the inclusion of sustainable practices (termed sustainable construction project management) are in a slight variation in terms of the number of stages or modules, as considered in different literatures[87,88,94,95], the objective and spirit being the same irrespective of the number of stages (6, 7 or 8). For a better discussion of every stage, six stages of SCPM have been considered herein on the presumption that the PC for the project has already been engaged by the Developer concerned. The *'method of selecting a consultant'* is also a broad topic for discussion, and for this discussion, this topic has been treated as *'outside the scope'*. These stages are given in the flowchart of figure 5.1. The treatment of these stages will vary depending on the type of the project. A detailed discussion on each of these stages has been taken up with specific reference to buildings in the subsequent articles.

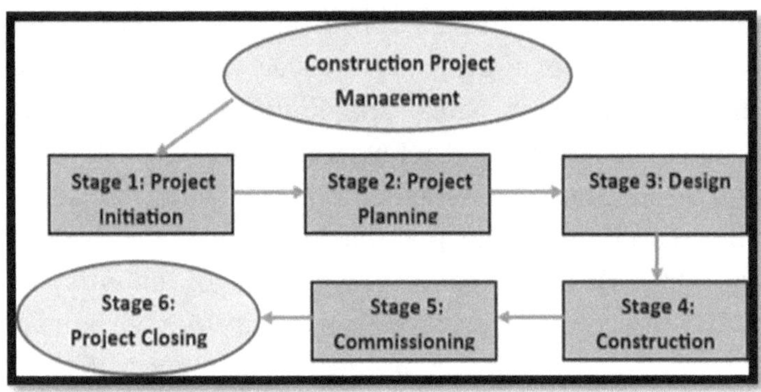

Figure 5.1: Flowchart Showing the Stages of Construction Project Management

5.3.1. Stage 1: Project Initiation

This stage is the most important one since a clear understanding of the project with respect to Terms of Reference (ToR) and activities involved for the project assigned to the Project Consultant (or the Project Manager) needs to be achieved. The ToR is a document signed between the PC and the Owner (the Client) at the time of the appointment of the PC. Obviously, the ToR will depend on the type of the project. The important aspects such as implementing agencies, implementation strategies, procurement plans, time of completion, cost limitations (if imposed by the Owner), etc., as desired by the Owner of the project, have to be clearly defined at this stage. In addition, a list of major stakeholders involved in the project needs to be defined by the Owner so that the PC may conduct consultations with the relevant stakeholders at different stages of project management to achieve the targeted objectives of the project on time. Summarily, the PC, during this stage, has to develop a clear understanding of the roles to be played by it (PC) in the whole process of sustainable construction project management before entering into the second stage.

This is the stage in which all steps of the project, from the planning stage to the commissioning stage, are clearly analysed, and the detailed working out of the scopes of works involved is carried out, and a Project Implementation Document (PID), which is also called an Initial Scope Report, is prepared. In fact, the ToR normally includes the condition to such an effect that the final assignment is subject to the approval of the PID by the Owner. The preparation of PID needs to be based primarily on the tasks covered in the ToR, which forms the basic document already signed between the Owner and the PC. A detailed analysis of the activities has to be carried out, and the deliverables and sub-deliverables at different stages of the project have to be duly identified. In addition, the due stress on the identification of methodologies to be adopted for each of the deliverables needs to be laid at this stage. There are primarily three components of a project assigned to a PC for construction project management (as conceived by the author of this book), namely:

- Component A, which includes all activities necessary for preparing the Detailed Project Report (DPR), including preparation of bidding documents,

- Component B, which includes all activities, including the project execution, commissioning and closing, and

- Component C, which includes Project Maintenance after commissioning (optional to the Owner) during the lifecycle of the project (by lifecycle, the whole life of utility is meant).

Component A is completed in Stage 1, Stage 2 and Stage 3 (as shown in figure 5.1), while Component B is completed in Stage 4, Stage 5 and Stage 6 (as shown in figure 5.1). Component C has not been included in the standard stages since it is optional for the Owner. However, it is an aspect deserving due consideration in the case of sustainable construction project management. As already stated, the PID to be prepared during this stage (Stage 1) is primarily based on the terms and conditions included in the ToR. Some of the Owners (organisations or individuals) engage PC only for Component A (stated above), some Owners go only for Components A & B, while some others may do so for all the three components, depending on their (Owners') own capabilities of handling the project and also depending on the type of the project. However, in this discussion, it is presumed that the two components (Components A & B) are covered in the ToR in variable measures *(to be discussed while dealing with the subsequent stages in detail).*

The first major step with respect to the preparation of the PID is the analysis[96] of the stakeholders. The list of stakeholders (as obtained from the Owner) needs to be critically analysed with the broad objective of deciding clearly as to *'whom to consult'* at different stages of the project management to avoid foreseeable *'roadblocks and delay'* during the process of completing the project in hand. As stated by Asana[96], the key stakeholder is obviously the Owner, with whom the agreement has been signed and who is responsible for according to the final approval of the PID and subsequent documents relating to project management, including the release of payment to PC. The other stakeholders have to be analysed with respect to their roles to be played in different stages of the project. Once their roles are clearly understood, the data and resources necessary for different stages of the project may be collected (by the PC), and timely consultations with appropriate and relevant stakeholders as and when it is necessary for proceeding with works of this stage and the subsequent stages of project management may be taken up. In the case of sustainable construction project management, the aspect of Environment Management Plan (EMP) constitutes an important component of the PID, which will depend on the type and location of the project. *(The details of EMP with reference to a specific project will be discussed at a later stage).*

The second step in pursuit of the preparation of PID consists of a detailed study of the feasibility of the project basically with respect to:

- Part A1*:* The availability of manpower, including specialists, as required for completing the projects based on the items of ToR within the time projected by the Owner with the desired quality of the project,

- Part A2: The assessment of financial resources required (on the part of the organisation of the PC) for completing all stages of the project management, as conceived in ToR and
- Part A3: The assessment of the return on investment (by PC).

For looking into all these three aspects, the PC needs to have adequate knowledge and experiences (both technical and administrative), skills, tools and resources to carry out the study of different aspects of feasibility, depending on the type and scope of the project as assigned to it (PC).

To complete Part A1, a list of major activities involved in each stage of the project *(Stage 2, Stage 3, Stage 4, Stage 5 and Stage 6 to follow)* has to be prepared. Thereafter, the requirements have to be worked out for tools (such as equipment, software, etc.) and manpower, including a specialist (who will work as the leader of the team) for each of the activities under each stage as per the list of the activities prepared. While doing so, the PC may need to consult with the appropriate stakeholders of the project so that no major activity (as conceived in ToR) is left out of the PID. At this stage, a major consideration needs to be given to the requirement of specialists for the project in hand. The PC (which is an organisation) may not have all the specialists as required. For example, the case of a specialist for EIA and SIA may be taken. This is an absolute necessity for *sustainable construction project management.* If the PC does not have a specialist in its organisation, it has to naturally go for hiring from outside. Normally, the specialist services under this type of situation are taken by the PC through the engagement of a sub-consultant subject to the due approval of the Owner. This is an important aspect to be covered in PID. Thereafter, the assessment of the time required for completing the activities under each stage of the project will be assessed, as the time period required for completing the whole project, as assigned through the ToR, has to be eventually arrived at. While assessing the time period, a clear assessment of the risks involved has to be taken into account. (*The aspect of risk management in construction projects will be dealt with in greater detail at a later stage*). Once the time required for each activity has been duly assessed, the total time required for completing the whole project, as assigned, will be calculated, and the distribution of the time so arrived at will be proportionately made over the subsequent stages of the project. The assessment of the total time of completion is a very important parameter for achieving the success of a project. There are many cases of complicacies *(delay, dispute, cost overrun, failure, etc.)* given rise to by inappropriate assessment of time for the completion of the projects. Therefore, the PC has to take all care by conducting consultations with the stakeholders as many times as necessary to understand, in clear terms, the activities involved in the project. At times, depending on the type and magnitude of the project, a flowchart for different activities becomes helpful in preparing the PID.

The next part of the work for PID *(PartA2, as noted above)* is the assessment of the total cost to be incurred by the PC for carrying out work under each stage of the project assigned to it. This cost basically involves the cost of manpower (to be required for all stages of the project) and resources for completing the assignment. Therefore, at this stage, the roles to be played by the PC have to be clearly understood with respect to Component B (as noted above), which includes implementation, commissioning and closing of the project. There are broadly two components of a project: Component A and Component B (as stated above, with Component C being optional). The PID must define in clear terms the works to be done by the PC with respect to Component B, i.e. in Stage 4, Stage 5 and Stage 6. There are again two broad parts of Component B as:

- *(Part B1):* Complete responsibility for the implementation of the project, which primarily includes allotment of works to contractors, quality control, cost control, control of time schedule, preparation of bills payable to contractors, etc. (In case the project is not on a turnkey-basis), and

- *(Part B2):* The involvement of the PC only with respect to giving design-clarifications during implementation stages, as and when required by the Project Management Unit (PMU). Normally, these aspects are well-defined in the ToR. If it is not included, a revision of the ToR will be necessary through discussion with the Owner. Therefore, the broad types of assignment of the project to a PC may be:

> Type A, which includes only Component A and Component B2 and

> Type B, which includes Component A and complete Component B (i.e. Components B1 and B2).

(The Pvt. Ltd. Company of the author of this book has the experience of handling projects of smaller size (of both types as PC under his leadership)).

Irrespective of the magnitudes of the projects, the basic concept of project management remains the same as far as the approach to PID is concerned. The assessment of the total involvement of finance for the completion of the project is, therefore, dependent on the type of assignment, as briefly discussed above.

Once the total cost involved on the part of the PC has been duly assessed, the return on investment (RoI) (Part A3) will be calculated and analysed to find if the project in hand is financially viable for it (the PC). If it is considered to be unviable in light of consultancy fees receivable from the Authority, before finalising the PID, the PC needs to negotiate with the Authority to make it viable through mutual discussions for achieving the financial viability of the project.

Before coming to the end of the PID, the consideration of some additional aspects appears to be of importance. These are:

- The terms of payment of the total consultancy fees due to the PC. It needs to be spelt out well, basically based on the completion of different parts of the work of the project. This has a bearing on the progress of work in different stages of the project,

- The aspects of approval with respect to completed parts of works at different stages of the project (to be discussed in detail while dealing with the relevant stages).

- The project may need clearance in some respects, such as environmental clearance, planning permission, construction permission, safety permission, etc., from different government and statutory bodies. The approach to be adopted for obtaining these clearances and permission has to be duly taken care of in the PID itself so that no 'roadblocks and delays' are caused on the timely completion of the project.

The PID should have an Executive Summary (or an Abstract) at the beginning of the PID (Initial Scope Report). The purpose of an Executive Summary is to give an overview of the project so that it facilitates the readers (the stakeholders and team members of PC) to know the salient aspects of the project (as discussed above) without devoting much time. In addition, it facilitates a stakeholder or a team member (of the PC) to quickly identify the area of the project in which the reader (the stakeholder or the PC's team member) is predominantly involved. A detailed discussion on the aspect of an Executive Summary of PID has been appropriately given by Asana[97].

At the end of this stage, the final PID is submitted to the Owner for approval. The PC enters into the next stage of construction project management by getting the approval of the Project Initiation Document.

5.3.2. Stage 2: Project Planning

This is the most critical stage in the process of construction project management. The planning of all activities involved has to be judiciously done with respect to the required 'manpower and tools' for achieving the targets with quality and within the time schedule (as conceived in the PID, already approved under Stage 1). As stated by Kumar[94]: *'...no error or fault is acceptable. A single error or mistake can cause a considerable loss.'* Therefore, initially, the task under this stage is to finalize a specific Project Leader/Project Coordinator/Project Director/ Project Manager/Any other (a designation as desired by the PC's organization based on its own standard practices). For this discussion, the designation of Project Director (PD) has been adopted. The PD must be a capable person with respect to 'technical knowledge, skills and leadership qualities' relevant to the project in hand. If the PC is a small organization *(say a small Pvt. Ltd Company like the one the author has)* handling a small number of projects, the Managing Director himself (subject to his expertise) becomes the PD. Since sustainability is a major consideration in today's construction project management, the PD of the project needs to be well-versed in sustainable principles and practices, as briefly dealt with under the preceding subheads. The basic document for detailed planning for the project in this stage is obviously the PID, as already prepared under Stage 1.

It is always convenient to carry out the project-planning with a flowchart for the different activities of the project. Naturally, the flowchart will depend on the type of the project. On the other hand, there are various construction project management software applications today that can be judiciously adopted for different purposes in the process of management. *(A detailed discussion on different software available today is outside the scope of this discussion).* It is up to the PD to decide what is required for his project. The basic concept of planning at this stage is obviously 'Organizing the work and establishing accountability'. To organize the work based on the activities, the PD initially has to mobilize the teams (including the team for EMP) required to complete the tasks at each stage of the project. For each of the teams assigned with a specific set of work, a team leader (TL) has to be chosen. It is the TL who will have the required knowledge and experience in the relevant domain of the activities, coordinate the work assigned to his team among his team members, and complete the tasks as per the fixed schedule. The TL is accountable to the PD for the work of his team. It is the responsibility of the TL to collect the necessary details for the work of his team from the PD.

The success of a project is absolutely dependent on the quality of the teams involved at different stages of the project. Therefore, it is necessary to place the team members in the right position in relation to relevant experiences and skills. The PD (if he is not the head of the PC's organization) will have to organize his teams with the head of the organization. Once the teams have been organized, a well-defined system needs to be developed for communication with and within the team members for interactions required regarding data, progress of works, etc. This system broadly depends on locations where different teams work. In the case of teams working at different locations, the appropriate tools (may it be emails, Google Docs. or any other management software) have to be finalized and communicated to all the team members. Now, the PD is ready to enter into the subsequent stages of the project. For the convenience of a discussion on the remaining stages of sustainable construction project management, the specific case of a building project has been considered since a specific treatment of different aspects depends on the type of project.

5.3.3. Stage 3: Design (For a Building Project)

This stage basically includes two phases:

- Phase A: Architectural Design (or Concept Design) and
- Phase B: Structural Design (also called Engineering Design).

In the case of sustainable construction project management (which has now become mandatory[91,92,93] in India), all environmental and social aspects need to be taken into account with due regard to the existing rules and regulations (as applicable to the project in hand and to the location of the project) while working on Phase A and Phase B by preparing an Environment Management Plan (EMP). In addition, this stage has to pay attention to the aspects of energy-efficient design of buildings[98] as well. Another aspect to be duly accounted for in this stage in India is obviously the Seismic Design[25,99,100] depending on the location of the site for construction. In summary, the work involved in this stage requires multidisciplinary professionals, depending on the complexity and magnitude of the project. These two phases (Phase A and Phase B) under this stage are dealt with in greater detail.

5.3.3.1. Phase A

Architectural Design (or Concept Design): The team leader for this phase of work is normally an architect. In fact, for a good concept design, there has to be mutual interactions between the architect and structural engineer *(to be dealt with in detail at a later stage).* The TL has to understand clearly the documents to be prepared at this phase, which the PC has to submit to the Owner for submitting the application/applications to the Authority/Authorities, i.e. the statutory body/bodies controlling the construction in the location of the site of the project for obtaining the necessary permission for construction. The documents to be submitted along with the applications normally include[92]: *Title of ownership of land/building, Key Plan, Site Plan, Subdivision/layout Plan, Building Plans including Elevations and Sections, Services Plans, Specification—general and detailed, certificate for structural design sufficiency, certificate for engagement of builder/constructor(s), where applicable and certificates for supervision.* The documents to be so prepared will fully conform to the rules and regulations, including formats, laid down by the statutory body/bodies of the location of the site.

The approach to sustainability[91,92] broadly covers three levels: planning level, layout level, and building level. The first two levels refer to the preparation of a master plan for a Real Estate/institutional/any other complex *(The aspect of preparation of a master plan for a complex is outside the scope of this discussion).* In this case, specifically, a building of any type *(for which a specific plot covered in a particular master plan of a city or a township or any other complex is given by the Owner to the PC for the purpose of construction project management)* is considered for the discussion. Therefore, the parameters covered under 'Building Level' are of primary importance for this discussion. These parameters[92] are: *Building siting and orientation, Envelope optimization, Building-services optimization, Lighting and ventilation, Sustainable materials, use of alternate and local construction materials employing low-energy consumption, maintenance and safe construction and Solar energy.* The TLs for this stage have to be well-versed with the implications of all these parameters and then proceed with the actual task of preparing the documents (as stated earlier) in sequential order.

It is presumed that *'Title of ownership of land/building, Key Plan and Site Plan'* are available. Therefore, the first task under Phase A is the 'conceptualization and planning' through which the preparation of the Layout Plan (prepared on the available site plan of the plot of the land meant for the building under planning) is taken up. The basic data for this part of the work is obviously the type of building, including the requirements of the Owner. This layout plan has to be prepared by giving due consideration to all development rules such as 'land use classification, requirements for subdivision and layout plan including means of access, open spaces, plot requirements, area and height limitations, including Floor Area Ratio (FAR) and set-backs, off-street parking space, etc.', as laid down in NBC[91,92] and also in the bye-laws of the relevant statutory body. It is felt that the consideration of only the bye-laws of the regulatory body alone is not adequate since there are scopes for improvement of bye-laws of some statutory bodies in light of provisions of NBC, particularly in view of the newly incorporated 'Approach to Sustainability (Part 11 of NBC)'. While preparing the layout plan, due consideration to the ground coverage and orientation (based on the sun path) has to be judiciously given. However, on many occasions, the limitations with respect to the judicious choice of orientation of the building block are brought about by the location of the plot and the approach road in urban areas. In such a situation, greater emphasis needs to be laid on the aspects of orientation in the internal planning of the building. Another aspect warranting due consideration in preparing the layout plan of a building is obviously the shape of the plan when the location of the site happens to be in an earthquake-prone zone[100,101]. Once the layout plan has been so prepared, the next task of doing the internal planning of the building will be taken up on the basis of the due consideration of the requirements of the Owner, which primarily depend on the type of the building *(residential, institutional, hospital, commercial etc.)*.

The planning of a building needs to be based on different measures suggested in Part 11: Approach to Sustainability of NBC[91]. As observed in the Foreword of this code — *'The benefits of incorporating measures listed in this part are not only environment friendly but also result in much better health and productivity of occupants, at minimal additional cost over the cost of conventional buildings, while substantially reducing the life cycle cost. This minimal additional cost is offset during a few years of usage of the buildings, and a vast advantage in cost is accrued during the life cycle of the building'*. Therefore, the TL for this phase will try to incorporate the relevant measures of the suggested ones at the 'conceptualization and planning' stage itself to the feasible extent in the location of the site of the building.

The internal planning of different rooms is primarily based on functional necessity and optimum use of natural light and ventilation in addition to due consideration to wind effect. While doing so, considering the sun path and its seasonal variation becomes necessary. Other aspects, such as building volume, the location of the staircase, lift (if necessary), and covered parking area, have to be provided in conformity with the provisions of NBC and relevant by-laws of statutory bodies. *(A detailed discussion of different planning aspects is avoided in this discussion).* Once the tentative planning for each floor of the building has been done, a discussion with the team of Phase B (Structural Design) is desirable. The TL of Phase B will look into the basic aspect of structural design, which consists of the structural system (normally, a framed structure is adopted in the case of multi-storeyed buildings). The TL for structural design will place the position of the columns on the building plans tentatively prepared by the team of Phase A and will put its comment, if any, and send back the plans to the TL of Phase A for the finalization of the building plans after giving due considerations to the position of columns and comments of team of structural design. While finalizing the plans, care needs to be taken to avoid columns, as suggested by the structural team in the utility area of the floors. Necessarily, further discussion with the structural team may be needed to resolve issues coming up in this respect. This approach of mutual interactions between the teams of Phase A & B is normally followed by many of the reputed consultancy organizations in the country to avoid any possible complicacy during the structural design stage. *(The author had an opportunity to experience this type of approach in the early 1980s at Bhabha Atomic Research Centre, Mumbai).*

Once the plans at different floors have been finalized, the next part of the tasks under this phase will be to prepare the elevations and sections of the building. While developing these views, the broad approach to sustainability, as covered in Part 11 of NBC[91]— Volume 2 (with specific reference to 'Technology Options'), needs to be taken into due consideration. This is, in fact, the stage in which tremendous attention needs to be focused on the optimization of 'embodied and operational energy' in the building. In addition, the attention will be directed towards the minimization of the production of 'greenhouse gas' in the building (on completion). Therefore, to achieve this end to the possible extent in the given location and under the known climatic conditions, adequate emphasis will be laid on the choice of appropriate materials *(desirably sustainable ones)* to be used for the facades and roof of the building envelope in addition to those for the interior walls as well. The embodied energy of a building[88] *'covers the whole design and construction phase and includes manufacturing all individual building components and energy used by machinery and in transportation'*. On the other hand, the operational energy[88] refers to *'the energy used by a building in use. This includes all day-to-day running and maintenance activities, including heating, lighting, servicing of equipment and systems and ongoing upgrading and refurbishment'.* An attempt should be made to utilize some of the traditional materials and technology, if economically available, in the area concerned. The positions and sizes of doors, windows, ventilators, exhaust fans, etc. will be judiciously chosen. The views so finalized need to be discussed with the structural team again to seek their views, particularly with respect to materials chosen for walls (both for the interior and exterior) and positions of doors, windows, etc. The structural team will obviously look into the plans (including the tentative elevations) from the perspective of structural design, particularly with respect to the dead loads that will come on different floors. A structural engineer will always try to go for reduced DL on the upper floors for the obvious reason of reducing the seismic effect. The TL of Phase A will duly account for the points to be raised by the structural team, and thereafter, the plans will be submitted to the PD for discussion with the stakeholders of the project and to get the approval of the plans (not elevations) only at this stage. The areas of shortcomings and suggestions for further improvement, if advanced by the stakeholders, will be duly incorporated into the plan before proceeding with the subsequent tasks.

The next task will be to develop the elevations and sectional views with the proper provision of shadings on the building envelope, including architectural treatment for adding aesthetic values. Extreme attention needs to be paid to finalizing the building envelope. The building envelope is the separator between the interior and the exterior of a building, and it is this envelope that plays the main role in the security, internal climate and internal air circulation. There are many examples of buildings leading to problems of suffocation, high energy consumption, and adverse effects on the health of occupants, basically on account of the deficient design of the envelope. A detailed discussion on different aspects bearing on the design of a building envelope with respect to sustainability and energy efficiency is truly beyond the scope of this discussion. However, expectedly, the TL of this phase is adequately equipped with the required knowledge[88,91,92,98] etc. and experience in the task assigned to him. The provision of shades (both vertical and horizontal) on facades (exterior walls) over windows and ventilators, type (flat or pitched) of roof, roof ventilators, position for solar panel (to be placed for renewable energy), position of water tanks, stair headroom, lift headroom, roof gardens (if necessary) etc. are some of the important aspects demanding due attention in the preparation of elevations and sections. Plantations, particularly on the western and southern sides, have been found to be very effective in summer. A typical building with a plantation on the southern and western sides (with a creeper) is shown in image 5.1. While preparing the elevations and sections, views of the TL of Phase B will be taken again to avoid any issues during the structural design stage. In addition, the views of relevant stakeholders are also desirably taken through consultations to avoid any possible 'roadblock' in the process of getting the approval of the concept design from the Client.

Image 5.1: A Building with Plantations on Southern Face of the Building
Source: Photo Taken by the Author in His Own Residence

Once the layout plans, elevations and sections, including general specifications of materials (the detailed specifications of items of work involved to be prepared during Phase B), have been finalized, the PD will seek the final approval of the concept design from the Client of the project before entering into Phase B (the structural design). This approval is very essential at this stage in view of basically two reasons:

- Once the structural design is started, any change in concept design is not desirable for avoiding re-analysis of the structural system and
- To avoid reworks even during the execution stage.

On receiving the approval of the concept design, the PD is in a position to give a complete set of documents, as necessary, to the Client for putting up the applications to the Statutory Bodies for obtaining the necessary permissions for the construction of the project. Normally, for applying to the statutory body concerned, in addition to the concept drawings (as mentioned above), the additional documents necessary include the projected cost of the project (in this case, a building project), certificate of structural design sufficiency and certificate for supervision. These documents need to be provided by the PC to the Client.

The projected cost is worked out on the basis of the floor area rates given in the Schedule of Rates, as applicable to the location of the project. The detailed estimated cost will be worked in Phase B of this stage.

5.3.3.2. Phase B

Structural Design (or Engineering Design): This phase covers all the remaining activities of Component A, as noted under Stage 1. Now, based on the 'conceptualization and planning' finalized under Stage 1, all activities up to the preparation of the DPR including the bidding documents have to be completed. Broadly, these activities are covered under the subheads – Analysis of the structural System, Design of different structural elements, Design of non-structural elements, detailing of both structural and non-structural elements, detailed estimates for the Civil Works, detailed design of different services and detailed estimates thereof, preparation of bidding documents and finally the preparation (compilation) of the DPR. At this stage, the TLs have to plan the activities involved for their team appropriately in recognition of the involvement of the basic design activities covered broadly under two categories: (i) Civil works and (ii) Services. Therefore, the works under these two categories have to be distributed between broadly two sub-teams: (a) Sub-team PB1(for civil works) and (b) Sub-team PB2 (for services). The works of both the sub-teams may feasibly proceed simultaneously since the concept design of the building has already been finalized by now. A brief discussion of the activities covered under each of these sub-teams is presented below.

5.3.3.2.1. Activities of Sub-team PB1

Analysis of Structural System: The identification of the structural and non-structural elements in the concept design is the first step in the process of structural analysis, including the load transfer mechanism in both sets of elements. Since, as stated earlier, the building considered herein is a framed structure, the structural model needs to be developed with due consideration of the load transfer mechanism. An appropriate software needs to be chosen at this stage. A valid license has to be naturally held by the PC. A pirated version of any commercial software has to be avoided since it is normally obligatory to mention the license details in the design report to be submitted to the Client. The most commonly adopted software includes STAAD, SAP, ETAB, etc., though there are other software for structural analysis and design. All loads, including those from the non-structural elements, as specified in the relevant codes of practice (as applicable to the region covering the location of the building), along with the load combinations recommended in the applicable codes of practice, will have to be appropriately accounted for. The basic load cases considered in the analysis are dead load, live load, wind load, and earthquake load. The Wind Load is not normally considered in earthquake-prone zones— particularly in zone V of India, since its effect is normally less than that of EL. The load combinations considered are those as given in IS code[25]. Extreme care needs to be taken when specifying assumed dimensions of structural members, including material properties while providing the data input to the software. From the frame analysis, the displacements of the mass center of each floor are obtained. Based on these displacements, story drift will be checked[25]. If the configuration is not the same in both the directions, story drift in either direction will be checked. In addition, the stability index, as given in Annexure E of IS 456—2000, should also be duly checked.

Design of Different Structural Members (including Detailed Structural Drawings): The design of different structural elements, including detailed structural drawings will be done by the design engine of the software on the basis of material specifications, as provided through input. However, the design of the foundation becomes simpler if it is done manually. The quality of foundation design under any situation is fully dependent on soil classifications and the SBC (Safe Bearing capacity), as obtained through appropriate soil investigation of the plot of the building. In earthquake-prone zones, special care has to be taken to ensure the ductile design of the joints. Once the detailed structural drawings for the structural members have been made available by the design engine, critical scrutiny of aspects such as joint detailing with respect to ductility, anchorage lengths, etc., needs to be carried out for refinement, if considered necessary. Thereafter, the salient non-structural members will be manually designed and detailed.

Detailed Estimates for All Items of Civil Work: All items of work (excluding all those required for Services) will have to be covered when working out the estimate. The initial requirement for this part of the work is the Schedule of Rates (SoRs), on the basis of which the estimates will be worked out. The SoRs to be adopted will be finalized in consultation with the Client. The PD has to seek formal approval of the Client to this effect. For any region of India, normally, the latest CPWD SoR (DSR—Delhi Schedule of Rates) is applicable. However, the SoR of other agencies, as available in the region concerned may also be chosen, depending on the desire of the Client. In either case, the detailed specifications for each item of work are given in the SoR (as approved by the Client). Generally, there is a provision for the application of Cost Index (CI), depending on the year of preparation of the SoR. The TL of this phase needs to duly account for this aspect, as applicable, when working out the estimated cost of civil works. There are normally some items of work which are not covered by the adopted SoR. For these non-scheduled items of work, naturally, the rates to be adopted will have to be duly worked out based on the standard rate-analysis practices. The rates so finalized with complete specifications (for each non-scheduled item of work) are subject to approval by the Client. Thereafter, the quantities involved for all scheduled and non-scheduled items of work will be worked out manually or by adopting appropriate software. Once the quantities have been calculated, the estimated cost of civil work will be worked out on the basis of the rates and finalized as stated above. The estimated cost will be summarised in the standard format in a tabular form, indicating the detailed specifications, quantity, rate, item-wise cost, and total cost of civil work, including cost index impact, if accounted for.

5.3.3.2.2. Activities of Sub-team PB2

Planning and Design of Building Services: The TL of Phase B of Stage 3 will prepare a list of services to be designed and estimated for. The building services may include a number of facilities and installations such as energy supply (gas, electricity and renewable sources such as solar, etc.), fire safety (detection and protection), Escalators and lift, Heating, Ventilation and Air Conditioning (HVAC), Lighting and lighting protection, security and alarm systems, water, drainage and plumbing, etc. The requirements of different building services basically depend on the type of the building and the requirements of the Client. Therefore, the preparation of the detailed list of different building services to be included in a particular building initially requires a detailed discussion with stakeholders concerned. Expectedly, the broad aspects of building services might have been covered in the PID, as approved (covered under Stage 1). The TLs of this phase of work expectedly understand the critical role of building services in the design of the building. It is truly in this context that planning and design of the building services have to be integrated into the overall building design from the early stage of the design process (Stage 3). As implied, the planning and design of building services do require the services of specialists in the area of HVAC, electrification works, plumbing works, etc., depending on the building services required. The activities of these specialists have to be appropriately integrated into the overall design process at early stages (as mentioned earlier) to avoid any possibility of clashes between building services and any building component. This type of clash, if caused, will result in delays and, at times, in reworks during the execution of the project. Therefore, timely interactions between the TLs concerned and the stakeholders on the one hand and among the team members (including specialists of building services) on the other will be of absolute necessity. Once the layout plans are prepared for different services, the same will have to be submitted to the Client for the necessary approval before taking up the work of design to be followed by item-wise cost estimation. On receiving the due approval of the layout plans from the Client, as in the case of Civil Work, the specifications will be finalized based on detailed design and on item rates available in relevant SoRs. For non-scheduled items of work, the rate analysis will be carried out, and the rates so achieved (subject to approval by the Client) will be adopted for the cost estimation. The schedule of items of work, along with respective quantity and rate (for each item), will be prepared in the standard format for each set of building services corresponding to each set of layout plans.

As stated in Stage 1, the task of preparing the Environment Management Plan (EMP) has to be taken up now (under Stage 3) since a sustainable project is under consideration herein.

5.3.3.2.3. Preparation of Environment Management Plan (EMP)

The necessity of a Construction EMP (CEMP) was briefly discussed under Stage 1. There are many standards, rules and regulations[90,91,92,93] for the management of the environmental impact, including the social impact created by construction at a particular location. As stated earlier, it is an area which requires specialists in this domain to be managed. There is the necessity of an independent team for the preparation of the CEMP for any particular building project. All necessary details finalized through Phase A and Phase B (under Stage 3—as discussed above) will be given to this Environment Assessment Team (EAT) for a detailed study and analysis of Environment Impact Assessment (EIA) and Social Impact Assessment (SIA). Based on the results of the impact assessment, the EAT will prepare the CEMP, giving due regard to standards and rules set by the governments and local statutory bodies, as applicable. The CEMP to be so prepared will broadly include the responsibilities of the client, the contractors (to be engaged) and the EAT (which is a part of the PC) with respect to monitoring and mitigation measures during the execution of the project. Once it has been finalized, it will be submitted to the Owner for its endorsement and for follow-up actions to get necessary environmental clearance from the Authority concerned. The last part of the work under Stage 3 of CPM is obviously the preparation of (a) the DPR and (b) the Bidding Documents, which are briefly discussed below.

5.3.3.2.4. Preparation of the Detailed Project Report (DPR)

The preparation of the Detailed Project Report (DPR) for any project is a very important task and needs a variety of considerations. The first and foremost is obviously the consideration of the template (or guidelines), if any, from the side of the Owner (Client) of the project for the DPR. If the owner plans to arrange funds from any financial institution, the DPR will then have to conform to the guidelines of that financial organization. The financial source may be the Owner itself, a government, a nationalized bank or any other financial organization such as WB, ADB, etc. Normally, financial organizations do have a template for the DPR. Under any situation, a DPR will broadly include salient features such as an executive summary, project background, site surveys and investigations, conceptual design, engineering design, financial estimates, risk assessment and mitigation measures, project implementation aspects, statutory clearances, quality management aspects, etc. After the Design stage (Stage 3 — Design), the project will enter into the construction (Stage 4). Therefore, different aspects of the project implementation *(to be discussed in greater detail under Stage 4)* will have to be finalized. The salient aspect is the role to be played by the PC. The PID prepared and duly approved under Stage 1 will be the guiding document in the preparation of DPR. As stated earlier, the PC is engaged for both Components A & B. So, it is presumed that it will be the responsibility of the PC to manage all activities relating to different aspects of the construction of the project *(the methodology to be adopted for execution will be dealt with under Stage 4)*. However, the broad elements of the project implementation strategy to be adopted will have to be included in DPR, as already stated above.

5.3.3.2.5. Preparation of Bidding Documents

The Tender Document (TD) (or bidding Documents) basically contains three parts. The first part (Part I) covers Notice Inviting Tender (NIT), Affidavit for Tender, Letter of undertaking, Form of tender, Memorandum, Special instruction to bidders for e-tendering (optional), Bidder's information, Bid Security Proforma, Site visit declaration, etc. The NIT has to duly incorporate the specific conditions for qualifying in the Technical Bid. Normally, the price (financial) bid is considered only when the bidder qualifies for the technical bid. Therefore, the basic requirements of technical bid have to be duly formulated depending on the complexity and magnitude of the project. The second part of the TD covers normally General Conditions of Contract (GCC), Special Conditions of Contract (SCC), Technical Specifications (for both Civil Works and Services), Approved makes, Drawings (concept and structural drawings for Civil Work and Layout drawings for Services), etc. The third part of the TD will contain the formats of both the Technical Bid and Financial Bid. In most cases of institutional/organizational owners, bidding documents exist in general forms. In such cases, the PD has to get those documents from the Owner, and based on that format, the TD for their project will be developed. During the process of developing the TD, consultations with the project stakeholders (particularly with those who will be involved in the implementation of the project) need to be conducted by the PD. The salient points in the NIT are the total cost of the project (as estimated and included in DPR) and the time required to complete the project as it arrives through the proper scheduling of different activities involved in the project. The appropriate scheduling of different activities is a specialized aspect and has to be done by the teams involved in the work of Stage 3. *(The different aspects of scheduling will be discussed in greater detail under Stage 4).* Similarly, there are some aspects that require special attention in the formulation of both the GCC and SCC. In the case of GCC, two clauses need special attention. These are the clause for price escalation and the clause for quality control (testing and inspection). In the case of the first one, the basis for the calculation of the Cost Index needs to be well-defined, including the base year. For quality control, apart from standard procedures and intervals of different control tests, the aspect of the supply of basic materials such as cement and steel may be given special consideration in consultation with the stakeholders. The author of this book derived good results in control of quality in many of his projects by incorporating the condition of supply of these materials from the Owner's side. This type of approach may be incorporated to avoid variation in the qualities of materials. However, the basic prices of these materials based on which the bidder quotes their rates of the items involving these materials will have to be stated clearly in the Financial Bid to recover the cost thereof from the bills payable to contractors.

Similarly, there are some aspects that require special attention even in the case of formulating the clauses of SCC. These aspects basically relate to the adoption of a sustainability approach (as briefly discussed earlier) and to the responsibilities and obligations of the bidder (contractor on allotment) for the appropriate implementation of measures clearly covered in the EMP.

Once completed in all respects, the DPR with all enclosures will be submitted to the Owner, and then necessary follow-up actions will be taken, including detailed discussions with stakeholders. The points on any aspect of the DPR, if raised by the Owner's side, will be duly incorporated in the DPR for its final approval (by the Owner). It is only after the due approval of the DPR that the project will go for bidding, and the PC will enter into the next stage.

5.3.4. Stage 4: Construction

5.3.4.1. General

This stage primarily includes two parts: procurement and construction (the physical process of construction from start to completion). Therefore, at times, this stage is named 'Procurement & Construction'. Earlier, it was stated that the PC is engaged for Component A and Component B. Therefore, the role of the PC is dependent on the Owner's desire (as presumably covered in clear terms in the approved PID). There are basically two types of involvement (in general) of PC in this stage, depending on the capabilities of the Owner to execute the project. The first type (Type A) arises when the Owner has its own competent Project Implementation Unit (PIU). For example, the case of the Government being the Owner may be cited. The government normally has its own capable departments (such as PWD) for implementing a building project on its own with the help from PC only with respect to design clarifications, as and when required. In this type of situation, the responsibility of the PC will be limited to providing only the design clarifications necessary, and no further responsibility for this stage (Stage 4) will be practically there for the PC. On the other hand, the second type (Type B) of involvement of the PC arises when the Owner (or Client) does not have its own capable PIU. In this situation, the PC will have the responsibility for all salient aspects of procurement and physical construction of the project, as briefly discussed below. In case of the non-existence of a capable PIU of the Client, a separate mechanism for control of all activities under this stage is created by the Client. It (the Client) has a number of options for creating a PIU only for the project. Normally, two approaches are seen to be used in the formation of this PIU. One approach is to constitute a body with relevant stakeholders and competent technical persons, including the PC. This body is normally named Technical Advisory Committee (TAC). The PC is entrusted with the primary responsibility of construction management (Covered under Type B, as discussed above) under the overall advisory control of TAC. The second approach consists of appointing a third agency (maybe a Project Manager (PM)) to oversee the PC activities. Depending on the complexity and magnitude of the project, the Client will choose the appropriate approach. For a systematic discussion in this chapter, it is presumed that the Client has chosen the second approach and placed in position the TAC and a PM in addition to the PC having the primary responsibility of all aspects of the execution of the building project under discussion. The PM may be an individual, a firm, or a company. The choice is entirely up to the desire of the Client, depending on the nature and volume of activities of the project. There has to be a well-defined norm of coordination among the Client, TAC, PM and PC for a successful completion of the project. If the Client desires, the TAC and PM may be organized even before the approval of DPR so that it (DPR) is approved on being routed through PM and TAC.

5.3.4.2. Procurement

The different aspects of procurement may be better appreciated with a clear understanding of different project delivery models adopted (for construction management), as internationally in practice, depending on the type and complexity of the construction project on the one hand and on the other, on exigencies and preferences of the Owner. The types[92,95] are: Design-Bid-Construct, Design-Construct,

Fixed-Sum Contract, Cost-Plus-Fee Contract, etc. In this discussion, the 'Design-Bid-Construct' approach has been considered since it is a common practice in our county. However, in the case of some projects such as roads and bridges, the second model, 'Design-Construct', is nowadays being adopted. Other types are adopted to a limited extent, particularly in private sectors, including individual constructions. The discussion on procurement in this chapter is, therefore, limited to the model 'Design-Bid-Construct'. The design in all respects of the building project considered herein has been completed by the PC and already procured by the Owner at the initial stage of project management, as discussed earlier. All the work up to the approval of the DPR (by the Owner) has been completed before entering this stage. The procurement has to start with the 'bidding' for the selection of contractor(s) for the construction part of the model considered herein. It may be stated that the bidding documents, also called tender documents (as discussed under Stage 3), will naturally vary if the model adopted is other than the "Design-Bid-Construct" model (as discussed above).

There are primarily two approaches for bidding. The first approach is to adopt the bidding for selecting only one contractor (may it be a company, a firm or an individual) for both the two groups of construction activities: (a) Civil Works and (b) Services. The second one is to go for bidding to select a Primary Contractor for the works of the first group (Civil Works) only. Then, a number of secondary (or sub) contractors will be selected through secondary bidding to execute the works of the second group (services). The choice of the bidding approach is entirely dependent on the will of the Owner. There are both advantages and disadvantages of the two approaches of bidding. The major disadvantage in the case of the second approach, i.e., the case of selecting separate contractors for civil works and services is the possibility of development of clashes during execution. On the other hand, there is an advantage of buying time in allotment because the tender evaluation and award only for civil works normally will be faster than that involved in the evaluation and award of works of both the groups (civil works and services) to a single contractor. The author's own experiences suggest a preference for the second approach over the first one in view of better control (by the PIU) with respect to selecting secondary contractors of higher qualities for the services, leading to more effective and economic execution of the works of services apart from an advantage of utilizing the services of those secondary contractors during the stage of maintenance of services, as and when required.

5.3.4.3. Bidding, Evaluation and Award of Contract

This is the most critical phase of Stage 4, since the salient aspects of construction, such as completion of construction within the stipulated time, with the quality, as conceived in the design and within the estimated cost of the building with due honors to the EMP, is dependent on the judicious award of the contract for construction. Some of the Clients have standard norms for these activities, and some do not. If the Client happens to be a borrower from any financial institution for the finance required for the project, then obviously, the norms set by the concerned financial institution for this phase of work will have to be strictly adhered to. For example, if the World Bank (WB) is the financer, the norms set by it (WB)[102] will be adopted for the award of the contract. In the absence of set norms for these activities, the standard norms of advertising the NIT through web portals and newspapers are normally taken recourse to. A pre-bid meeting with the prospective contractors may also be arranged to give clarifications for issues such as specifications, site visits, conditions of the contract, etc., before the closing date of bidding.

At this stage, due consideration has to be given by the Client to the aspect of the 'Bid Evaluation Approach', which is a very important aspect and, in fact, it should constitute the first step in the whole process of 'bidding, evaluation and award of contract'. This approach has to be developed on the basis of a set of criteria to be judiciously chosen depending on the nature of the work for which the bidding is to be evaluated. Normally, the criteria should include parameters[103] like *"technical capabilities, price, quality of deliverables, project management plan, environmental sustainability, financial stability, and compliance with tender requirements."* This list of parameters is not exhaustive; more parameters, such as past performance of similar projects, experiences of the bidder concerned, market conditions, etc., may also be included, as per the type and location of the project. As suggested by the World Bank[102], the weightings and score thereof may also be established for different parameters included in the 'bid evaluation approach'. The approach so finalized may be included in the bidding documents. This document (Bid Evaluation Criteria BEC) takes care of Transparency, Value for Money and Integrity[102]. If the Client concerned does not have an appropriate BEC in place, the same needs to be established for the project in hand. Normally, this will be jointly prepared by the PM and PC (PD) and duly placed before the TAC. Once it is approved in the TAC, it will go to the Client for its final endorsement (or approval), after which it will be included in the bidding documents. It may be restated that the PIU for this discussion has been assumed to consist of the Client (the final authority for approval of all documents relating to project management other than those of clearances from statutory bodies), the TAC, PM and PC. The PIU considered herein may be in slight variation depending on the choice, source of funds and capability of the Client. The next step consists of creating a Bid Evaluation Team (BET). There are a number of approaches to the creation of a BET. It truly depends on the choice of the Client. Normally, the ideal approach will be to constitute a team comprising the PM, PC, Financial Manager (FM) or Accounts Officer of the Client and one or two technical members of TAC, as desired by the Client.

There is another aspect to be duly taken care of in the bidding process. This aspect emerges from the question as to what the eligibility criteria will be for the issue of TD. If the Client is a Government Department like PWD, there is apparently no need for such an eligibility criterion since it has a set of registered contractors categorized into a number of classes. For each of these categories, the limiting project value is well-defined. Therefore, for such clients, TD will be issued only to the eligible category as long as no financial institutions, such as ADB, WB, etc., are involved in funding the project. The financial institutions have well-set Prequalification Criteria[102] for the issue of TD to prospective bidders. Otherwise, the Clients normally develop Prequalification Criteria for the issue of TD, based primarily on factors such as proofs of financial capabilities, average turnover for the past few years (to be specified), experiences of successful completion of similar projects, etc. The TD is issued only to those who submit the necessary documents and substantially meet the requirements of the set criteria along with the request for TD. Then, all the parties receiving the TD are eligible to submit the bids by the closing date and time, as contained in the NIT. At the expiration of the closing date for submission of bids, the evaluation process for the bids received has to start immediately.

Process of Evaluation of Bids: The complete process of evaluation of bids comprises basically three steps[102]: the opening of bids and preliminary evaluation, the technical evaluation and the financial cost evaluation. As discussed above, the whole process of evaluation of bids will be carried out by the BET in place.

For the first step (for the opening of bids and preliminary evaluation), the bidders may also be invited. Immediately upon opening the bids, the preliminary evaluation is carried out. The objective of this evaluation is to examine if:

- All the bidding documents have been duly submitted or not with signatures of the authorized person(s) of the bidders,
- The technical and financial bids are in separate sealed covers or not.

The shortcomings, if any, have to be duly noted, and then the BET has to judiciously decide whether the shortcomings noted are adequate for the rejection of the concerned bid or not. Necessarily, TAC's and, subsequently, the Client's views to this effect may be taken by BET. If, eventually, any bidder is rejected at this stage, the decision to that effect may be notified formally to the bidder(s) concerned (including the refund of earnest money, if given in any form with the bid).

The second step of the evaluation process is the opening of the technical bids by the BET, which is only for the bidders qualifying in the preliminary evaluation (as stated above). The basis for evaluating the technical bid will obviously be the BEC covered in the bidding documents, including the bidding format given therein. The first part of this evaluation process will be to examine if all the parameters in the format given have been completely and duly furnished, along with the necessary supporting documents. If there is any shortcoming with respect to any parameter and/ or to any supporting document, it may be noted as a possible reason for rejection of the technical bid. Secondly, the technical bids have to be critically examined, and the proper weightings (presumably previously finalized) are awarded for each of the salient parameters of the technical bids. The weightings may be valued through scores (as previously decided). This is indeed a very complex stage in the evaluation process, and it does warrant a high degree of reasoning with integrity on the part of BET since any wrong or biased decision, if taken, is liable to be challenged by the bidder(s) to be affected. Each member of BET will give the allotted score to each parameter, and the total for all parameters thereof from each member is calculated. Subsequently, the average of all the total scores forms the basis of preparing the ranking list of bidders for the technical bid. Based on this ranking and the shortcomings, as noted in the first part of the technical evaluation, a final decision to reject any technical bid will be taken. This type of approach takes care of the *'Conflict of Interest',* if any (among the members of BET), to a great extent. The 'Conflict of Interest' is a phenomenon commonly found in many construction projects internationally, more so in the case of developing countries. It is in this context that organizations like WB[102] place adequate emphasis on 'Maintaining Integrity of the Evaluation Process'. Even in our country, there are many cases of construction projects facing problems like disputes, delays, cost overruns, etc., leading to 'Conflict of Interests'. The author himself, being PC for some projects, has the experience of fighting this type of conflict in the construction sector. There is an aspect of maintaining confidentiality till a final decision on the award of the contract is taken to avoid disruption in the process of evaluation. The anomalies in the process of evaluation and award of contracts, particularly in public-funded projects, are commonly observed. In support of this contention, an observation of Comptroller and Auditor General (CAG) of India[104] may be quoted as — *'Audit examined 802 contract bonds (1) costing Rs.4,857.57 crore executed by SEs and EEs, PWD in selected districts and found large scale deviations from laid down criteria in technical evaluation of bidders with majority of tenders (73 Percent) were not competitive where only one or two bids were received...'* Therefore, maintaining high integrity is an essential component based on the pre-determined criteria in the bid evaluation process so that the debriefing to an unsuccessful bidder (in the technical evaluation) may be necessarily given convincingly. The WB[102] has dealt with this aspect in greater detail with examples of scores on weightings. *(Interested readers may please refer to this reference).*

The third step in the procurement process is obviously the opening and evaluation of the financial bid. The bids of only those bidders who qualify in the technical bid, as discussed above, will be opened. In this case, the first task is to open the financial bids and then carry out the preliminary evaluation. The basic objective of this evaluation is to examine if all the formats, as contained in the bidding documents (for the financial bid), are duly filled in and signed (on every page) by the bidder (or their duly authorized person(s)). The bids that are incomplete with respect to some parameters (or documents) are rejected with justifications thereof. The remaining ones are considered for final evaluation. At this stage, the BET has to consider the total number of financial bids qualifying in the preliminary evaluation. If the Client is a government organization, the rule of at least three bids needs consideration, as recommended by the CAG[104]. In case of valid financial bids being less than three, the re-tendering is normally taken recourse to (in the case of government clients). However, in cases of other clients, the approach of re-tendering will be guided by other factors such as exigencies of work, norms of fund providers (if applicable), etc.

Before evaluating the financial bids, two important points need to be ascertained at the level of BET. The first one is the target cost up to which the Client desires to go in relation to the approved project cost (based on the project cost as estimated and duly approved), and the second one is weightage and scoring criteria (as discussed earlier in this chapter). Different pieces of literature are available on both of these points. The award based only on the lowest financial bid, as practised in many cases, has led to problems such as poor quality of construction, delays in completing the project, disputes, etc. Therefore, the approach for award recommendation based on combined weightage and score allotted to both technical and financial bids has been internationally popular[102] in recent times. Apparently, the effectiveness of an approach of combined scoring is dependent on to what extent the allocation of weightage and scores to different parameters of both the technical and financial bids made by the BET is judicious on the one hand and, on the other, on how honestly and appropriately the relevant parameters are evaluated and scored. This aspect has been elaborately dealt with, including examples from the WB[102]. Once the rankings of the bidders are finalized on the basis of combined scores, as discussed above, the BET has to place the ranking report with a detailed evaluation report before the TAC for detailed discussion in the meeting of the latter. It is normally the TAC that will decide whether a negotiation with the bidders is necessary or not in view of the total project cost arrived at through the evaluated financial bids. There are, again, different views on the ways and objectives for the conduct of negotiations. As per the World Bank[105]: *Negotiations may involve negotiating terms and conditions, price, social and environmental aspects and innovations providing they do not change the minimum requirements set out in the Procurement Documents. The negotiation is about creating extra value for the borrower and the Bidder/Proposer. It is not solely about trying to reduce the price'.* One way to conduct a negotiation is to call the top-ranking one or two bidders for negotiation, the basic objectives of negotiation being to bring down the cost as close as feasible to the lowest financial bid or necessarily even lower than that so that the final approved cost comes closer to the Client's target cost and others, as stated by WB (stated above). The other way is to call all the bidders (as per the ranking list), the objective being the same as given in the first case. In this case, a revision of the final ranking list will be necessary. Whatever approach is adopted, the basic necessity is the ethical values for a successful negotiation. The final award recommendation, along with the evaluation report, including the details of negotiations, if conducted, will be placed before the TAC. Once it is approved by TAC, the same will go for final approval (by the

Client) and final award of works will be given to the successful bidder and the award of the contract will be duly notified to all the bidders. The Earnest Money, received along with the bids, will be released to all bidders other than the one receiving the award of contract.

The letter of the award given to the selected bidder must include the condition(s) to the effect that the contractor (or their authorized representative) is required to come to the office of the Client for execution of contract documents, as detailed in the bidding document within a specified period. The contract agreement will be entered into only after the due submission of all necessary documents as applicable to the contract. Failure to do so within the specified time may result in the awardee abandoning the contract. In case of abandonment, the client has the option either to award the contract to the bidder in the second position of ranking list of bidding evaluation or to go for re-tendering debarring the one abandoning the contract. Normally, this type of condition is covered in the GCC, given in bidding documents.

Once the contract has been awarded, the project reaches the phase of entering into the physical construction.

5.3.4.4. Construction (Or Execution of the Building Project)

5.3.4.4.1. Organization Set Up

The broad guidelines for the management of this stage of activities are set by Part 7 of NBC[91]. The basic requirement for the physical construction of the project is a clear understanding of the organization set up on the parts of all the stakeholders with reference to the control of the activities of construction relating to construction practices. The Organization Set up (OSU) adopted for this project is diagrammatically represented in figure 5.2, given below for the delivery model of 'Design-Bid-Construct,' as stated earlier.

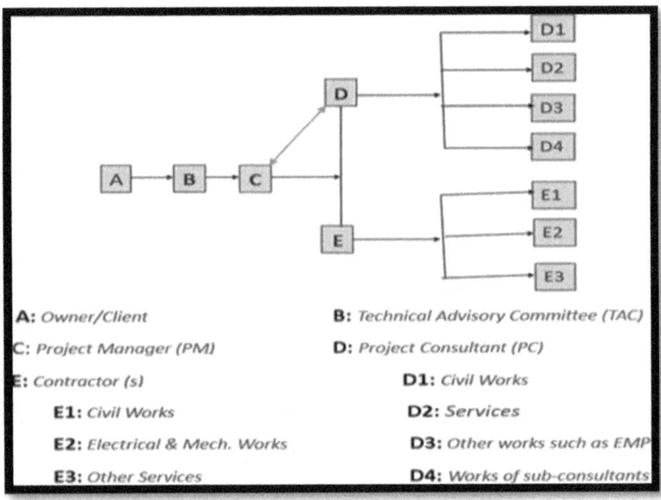

Figure 5.2: Organization Set up (OSU)
(Prepared by author with due regards to NBC[91])

This 'Organization Set up' is responsible in general for the physical construction of the project by ensuring the implementation[91] *'within the estimated cost and planned period to the required quality standards and in a safe and sustainable manner'*. Therefore, the coordination and mutual support among the different constituents of OSU is the basic necessity. The primary responsibility for developing this basic requirement lies with PM, PC, and the Contractor(s). In some of the projects, the provision of TAC is excluded. However, the author's own experiences indicate a number of its (TAC's) benefits, including a check to the 'conflict of interest' on the one hand and, on the other, maintaining the desired degree of transparency of different activities. In fact, there are many projects completed successfully with the inclusion of a suitably constituted TAC and by avoiding the engagement of an additional PM, the role of PM being played by the PC(PD) itself. Truly, the type of OSU is dependent on the choice of the Owner/Client. In either case, the 'coordination and mutual support' among all the constituents of OSU has to be ensured for the appropriate implementation with due regard to the relevant recommendations contained in Chapter 7 of NBC91, Volume 2 (for projects in India).

As discussed earlier, all activities involved up to the finalization of the DPR (followed by the Client's approval) have been completed by the PC (PD). Before entering into the phase of the physical construction of the project, it is obligatory to obtain all the necessary permissions and clearances of all the relevant statutory bodies concerned and as per the applicable laws of the land (discussed earlier in detail). As evident in the OSU (Figure 5.2), the constituents, the Client and the TAC are not directly involved at the construction site. All the remaining constituents of OSU are those directly involved in the production process of construction activities at the site, and they truly constitute the Production Team (PT). The main members of this PT are obviously the PM, PC (PD) and the Contractor(s). Once the contract has been awarded, there will naturally be pressure on the PT to get on with the work of actual construction activities. Therefore, the PT has to sit immediately to finalize the first task of construction planning.

5.3.4.4.2. Construction Planning

Normally, there is confusion between 'project planning' and 'construction planning'. The former is the planning of the whole project at the macro level, while the latter is the planning of the construction activities at the micro level. Construction planning (also internationally, at times, called production planning) basically *'establishes the methods to be used, assignment of personnel, the movement of material to the workforce, and the process of assembling the pieces*[95]*'.* The PT has to initially understand all technical, legal and administrative aspects, as contained in DPR and related contract documents. On detailed inspection of the site, a site layout plan for different utilities such as storage facilities for materials (like cement, steel, shuttering materials, etc.), storage of equipment, sanitary and water supply arrangements, electricity arrangement, site office, site laboratory facilities, workers room, shed for fabrication works, site security arrangements (including enclosure for the site boundary), etc. has to be prepared. Since it will take a few days for all the aspects of construction planning to be completed, the site preparation team may be immediately put to work at the site to complete all works based on the site layout, as prepared by PT. This type of approach will result in saving time on the one hand, and on the other, it will mean that the construction activities have already taken the initial start. Special care has to be taken for drainage of wastewater, collection of waste materials, control of dust and sound, etc., during the phase of site-preparation activities since sustainability is a major consideration, as contained in EMP. For a building project, the different salient aspects to be considered for construction planning, as recommended by NBC[91] are: (a) Sequencing of project components, (b) Planning tools, (c) Resource planning and (d) Time cost trade off. These aspects are dealt with in greater detail below:

Sequencing of Project Components: It may happen that people involved in the PT have never worked together before. For them, the process of construction planning may be treated as an opportunity to begin the *team-building process[95]*. It is in this context that all the salient member(s) of each PM, PC and Contractor(s), including suppliers of materials, subcontractors and sub-consultants, need to get involved in the whole process of construction planning (in all sessions to be held). This type of approach contributes immensely towards the desired team spirit, as required for a successful implementation of the project in hand. It was appropriately observed by S. K. Sears[95] *et al, 'an individual's expertise can identify future problems and solution'.* The task of sequencing different components (both for civil works and services) is, indeed, a complex one, and it truly requires expertise and experience in the relevant areas and involves individuals in a number of joint sessions of PT (including all members, as stated above). The two factors[91] governing the process of sequencing are 'the methodology of construction' adopted and 'the availability of resources'. The next phase of construction planning is obviously the task of 'Scheduling', the effectiveness of which is predominantly dependent on how appropriately the sequencing of project components is formulated.

Project Scheduling: The planning tools are adopted for scheduling different components of the project, identified and sequenced in the preceding phase of construction planning, the basic emphasis being predominantly laid on the targeted period of time for completion, as covered in the contract documents. There are cases of projects in which scheduling in different standard forms is done in the design stage and in the stage of bidding by the contractor(s) in the form of 'a construction plan'. However, at this stage, a final schedule has to be developed by the PT by giving due consideration to those, if available, as stated. The first part of the works involved in the process of developing the work-schedule is naturally the 'breaking down' of the total scope of projects into divisions such as foundations, sub-structure works, etc. to be followed by further breaking of each division into subdivisions. For example, the foundations will be divided into subdivisions, such as laying the foundation (whatever type of foundation), erecting the column, laying tie-beam/grade beams, etc. Thereafter, each subdivision will be further broken into a set of items of work on the basis of structural drawings and detailed specifications of items of work (as covered in the schedule of items of work). This stage of work is called the *Work Breakdown Structure (WBS)*[91]. Once this task has been completed, the task of preparing the 'Project Scheduling' has to be taken up.

Time, cost, and scope are the main constraints that the PT has to manage for any construction project. The major tools available today for the effective management of these constraints are the Gantt Chart, Pert Chart and Network Diagram. The Gantt Chart (traditionally known as the Bar Chart) has developed significantly nowadays; there is cloud-based software even for Gantt Charts with the inclusion of features like the addition or omission of tasks and defining dependencies, which parameters account for the shortcomings of traditional Bar Charts. A detailed discussion on a comparison of all these three tools is outside the scope of this discussion. What is attempted herein is a discussion of project scheduling with specific reference to the Critical Path Method (CPM*) of Network Diagrams. *(The star (*) on CPM has been used to distinguish it from CPM adopted for Construction Project Management).* The basics of CPM* are available in different textbooks and, therefore, avoided herein. Only the salient points of CPM* in relation to the scheduling of construction projects are briefly discussed. The Program Evaluation and Review Technique (PERT) is somewhat different from CPM*, and it (PERT) has been normally applied to research and development activities. This is because, as stated by Sears[95] *et al.: 'research is generally highly exploratory in nature; historical experience and background are rarely good measures for future time estimates, and make reasonably accurate time estimates difficult to establish. As a result, researchers have developed PERT as a method of statistically evaluating project duration over a time-sensitive domain.'*

Primarily, there are eight steps[95] in the process of developing the scheduling by CPM*. They are: estimating the time required for each network activity (project activities, as listed out in WBS), computing the time period required for overall project completion (not exceeding the time for completion as included in contract documents), establishing time intervals (time required between start and finish) for each activity, identifying the critical activities needing expedient execution, shortening the project duration at the least possible cost, adjusting the start and finish times of the activities with the main objective of minimizing the total execution period of the project by keeping in mind the absolute necessity of reducing resource conflicts and requirements of manpower and construction equipment, making a working project schedule that will show the anticipated dates for start and finish for each of the activities, as included in WBS and finally recording the assumptions made and the boundary conditions of the schedule so prepared. In this process of scheduling, the most important aspects are the allotment of time to each of the activities on the one hand and, on the other, the choice of the start and finishing time for each activity in judicious consideration of the interdependencies of activities. It is in this context that the experiences of the members of PT come into play in respect of assessment of time required for each activity with reasonable accuracy. To achieve this end, a number of discussion sessions of all the members of PT (as discussed earlier) will have to be held. Necessarily, the use of commercial software may be taken recourse to. Some available pieces of literature suggest a number of rules that may be useful when finalizing the time assessment for individual activities. Based on the network diagram so prepared, the Critical Path will be determined by following the standard procedures. There will be a number of paths to traverse from the starting node to the finishing node of activities. These paths do not represent alternative ones, and in fact, each one of the activities represented by these paths needs to be completed. Therefore, the longest path (in terms of durations required) will be the Critical Path (CP), and the total time required to traverse the CP will be the total duration of the project execution. *(A detailed discussion on the method of finding the CP has been deliberately avoided herein).*

The total time required to complete the execution of the project, as determined from CPM* (as briefly discussed in the preceding paragraph), does represent the actual time required to complete all the activities of the project. However, no project can be completed within this projected time, as everywhere and in cases of projects of any type, some days of working time, as considered in the scheduling through network diagrams, are bound to be lost on account of weather effects and other unforeseen situations leading to shortage of materials, delays in delivery of materials and equipment depending on locations of site of construction. A realistic assessment of the extent of loss of time accountable to this type of situation cannot be made. Therefore, the normal practice is to account for a Contingency Time computed on the basis of experiences gathered in similar projects executed in the recent past in the location concerned. Once this contingency time is duly assessed, the same will be added to the completion time suggested by the CPM* to get the final project completion time period. The contingency time so accounted for may go on being adjusted judiciously in the schedule periodically depending on the period and extent of working days to be lost during the period of physical construction.

Resource Planning: Manpower, Equipment, Material and Money are the predominant resources for all construction projects in varied proportions depending on their (projects') magnitude and complexities. The successful completion of the project within the scheduled time and cost with the conceived quality of construction is entirely dependent on how well these resources are managed. Therefore, the planning and management of these resources for any construction project require the deep attention of the PT, which has prepared the 'Project Scheduling' with the adoption of the Critical Path Method. This method leads to the total time required to complete the project, as agreed upon by the contractor(s) in the contract agreement. However, this project scheduling does not consider the very important aspect of managing resources required to complete each activity within the specified time. It is now its (PT's) responsibility to prepare a well-conceived Resource Management Plan (RMP), basically based on the project scheduling already prepared. The basic objective of the RMP will be to ensure the optimal availability of requisite manpower, material and equipment at the site for efficient execution of the activities within the time set in the construction schedule. It (RMP) will primarily include: the manpower scheduling (inclusive of technical staff, skilled workers and unskilled workers), equipment scheduling (depending on the methodology adopted), material scheduling and cash-flow scheduling. The assessment of requirements of all these resources has to be based on the 'Project Scheduling". In the absence of appropriate resource planning, two problems, as duly stated by A. Alhady[106] et al., will crop up. These are: Resource Allocation Problem (RAP) and Resource Levelling Problem (RLP).

Resource Allocation Problem & Resource Levelling Problem and Solution: The objective of solving these two problems is, as observed by Alhady[106] et al., *'to have a stable working site with no conflicts and also to balance the amount of work wisely throughout the construction project'.* The non-solution of these problems might lead to a situation of 'hiring and firing' of the workforce, which may eventually result in problems like delays, cost overruns, etc. A number of methods (including software thereof), as developed by researchers around the world, exist today to solve these problems. They include heuristic, metaheuristic and optimization approaches. By adopting a suitable approach, these problems can be solved, and the Project Scheduling prepared earlier is then readjusted to get the final Project Schedule. Based on this final scheduling of the project, the manpower schedules, material schedules, equipment schedules, cash-flow schedules, etc., will be prepared with due identification of parties (Client, contractors, consultants) responsible for delivery and supply as per the conditions of the contract.

Time-Cost-Quality Trade-off: This is a relatively new concept in construction project management and is included in NBC[91]. A number of research activities have been conducted around the world on this topic, as evident from the research paper of A. A. Galagali[107]. An account of time, cost, and quality is available for each construction project activity in the Project schedule, as discussed above. The concept of "trade-off" consists of making an analysis of the final project schedule with a view to deciding if there is a justification for reducing project completion time in due consideration to the impacts to be caused on the cost and quality of the activities of the project (by the reduction, if made). This 'trade-off' is indeed a complex problem and truly demands experiences and knowledge on the part of the PT concerned on the one hand, and on the other, it depends on the extent of the urgency of the project on the part of the client. The reduction in the total project time *(the process of this reduction is called 'Crashing' of the project)* will lead to an increase in the total cost of the project, the increase of cost being dependent on the percentage of this reduction. On the basis of their detailed study, A. A. Galagali[107] concluded—*"Crashing of any project must be taken only when the benefit received from crashing is more than the actual cost of crashing."* Therefore, a decision as to whether a project needs to be crashed or not has to be made judiciously by the PT concerned.

5.3.4.5. Physical Construction (Or Project Execution or Simply Construction)

This phase comes under Stage 4 of the CPM and is the longest and the most crucial phase of the activities involved in the whole *project life cycle.* During this phase, the deliverables to the Client are executed and completed in all respects, as duly covered in the Project Schedule, and finalized prior to reaching this stage *(discussed under the preceding heads and subheads).* All the activities at the site will basically have to be handled by the PT *(comprising PM, PC, and Contractors, as stated earlier).* Technical representatives of each of the parties of PT (called Site Engineers or Supervisors) with requisite qualifications and experiences in the domain of activities will be placed at the site, the supply of workforce being basically the responsibility of the contractors concerned with the divisions of activities as per contract conditions of the delivery model *(in this case, the model considered being 'Design-Bid-Construct).* All matters requiring the Client's approval will be routed through TAC. The primary objective to be targeted by the PT during this phase will be to complete the project within the time and cost (as per the Project Schedule) by ensuring the conceived quality and by satisfying all the stakeholders of the project. To achieve this end, as recommended by NBC[91], the different management functions warranting proper attention of the PT during the execution phase are: *Scope Management, Procurement management, Time management, Cost management, Quality management, Risk management, Communication management, Human resources management, Health and safety management, Sustainability management, Integration management and other management processes.* These functions are briefly discussed below.

5.3.4.5.1. Scope Management

It fundamentally means how the scopes conceived in the 'Project Schedule' finalized under phase 'Construction Planning' will be managed during the period of physical construction. The basic premises of the Scope Management Plan[91,107,108] are defining the roles and responsibilities, scope definition, project scope statement, work breakdown structure, scope verification and scope control.

For the project considered in this discussion, the OSU and the PT have already been dealt with in figure 5.1. The PT, which comprises the PM, PC, and Contractor(s), is directly responsible for physical construction. Therefore, the PM and the PC(PD) are basically responsible for the management of the scopes, as clearly formulated and included in the project schedule with the provision of *minor changes and/or authorized variations*[91]. There is an absolute necessity of close coordination between the PM and PC. The contractor concerned will execute the scopes under the direct guidance of the PC to be overseen by the PM, who is directly responsible to the Client *(the PM may be considered a direct representative of the Client).*

Therefore, the PC has the direct responsibility of managing the scopes, and the responsibility of executing the scopes obviously lies with the contractor as per the conditions of the contract *(discussed earlier)* under the joint guidance and supervision of the PM and the PC *(based on OSU considered herein).* However, the indirect role and responsibility of scope management lie with all constituent members of PT. Table 5.1, given below, has been prepared with respect to the roles and responsibilities for scope management.

Name	Role	Responsibilities
OSU	Client	To accept project deliverables
		To accept the completed project
OSU	Project Manager	To measure and verify project scope
	Project Consultant	To facilitate scope change requests
	(i/c their site engineers)	To facilitate impact assessment of scope change
		To place the scope change perspectives in TAC
		To get the approval on scope change from Client
		To update project documents based on changes
OSU	Contractor concerned	To communicate outcomes of scopes to workforce
	Site Engineers/Supervisors	To execute on the basis of updated schedule

Table 5.1: Roles and Responsibilities for Scope Management

The 'Scope verification' based on the scopes included in the project schedule has to be verified by the PM in association with the PC (PD). The deliverables to be handed over to the Client are listed on the basis of WBS, and the 'scope verification statement' that is prepared is to be endorsed by the client. During the execution period, this statement of deliverables (duly accepted by the Client) is the Project Statement Document, which will go on to be verified jointly by the PM and the PC (PD) to ensure that the project works remain within the scope of the project. It will be the joint responsibility of PT to 'control the scope' of the project, as covered in the scope verification statement already prepared. The change in scope, if any, has to be dealt with, as covered in table 5.1.

5.3.4.5.2. Procurement Management

The different aspects of procurement management depend basically on the type of delivery model adopted for the project in hand. In this discussion, the adopted delivery model is 'Design-Bid-Construct'. As such, the major responsibilities of procurement management lie with the contractors to whom the works under both the categories, i.e. Civil Works and Services, are awarded *(as discussed at the beginning of Stage 4)*. The procurement management plan has to include the process of procuring materials, equipment and products required for the production of different deliverables of the project, as covered in the Statement of Deliverables and also in time, as conceived in the Project Schedule. In the delivery model of 'Design-Bid-Construct', this Procurement Management Plan is normally developed by the PM, PC and the Contractors concerned. If some materials, such as cement, steel, etc., have to be supplied by the Client *(the cost thereof is recoverable from the concerned contractor, as discussed earlier)*, the schedule for the same has to be taken care of by the PM. Many aspects relating to procurement management are exhaustively discussed in different publications[95,105,107,108,109,110].

5.3.4.5.3. Time Management

The basic objective of time management is to complete the project activities as per the project scheduling (the baseline schedule) and the WBS, which define the duration of time for each of the activities of the project. During the stage of construction, the PT has to develop a plan for monitoring, reviewing and revising the baseline schedule depending on the actual progress of work and analyzing the time taken to achieve the recorded progress. The basic objective of this analysis is to ascertain 'deficiencies and slippage', if any. In case of slippage, measures such as adopting an increase of resources, including workforce, improved technique of construction, etc., will have to be taken so that the slippage may be taken care of by reducing the allotted time for the remaining activities. These tasks of recording the progress and reviewing and updating, including revising the project schedule, as necessary at a regular interval (may be daily or weekly or fortnightly) have to be planned by the PT. The detailed guidelines are available in BIS code of practice[110].

5.3.4.5.4. Cost Management

The cost management of a construction project primarily depends on the delivery model of the project. In this discussion, as stated earlier, it is the 'Design-Bid-Construct', and the basis of bidding has been the 'item rate'. Therefore, the baseline for cost management is naturally the *'Schedule of items of work with the accepted rates and quantities of each item of work'*, as included in the contract documents for each category of contractors (civil works and services). It is presumed that the quantities estimated for each item of work, included in the schedule of quantities and specifications during the stage of design, are correct. Therefore, the responsibility for the correctness of the quantities involved for each item within an accepted range of variation lies with the PC concerned. This accepted range of variation in quantities is normally included in the conditions of the contract under the cost-escalation clause. The author, playing the role of PC in many projects, has the experience of working in the variation range of ± 10 Percent of scheduled quantities, beyond which the contractor concerned has a valid reason for claiming escalation of the accepted rate of the item concerned. At times, this range of variation is linked to the total cost of the project. During the phase of physical construction, the total cost of the project, the schedule of accepted rates, project schedules, other management plans, etc. are available. As such, the cost management approach basically consists of monitoring the progress and finding the cost thereof based on the accepted rates and quantities (as contained in the accepted schedule of rates and quantities). In line with the recommendations of NBC[91], this approach includes recording measurements of works completed at a certain stage (to be decided by the PT, normally on the completion of certain activities), working out the cost of measured activities based on the accepted schedule of items of work, comparing the cost and quantities so obtained with those of corresponding items of work on the project schedule. Based on a critical analysis of this comparison, a realistic assessment of its impact on the total cost of the project will be made to decide whether any corrective measure within the limits of contract conditions is necessary. The broad guidelines given in code[111] may be adhered to.

5.3.4.5.5. Quality Management

Total Quality Management (TQM) has been defined in the Govt. of India Manual[112] as— *'the management approach of an organization, centered on quality, based on the participation of all its members and aiming at long-term success through customer satisfaction, and benefits to all members of the organization and society'.* In this case, the customer is any person from OSU who is receiving a particular product. The objective of TQM is to involve everybody from all levels and across all activities of the project. The preparation of the quality management plan is a prerequisite to the start of the physical construction. It covers three basic components[91]: *quality planning, quality assurance and quality control.* A part of the quality planning is completed during the process of project design, including scheduling while finalizing the specifications and drawings for different project activities. Now, a critical analysis of the specifications for each activity is done for the identification and preparation of a comprehensive list of different tests for different activities, to be conducted for conformity with quality standards, as laid down in the relevant codes of practice and as conceived in design. Quality Assurance, on the other hand, is: *"essentially a preventive activity and is therefore to be systematically planned in advance".* The activities normally include planning for different tests to be conducted, including identification of laboratories, interval of different tests, acceptance criteria in conformity with code provisions, aspects of inspection and control processes, assignment of roles and responsibilities of the PT, etc. Quality control relates to activities to be taken care of during the phase of physical construction, as contained in manual[112]. It (Quality control) broadly involves (a) control of methods of construction depending on the type of each activity and (b) control of end products (quality of materials brought to the site, field, laboratory tests, etc.).

The quality control has to be based on the system responsibilities set in the quality assurance plan. *(For details, the interested viewers may refer to guidelines as contained in manuals and codes[91,113,114])*

5.3.4.5.6. Risk Management

There are different sources that create risks that might impact the execution of project activities. The impact may lead to many issues, such as delays in construction, cost overruns, disputes, etc. Therefore, the development of a risk management plan is an important component of the construction planning. The primary areas to be analyzed and the possible risks to accrue thereof are the safety of the project team, financial safety, safety against legal risk, safety against lapses in proper resource management, safety against environmental risks, etc. The risk management process consists of developing a risk management plan that will include all necessary measures for identification, monitoring and mitigation, the basic thrust being laid on assigning the responsibility of risk management to appropriate team member(s) *(in case of occurrence of any risk during execution).* The broad guidelines are given in IS code[114].

5.3.4.5.7. Communication Management

The basic requirement for communication management is to establish a communication system, which is the Management Information System (MIS), depending on the complexity of the project on the one hand and, on the other, on the structure of the OSU for a particular project. The different agencies are involved in a construction project, and therefore, MIS to be established has to integrate[91] – *'the work and information flow within each agency and flow of information between different agencies.'* To facilitate the flow of information, the fundamental necessity is to establish the communication chain by including the key persons of different agencies involved in the project. Normally, all the constituent members of OSU, including their site representatives (site engineers/supervisors of PM, PC and Contractors), are included in this chain. The appropriate tools and technology, as available, will be used. The MIS so developed has to incorporate two-way communication for saving time in exchange of information. The MIS is configured in such a way that all the data relating to the progress of activities, value of works in terms of cost, quality control aspect, updated schedule of activities as compared to the targeted project schedule, etc., are duly incorporated. The broad guidelines are given by NBC[91].

5.3.4.5.8. Human Resources Management

The quality of a construction project at the level of physical construction substantially depends on the skills and knowledge of the workforce, including both skilled and unskilled ones. Therefore, the essence of human resources management lies in engagement of workforce with the required level of skill and knowledge in the respective domain of activities. It is in this context that the job-specific orientation/training program needs to be conducted at the site by the competent members of the PT. In addition, the engagement of the workforce in adequate numbers for each activity is also an aspect to be duly managed so that, as far as possible, the culture of overtime work in any shit is not encouraged. A mechanism for regular checking of the workforce on the basis of the human resource schedule prepared earlier has to be established. The broad guidelines are given by NBC.

5.3.4.5.9. Health and Safety Management

The management of health and safety is an essential requirement at construction sites since, historically, there have been many cases of incidents leading to the suffering of the workforce in different forms, including loss of limbs and life. These sufferings can be prevented by adopting an appropriately formulated management plan based on the available regulatory laws and standards applicable to the country where the site is located. In India, as suggested by NBC[91], standards and provisions set in *the Building and Other Construction Workers (Regulation of Employment and Conditions of Service) Act, 1996* have to be duly honored by due incorporation of necessary measures into the management plan to be followed by its (plan's) due implementation at the site during execution. The broad guidelines for the preparation of this plan are given by NBC.

5.3.4.5.10. Sustainability Management

The different aspects of sustainability in construction have been already dealt with during the phases of planning and design, including the development of an EMP. Sustainability management consists of developing a mechanism for taking care of all the parameters, including those of EMP, during the phase of physical construction. This mechanism is based on the specific identification of specific areas involved, assigning responsibilities, formulating a system for monitoring and reporting, and facilitating reviews by statutory bodies concerning sustainability, environment, etc. *(as discussed during the phases of planning and design).* The broad guidelines for sustainability are given by NBC.

5.3.4.5.11. Integration Management

The primary objective of integration management is to ensure coordination among the different agencies (or the project teams) involved in the project during the construction phase. There are interdependencies of different activities, and therefore, the failure of any team to complete a particular interdependent activity will adversely affect other activities that are dependent on it. Therefore, these teams will have to work for their mutual interest. The failure on the part of any team of interdependent activities may lead to conflicts among the affected agencies. This is where the processes to be covered in the integration management plan will resolve issues in the interest of all parties involved. The primary responsibilities of ensuring the desired integration through the processes as conceived in the plan will naturally lie with the PM and PC (PD). The broad guidelines for this integration management plan are covered in IS 15883 (Part 12).

5.3.5. Stage 5: Commissioning

The commissioning of a construction project is a vital and critical process for ensuring that it (the project) functions efficiently, safely, and economically with respect to all components of civil works and services, including all equipment. Two basic necessities for commissioning are:
- Constituting a commissioning team and
- Preparing a checklist of items for checking.

The team will include members of the Client, PM, PC and Contractors concerned. The checklist is based on the as-built drawings for both civil works and services and will depend on the uniqueness of the structure. In the case of a building, too, it (the checklist) depends on its type (residential, commercial, industrial, etc.). If any defects or shortcomings are noted during the process of commissioning, immediate measures will be taken by the parties concerned for corrections. On the completion of the corrective measures (if required), a commissioning report will be prepared and will be duly signed by the relevant members of the commissioning team. There is another aspect of commissioning, which is called ongoing commissioning. This relates to the defect-liability period, as covered in contract documents. The subsequent defects, if noted by the Client within the defect-liability period, will have to be taken care of by the contractors concerned at their (contractors') own cost as per the provision of the contract documents. This is an important aspect to be included in the commissioning report.

5.3.6. Stage 6: Project Closing (or Project Closeout)

This is the last stage of construction project management. This stage primarily includes the handing over of the project to the Client and closing of all the construction activities at the site of the project. Apparently, the stage appears to be simple from a distance. However, it is truly not so, and it does involve a complex task of the documentation to be duly accounted for in the process of closing out a construction project, the degree of complexity being a function of the type and magnitude of the project. For a building project, the salient documents, including those stated in NBC[91] are: a list of inventories such as equipment, fitting, etc., certification and settlement of final bills for all contractors and sub-contractors, etc., obtaining completion certificates as required from statutory bodies concerned, preparation of maintenance manual, commissioning report, all other documents, such as guarantees for equipment and salient fittings, all as-built drawings, list of all left-out materials, fittings, tools and equipment procured at Client's cost, record of orders for change in specifications (if any), etc. All the documents as per the list so prepared (both hard and soft copies) will be handed over to the Client through the channel as per OSU. The other activities necessary for closeout include restoring the surroundings of the building, completing site clearance, and obtaining a hand-over certificate from the Client.

5.4. Concluding Remarks

Having been at the end of the topic of this chapter, it has been strongly felt that it is, indeed, a very complex area in view of the fact that a very big volume of considerations is involved, as evidenced by the availability of literature on it (this topic) internationally today. This is because no two structures are the same in all respects bearing on project management, though the principles of stages involved are basically the same. For example, the treatment of the stages of project management of a building under a particular delivery model will vary substantially from that of the same building under a different delivery model. Similarly, the treatment will be different from one type of structure to another. This is the reason why, even today, this is a live topic for case studies and research. These studies have been facilitated by the availability of different commercial software worldwide. The treatment of the topic in this chapter has been specific to a building project. However, the author (of this book) is aware of the importance of the treatment of the same specific to an infrastructure project (roads and bridges) in view of the extensive volume of presently on-going construction activities under this sector elsewhere. It could not be taken up at this end because of time constraints. Interested readers/viewers may please refer to the book[95] under reference, in which the treatment of the topic in relation to a bridge project has been extensively made.

Chapter 6 | Maintenance of Buildings: Different Aspects of Its Management

6.1. Introduction

The maintenance of a building is an important area to be duly taken care of during its lifetime to keep the built environment in good condition so that it continues to serve the objectives for which it has been built. The maintenance management deserves the due attention of the owner. Today, different guidelines, including a number of software relating to maintenance management of buildings, are internationally available. In India, too, there are a number of standards[91,115,116,117] published by BIS apart from books and other publications. While thinking of this area of management, the first point striking the author's mind is the aspect of levels of ownership of buildings. There exist broadly two levels of ownership of buildings: individual and institutional (or organizational). However, the basic concept of maintenance management of buildings applies to both types of ownership, though there are obvious differences with respect to the ways they are treated. The experiences gathered by the author as an engineer responsible for the maintenance management of buildings and other infrastructure of a reputed organization *(Tocklai Experimental Station under Tea Research Association of India, a pioneer Tea Research Centre established during the British Era)* over a period of nine years (from 1978 to 1987) during his professional life speak of the volume of activities and aspects of management in this area on the one hand and on the other, of the importance of maintenance management of structures. The author gathered the most valuable experiences bearing on different aspects of maintenance management during that period when management technology was not as advanced as it is today.

The NBC[91] (Chapter 12) deals with different aspects of Asset/Facility Management. The building is only one type of physical asset irrespective of its type of ownership (an individual or an organization). An individual owner may own a single building or a group of buildings, while an organization owns a series of buildings used for different purposes. It is in this context that a difference in ways of maintenance management adopted by the two broad types of ownership of buildings comes in. An individual owner normally depends on hired service providers for different maintenance activities, while an organizational owner has a maintenance team of its own for regular maintenance activities and takes hired service-providers only for specialized activities.

As observed in NBC (Part 12)[91]: *'Maintaining a building is expensive; it costs many times more to run a building over its lifetime than to build it, yet maintenance is often not accorded the priority it warrants. A poorly maintained building will be a drain on resources and will impair building use, whereas a well-maintained building will function smoothly and represent an appreciating asset to its owners'.* Therefore, the importance of maintenance management does not need to be over-emphasized.

The NBC[91] classifies the management of Asset/Facility as *'Hard Services'* and *'Soft Services'*. In this discussion, only *Hard Services* are considered since they relate only to the maintenance management of buildings. The hard services basically include the Building Fabric and Building Services.

6.2. Phases of Maintenance Management of Buildings
The different phases involved in the professional approach to the maintenance management of a building may be broadly summarized through the flowchart given in figure 6.1a. These phases constitute the complete cycle of maintenance management of a building. The maintenance of a building is a continuous process and broadly covers two categories: the 'Building Fabric' and the 'Building Services', as shown in figure 6.1a.

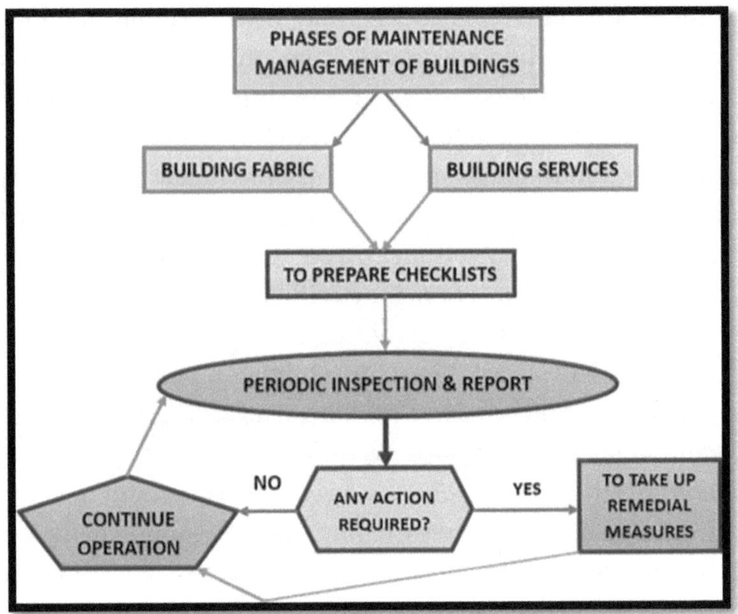

Figure 6.1a: Flowchart of Main Phases of Maintenance of Buildings

6.2.1. Building Fabric

The building fabric includes all elements and components (both structural and non-structural) of a building. In fact, all the primary items of civil works completed during construction, including addition/alterations and refurbishment, excluding the building services, are covered.

6.2.2. Building Services

The building services for maintenance include[91]:

- Plumbing and drainage,
- Air-conditioning, heating and mechanical ventilation (HVAC) services,
- Electrical installations,
- Lift and escalators and
- Fire-fighting detection and suppression.

6.2.3. Preparation of Checklists

The preparation of the checklists for both the building fabric and building services is the most important phase in the whole framework of maintenance management. The effectiveness of the whole management framework depends on how appropriately and accurately the respective checklists (for both categories) are prepared. The persons engaged for the task by the owner of the building must have the appropriate technical knowledge in the respective domain (building fabric and building services). For organizational ownership, the technical persons concerned (or the maintenance engineer) of the maintenance department will be responsible for preparing the required checklists and maintaining a register (or an inventory) for each of the buildings. However, the problem arises in the case of individual ownership. They have to seek the help of the hired technical persons to prepare the checklists for each of the elements of the two categories (figure 6.1a). The broad guidelines for the preparation of checklists have been given by NBC (Part 12)[91]. There are other publications as well dealing with the preparation of detailed checklists. The publication[118] by M. Ghambari *et al.* has exhaustively dealt with different aspects of the building management framework, including the aspect of the preparation of the related checklists. The importance of checklists for both the categories of a building consists of the fact that the owner remains organized in the maintenance activities for their building(s). They (the owners) can differentiate between the tasks to be done by themselves and the tasks to be done by hired service providers. The checklist for the building fabric should include items like roofs, floors, walls, doors/windows/ventilators, finishing items, etc. Under each of these items, there will be a number of sub-items. Similarly, for each type of service (as mentioned under building services given above), separate checklists are to be prepared. Different items and sub-items for both the building fabric and building services of a building appear in the Appendices to Part 12 of NBC[91].

6.2.4. Periodic Inspection & Report

The inspection of a building for the purpose of maintenance of elements/sub-elements of a building causes a complex issue with respect to its periodicity (or frequency of inspection). The degree of complexity is primarily dependent on the type of the building and its type of use. In addition, the type of ownership of a building has also a bearing on the frequency of inspection, since the organizational owners have their own maintenance teams. However, the individual owners normally do not have well-organized maintenance teams. In the codes[91,115], the frequency of inspection has been treated under three types of inspections for the purpose of maintenance measures of a building as Routine, General and Detailed ones. These three types are briefly discussed below.

Routine: Routine maintenance normally relates to different elements/sub-elements of building services. However, at times, it may relate to sub-elements of building fabric, such as roof leakage, wall dampness, floor dampness, and roof drains (or gutters). There cannot be a scheduled time for problems of this type. The maintenance measures have to be taken as and when the problems develop. In this case, obviously the problems have to be reported for actions to the owner or to the maintenance team of the owner (depending on type of ownership) by the users (in case the owner is not the user). In the case of institutional ownership having a maintenance unit, normally, there exists standard-forms (work-order sheets) given to the users of the building (irrespective of the type of use) through which the respective users report the problems to the maintenance unit. When receiving these work-order sheets, the relevant technician of the maintenance unit takes corrective measures. In solution to the problems, there is even a provision for taking the feedback of the users on the work-order sheet itself. However, if individual owners have no technical persons of their own, the assistance of hired technical persons is naturally taken.

General: The general inspection[91] of all elements and sub-elements of both the building fabric and building services has to be conducted by a technically competent engineer visually once in a year. The major objective of this inspection is to make budgetary provisions for a subsequent year in the case of an institutional maintenance unit for items of work involving substantial cost. These items of work involve items like painting the building fabric, some elements of building services requiring repair or replacements, etc.

This general inspection (once in a year) is necessary even for buildings owned by individuals for proper planning of major items of works mentioned above.

Detailed: The frequency of the detailed inspection of a building is truly a conditional one.

Generally, it is dependent on two considerations. Firstly, the report of the general inspection has to be critically examined to identify if any defect noted in the building fabric relates to any structural element likely to cause concern for the structural stability under any occasional event such as wind, earthquake, etc. If so, a detailed inspection has to be conducted by an appropriately qualified engineer. Secondly, a detailed investigation has to follow immediately after the occurrence of major events such as fire, earthquake, blast, etc. However, as suggested by codes[91,115], under normal conditions, a detailed inspection based on the prepared checklists needs to be conducted for the building fabric by a competent engineer at least once in five years.

Report: The inspection reports item-wise (based on checklists) have to be prepared for both the general and detailed inspections, as described above. For routine inspection, normally a report is not an absolute necessity, since the defects noted during this inspection are immediately attended to. As recommended by NBC[91]: *'The resulting information should be arranged in three categories: those matters requiring immediate attention, those that can be placed into a maintenance program and those that can be postponed but should continue to be monitored and reviewed'.* Based on the reports, it has to be decided whether the normal operation of the activity/activities concerned should continue or not before the remedial measures for the noted defect(s), if reported, are taken. The different aspects of remedial measures are discussed below.

6.2.5. To Take up Remedial Measures

The remedial measures have to be taken on the basis of the type of maintenance methods (also called the type of building maintenance[119]). The broad types[91,119] are: Planned Maintenance and Unplanned Maintenance. The different phases involved in the whole process of adopting the remedial measures are summarized in the flowchart shown in figure 6.1b, which is truly in continuation with the one shown in figure 6.1a.

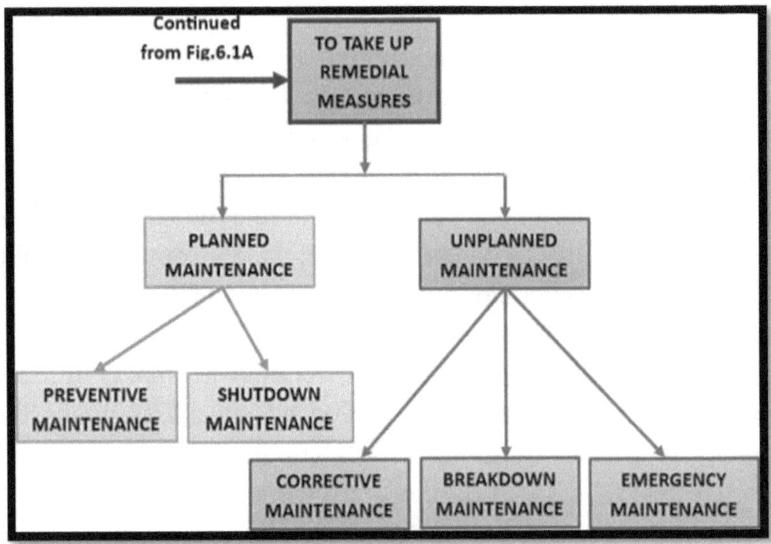

Figure 6.1b: Flowchart for Main Phases of Maintenance of Buildings

6.2.5.1. Planned Maintenance

The planned maintenance *(also called the scheduled maintenance)* of a building normally includes the maintenance works that are planned or scheduled for execution to keep the building in normal operational condition. It broadly includes two categories, as covered in NBC91:

- Preventive maintenance and
- Shutdown maintenance.

6.2.5.1.1. Preventive Maintenance

It is further split into sub-categories: (a) Condition-based maintenance, (b) Reliability-centered maintenance and (c) Total productive maintenance. The reports of the inspection *(only those of General and Detailed inspections, as discussed above)* need to be carefully examined by technically qualified persons to identify the items with regard to these three sub-categories. A brief discussion on each of these sub-categories is presented below.

A. Condition-based Maintenance

The inspections conducted, as discussed above, are a step taken as a strategy to monitor the actual condition of the building fabric and the building services. Therefore, a critical analysis of the reports thereof reflects the type of maintenance measures to be taken. Depending on defects, the preventive maintenance measures may include[91] *'Cleaning and servicing, Rectification & repairs and Replacements'*. The aspect of 'Rectification and repairs' relating to building fabric will be discussed in greater detail at a later stage in this chapter.

B. Reliability-Centered Maintenance

This method of preventive maintenance applies to facility systems such as HVAC systems in a building. An appropriate preventive measure is taken on the basis of data on the monitoring of parameters like operating efficiency with respect to energy consumption, comfort cooling, etc.

C. Total Productive Maintenance

The concept of total productive maintenance is apparently more applicable to industrial buildings, which house a lot of equipment and machinery. As far as the building fabric and building services are concerned, the application of this concept may be looked upon as a measure that will ensure appropriate cooperation between the maintenance team and the users in increasing the effectiveness of maintenance measures with respect to both aspects *(building fabric and building services)*.

6.2.5.1.2. Shutdown Maintenance

The shutdown maintenance is necessary when there is planned execution of major renovation/rectification works for the building elements. In this type of situation, the shutdown will mean stopping the normal operation of building activities for the purpose of which it is used.

6.2.5.2. Unplanned Maintenance

The unplanned maintenance works relate to the defects of a building (for both the fabric and services), which require immediate attention. These defects may include water leakage problems, major cracks in structural elements, failure of the functioning of the lift, settlement of the foundation, etc. For these types of defects, the measures to be taken have to be based on the views of the competent technical persons of the domain covering each of the defects concerned. The owner concerned has to act as per the recommendation of the relevant experts. As shown in figure 6.1b, the unplanned maintenance of different defects comes under three sub-categories[91]:

- Corrective maintenance,
- Breakdown maintenance and
- Emergency maintenance.

6.2.5.2.1. Corrective Maintenance

The measures necessary for corrective maintenance may be either planned or unplanned, depending on the exigencies of the measures formulated for correction. For example, the case of cracks observed in the case of the building element may be taken. One may prefer to observe the propagation of the crack for some time just to conclude whether it is a dead one or a live one before the measure to be taken is duly formulated as a planned corrective measure. However, defects like the failure of the lifts, roof leakage, etc., have to be taken as unplanned corrective measures.

6.2.5.2.2. Breakdown Maintenance

The breakdown maintenance relates mostly to building services. The most common example is the failure of the water supply system to a building or a group of buildings *(in the case of both types of ownership – individual or institutional)* having individual water supply systems. The breakdown may be accountable to the failure of the pumping system or the drying-up of the water source itself. The restoration measures become an immediate necessity.

6.2.5.2.3. Emergency Maintenance

The situation of emergency maintenance to a building is brought about by the incidence of an event. The most glaring example is the earthquake. The example of an apartment building (cited once earlier) suffering extensive cracks/crushing of concrete in the columns of the soft storey on account of the 2021 earthquake in the city of Guwahati (Assam) may be given. It warranted emergency maintenance measures to create a sense of safety among the occupants of the upper floors. In fact, this type of emergency maintenance has to be taken up with due regard to cost-effectiveness.

What has been discussed in the preceding pages of this chapter presents a broad approach to building owners for the maintenance management of its built-environment. However, many more aspects bearing on this broad approach are there. The salient ones, as covered in NBC[91] include cost effectiveness, other factors affecting maintenance, influence of design, maintenance planning, maintenance work programs, etc. NBC deals with all these aspects in detail. Therefore, a detailed treatment of these aspects has not been included in the scope of this chapter. However, the maintenance aspects relating to the building fabric alone are discussed in greater detail in the subsequent parts of this chapter under the broad heading of *'Maintenance of Building Fabric – Repair and Rehabilitation'*.

6.3. Maintenance of Building Fabric – Repair and Rehabilitation

The maintenance of the building fabric *(defined earlier)* broadly involves three strategies: Repair, Rehabilitation and Retrofitting. Understanding these three strategies in clear terms is a prerequisite for making a judicious choice of the strategies for the maintenance of a building, depending on its present condition, its type of use, its age and the extent of deterioration of its elements and components. The maintenance of a building fabric is an absolute necessity for ensuring the continuity of its original condition, which is the one achieved on completion of its construction with the specifications necessary for the intended life. As the building (in service) starts growing in age, the damage/distress of different types starts developing because of[121]: *'cyclic temperature variations, overloading, physical causes & aggressive chemical attack due to environment, etc.'*. Therefore, the task of regular maintenance through the adoption of one or more of the repair, rehabilitation and retrofitting strategies becomes absolutely necessary. The objective of regular maintenance is to keep the building in its original condition during its intended life. The maintenance truly does not cover any measure taken for buildings considered to be deficient with respect to the requirements of the current provisions of the applicable codes, including the seismic codes. Obviously, a building found to be deficient would require strengthening measures *(discussed in Chapter 2)* like rehabilitation and retrofitting. However, even the repairing measures might include strategies like rehabilitation and retrofitting (to a limited extent) depending on the type and extent of damage/distress suffered by the building fabric.

In this discussion, different aspects of repairing and rehabilitating an RCC building (only the building fabric) have been taken up. As stated in the previous para, only repairing and rehabilitating a structure to bring it back to its original condition is considered. The rehabilitation and retrofitting, as required for strengthening a building deficient with respect to strength and stiffness in light of the requirements demanded by the modern codes, are not covered herein. The different aspects of structures vulnerable to structural damages likely to be caused by events like wind and earthquakes have been dealt with earlier. For a systematic discussion of different aspects of *'repair and rehabilitation'*, as required for maintaining the building fabric in the 'original condition', the flowchart summarizing broad phases and sub-phases involved in the whole approach to the maintenance of the building fabric has been prepared as shown in figure 6.2.

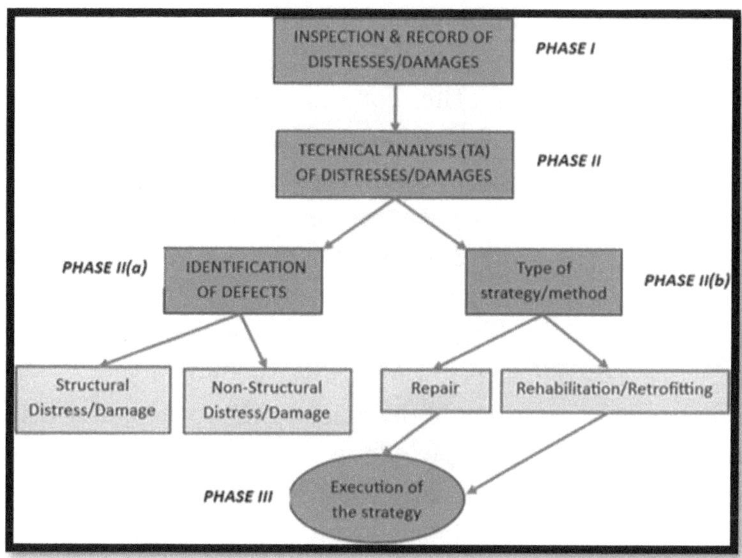

Figure 6.2: Flowchart Summarizing the Broad Steps in Maintenance of the Building Fabric

6.3.1. Inspection and Record of Distresses/Damages (Phase I)

The types of inspection *(Routine, General and Detailed)* naturally apply to building fabric. The reports thereof yield the items of distresses and damages in the building fabric, which need to be duly taken care of by the appropriate repair methods, rehabilitation and retrofitting. The technical analysis of the defects will lead to the identification of the category of maintenance measures, which may be covered either in (a) Planned maintenance or in (b) Unplanned maintenance. For the appropriate analysis, the identification of different types of distresses/damages developing in the building fabric is a prerequisite.

The commonly observed distresses and damages in building fabric may be broadly looked upon as—(a) those in structural elements and (b) those in non-structural elements, including finishing items. These distresses and damages are discussed herein with reference to an RCC building.

6.3.1.1. Distresses/Damages in Structural Elements

Since the discussion is limited to an RCC building, the major structural elements are of reinforced concrete occasionally, except for the roof *(because, at times, even in an RCC building, the roof consists of CGI/Dyna/Asbestos roof)*. The common distresses in reinforced concrete are cracks, crushing of concrete, disintegration and spalling *(or peeling off)* of concrete, erosion of concrete, corrosion in rebars, seepage of water, etc. There are different physical causes, including foundation settlement, responsible for the distresses of different types.

6.3.1.2. Distresses/Damages in Nonstructural Elements

The non-structural elements of the building fabric include walls (both outside and inside), doors/windows/ventilators, all architectural elements (horizontal and vertical fins) outside the building, and all finishing items, including floor finishing and painting. The salient distresses/damages include cracks in masonry walls, dampness in masonry walls of the ground floor, shrinkage cracks in plaster, green stains in brickwork, termite attack, etc.

The distresses and damages mentioned above do not represent an exhaustive list. These are considered salient ones for a discussion on the methods of repair in general.

6.3.2. Technical Analysis of Distresses and Damages (Phase II)

As observed by CPWD[121]: *The engineers responsible for maintaining buildings often begin repair activity without adequate understanding of the factors responsible for the defects.* There are many instances that corroborate this statement of CPWD. Therefore, an appropriate technical analysis of the distresses/damages (as noted above) is an absolute necessity for appropriate adoption of method of repair/rehabilitation. The engineer conducting this analysis has to be well-equipped with the knowledge and experience in both the design and construction of the building fabric on the one hand and, on the other, with appropriate knowledge of the methods/materials of repair and rehabilitation. The basic purpose of technical analysis is to identify the root cause leading to a particular type of distress/damage so that the required remedial measure can be suggested to the owner of the building. The salient points bearing on technical analysis are briefly discussed below.

The distresses/damages observed have to be initially analyzed to group them (the defects) into two categories: *'Structural distress/damage'* and *'Non-structural distress/damage' (both being under Phase II(a))* (Figure 6.2). The structural defects are those observed in the structural elements, which are caused by structural actions such as axial forces (causing either tension or compression), bending moment (causing bending tension and compression), shear (causing diagonal tension and compression), etc. These defects, if not duly attended to at the time, may lead to an adverse impact on the integrity and stability of the building. These defects are primarily accountable for deficiency in planning and design, poor workmanship during construction, poor quality control, poor maintenance, overloading, use of substandard materials, etc. Structural defects invariably appear in structural elements. However, structural defects are observed at times even in non-structural elements such as infilling walls placed between columns *(but its contribution to lateral stiffness is not accounted for in the design, as suggested in seismic code),* particularly when the building is acted upon by lateral forces caused by wind, earthquakes, etc.

Non-structural distresses/damages may occur both in structural and non-structural elements. These defects are primarily accountable to poor workmanship in the construction of elements such as brickwork, plastering, painting, etc., dampness (from sources like leakage from the plumbing system, rising dampness from the ground, poor waterproofing, etc.), chemical reactions on account of the use of faulty ingredients in the adopted mortar used in brickwork, etc. The non-structural defects in non-structural elements do not pose any risk to the integrity and stability of the building. However, they do reduce the lifespan of the elements concerned, apart from causing inconvenience and discomfort to the users. On the other hand, the same occurring in structural elements, if not corrected in time, will eventually pose a risk to the stability of the building.

The broad objective of technical analysis of the defects under both categories (structural and non-structural defects) is to identify the defects falling under planned maintenance and unplanned maintenance (as discussed earlier with reference to figure 6.1b). This identification facilitates the appropriate adoption of repair methodology and repair materials. The technical analysis is discussed below in greater detail with reference to defects in structural and non-structural elements.

6.3.2.1. Identification of Defects (Phase II(a))

As discussed in the preceding subhead, the defects observed need to be duly identified as (a) Structural Distress/Damage and (b) Non-structural Distress/Damage. Some of the aspects of identification are discussed below.

6.3.2.1.1. Structural Distress/Damage

The structural defects are those appearing in structural elements, which, in the superstructure of an RCC-framed building, are columns, beams, slabs, and shear walls (*if adopted*). In addition, the substructure, too, includes structural elements depending on the type of foundation. However, in this discussion, these foundation elements are excluded, though the effect of the settlement of the foundation is a consideration because of its impact on the elements of the superstructure. The appropriate identification of the structural actions responsible for the appearance of the defects is the basic objective of the technical analysis of the reported defects. It is, indeed, in this context that the due analysis can be conducted only by engineers having a clear understanding of the structural actions and the effects thereof. The structural defects in columns, beams and slabs are discussed below.

6.3.2.1.1.1. Structural Distresses/Damages in Columns

The salient structural defects commonly observed are shown in figure 6.3. The structural actions leading to different defects (as shown in the figure) are briefly discussed defect-wise as follows.

6.3.2.1.1.1.1. Horizontal Cracks

Cracks of any type in concrete (or reinforced concrete) are obviously caused by tension developing in the direction perpendicular to the line of the crack.

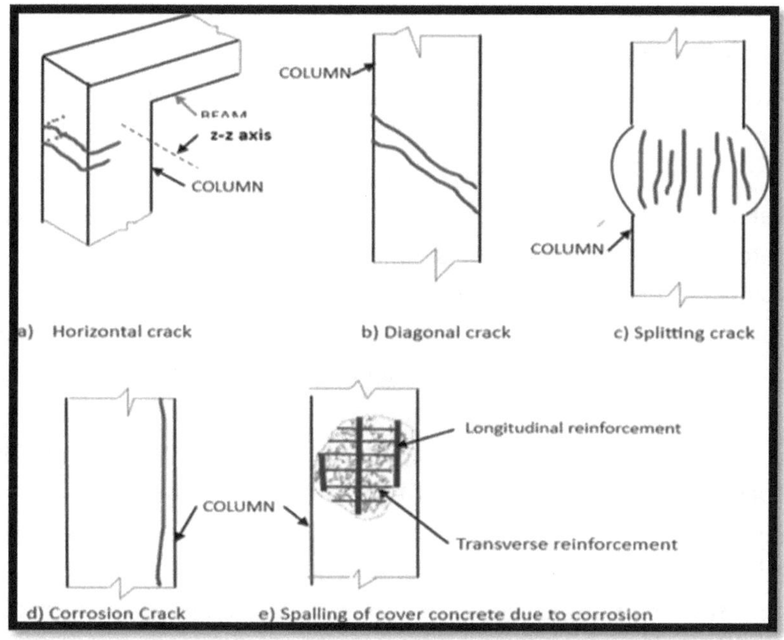

Figure 6.3: Structural Distresses in Columns of an RCC Building

The fundamentally striking point consists of proper appreciation of the structural action(s) producing this tension. These horizontal cracks invariably appear near the beam-column joint, as shown in figure 6.3 (a). The section fails to take this tension. There are a lot of factors leading to this situation, basically the flexural tension due to the bending moment about the z-z axis (shown in *the figure).* This bending moment may cause the crack under two situations - the first one being under normal loads *(DL + LL)* and the second one being under lateral load *(DL + LL + Lateral Load caused by wind, earthquakes, etc., causing tension on the face concerned).* The cracks are developed primarily for two reasons: deficient design and/or poor-quality control during construction. However, there may also be some secondary reasons, such as overloading (resulting from a change in the use of the building), poor detailing of required reinforcement, etc. The remedial measures for these types of cracks have to be natural and based on the correct assessment of the cause of the development.

6.3.2.1.1.1.2. Diagonal Cracks

The diagonal cracks, as shown in figure 6.3(b), are naturally caused by tension developing in the direction diagonally opposite to that of the crack itself. Therefore, it suggests that the basic reason is the horizontal shear in the columns. The horizontal shear in columns is primarily caused by lateral forces (wind, earthquakes, etc.). Therefore, the diagonal cracks in a column pause a serious issue requiring immediate measures to avoid the risk of collapse of the building, particularly in our country, where the whole of the land mass is earthquake-prone with variable zone factors. The primary reasons for these types of cracks are attributable to the deficiency in design with respect to providing both transverse and longitudinal reinforcement with due regard to the adopted cross-section and/or poor workmanship in construction. The diagonal cracks may appear anywhere in the height of columns in a storey (more likely in the ground floor columns) since the horizontal shear in a particular column is nearly uniform.

6.3.2.1.1.1.3. Splitting Cracks

The splitting cracks are vertical ones having variable widths, as shown in figure 6.3(c). The section obviously splits under heavy compressive stress due to which the longitudinal steel tends to buckle, causing thereby a tension along the plane of the cross-section on the cover-concrete. The reasons, thereof are attributable to a number of factors such as overloading, low reinforcement ratio, less transverse reinforcement, poor concrete-quality, smaller cross-section, etc.

6.3.2.1.1.1.4. Corrosion Cracks

Apart from structural cracks caused primarily by structural actions (as stated above), there exists the possibility of the development of secondary cracks caused by environmental factors such as shrinkage cracking, thermal cracking, freeze-thaw, etc., during the service life. These cracks, irrespective of their widths, facilitate the ingress of chloride from the chloride-contaminated environment and initiate corrosion in the reinforcements (both transverse and longitudinal). This type of corrosion is called *chloride-induced corrosion*[122]. This type of corrosion is common in the sea coast because of the presence of chloride. The other type of corrosion, called the *carbonation-induced corrosion*[122] is caused by either moisture coming in contact with rebars through permeable concrete or atmospheric air (containing moisture) coming in contact with rebars through the secondary cracks. The cover concrete provided is less than the one recommended by the code, and it aggravates the inflow of moisture. The corrosion keeps on propagating with time and leads to vertical cracks along the outside of the longitudinal rebars, as shown in figure 6.3(d). The remedial measures have to be based on the extent and the type of corrosion.

6.3.2.1.1.1.5. Spalling of Cover Concrete Due to Corrosion

Because of the weakening of the surface concrete, the process of spalling occurs. It starts initially with the formation of surface cracks, and then the surface concrete starts spalling in small pieces, thereby exposing the reinforcements, as shown in figure 6.3(e). There are a number of reasons causing the spalling of the cover concrete. The basic reason is the corrosion induced in the reinforcement through the carbonation process, as briefly stated in the case of *corrosion cracks.* The rust, so formed, on the rebars, creates a pressure on the cover concrete and results in spalling. Other reasons for spalling are attributable to *'fire exposure', 'freeze and thaw cycles',* and *'alkaline chemical reaction', 'lack of adequate concrete cover', 'poor quality of cover concrete', lack of proper curing,' etc.* If adequate remedial measures are not taken to repair the localized spots of spalling immediately on appearance, the spalling will spread over greater area and pose a threat to the safety of the building, since the column is the most important structural element.

6.3.2.1.1.1.6. Crushing of Concrete

The crushing of concrete in a column relates to a failure mode for a concrete element. It indicates not only the loss of compressive strength of the section but also the exceeding of the capacity of the section to resist the compressive stress induced on the section by overloading, foundation-settlement, occasional events such as earthquakes, etc. The crushing of concrete in a column is not a generally observed stress for a building fabric in the service when regular maintenance is considered.

6.3.2.1.1.2. Structural Distresses/Damages in Beam

The structural actions causing structural distresses/damages in the beam of an RCC building are primarily bending moment, shear force and torsional moment. The bending moment is responsible for the development of flexural cracks in the tension zone and the crushing of concrete in the compression zone. On the other hand, the vertical shear and torsional moments are responsible for the development of shear cracks. The corrosion in rebars may also lead to structural distress, such as cracks and spalling. Some of these defects are briefly discussed below with reference to the distresses schematically shown in figure 6.4 below.

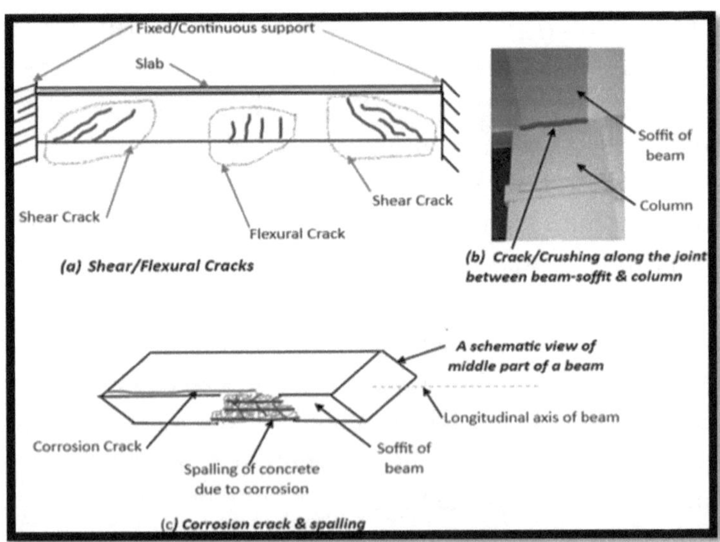

Figure 6.4: Structural Distresses in Beam of an RCC Building

Flexural Crack: The flexural cracks, as shown in figure 6.4(a), mostly appear near the mid-span of the beam, where the sagging bending moment becomes maximum (invariably under gravity loads). These cracks appear basically due to a deficiency in design or construction. The required tension-reinforcement is not available and consequently the concrete (being weak in tension) develops crack. The flexural tension may also be more on account of overloading at times as well. Therefore, it has to be observed critically for a reasonable period of time to monitor whether the cracks appearing are active or passive before making a choice for the remedial measures to be adopted. The tension near the support caused by the hogging bending moment is obviously very high. However, normally, a tension crack at the top of the beam (the tension zone being at the top) does not appear because of the presence of a slab. Against this situation, at times, the crushing of concrete at the bottom face of the beam along the joint between the beam and column occurs, particularly when the lateral force (either due to wind or earthquakes) produces compression in this zone, as shown in figure 6.4(b). The crushing occurring in this zone clearly indicates a deficiency in design. Similarly, in this zone, there exists the possibility of the development of tension crack as well (Figure 6.4(b)), particularly when the reversal of stress takes place on account of lateral forces. This tension crack (if it appears) is also primarily attributed to the deficiency in design in earthquake-prone zones or in zones with high wind speed.

Shear Crack: The shear cracks appear diagonally in an area close to the supports, where the vertical shear is maximum, as shown in figure 6.4(a). The cracks develop due to the diagonal tension produced by the vertical shear; the basic reason for development is the inadequate shear reinforcements (vertical stirrups and/or inclined bars). This type of crack in a new building is obviously accountable for design deficiency. However, the same observed in a sufficiently aged building may be attributed to overloading resulting from a change in use or to deficiency in requirements, as demanded by modern codes of practice—the seismic codes in particular. The diagonal cracks may also be caused by torsional moments developing in a beam. The diagonal cracks developing on account of torsion normally extend around the whole cross-section in contrast to the ones caused by vertical shear. The torsion in a beam is normally caused by secondary beams monolithically supported only on one side. Similarly, it (the torsion) is also caused by a slab monolithically connected on one side (as in the case of exterior beams). Therefore, these shear cracks need to be repaired before they reach the stage of impacting the stability and integrity of the building.

Corrosion Crack: The phenomenon for the development of corrosion cracks in a beam is exactly the same as the one described in the case of the same (corrosion cracks) for the column. The cracks develop along the longitudinal reinforcement, as shown in figure 6.4(c). In the figure, only one crack has been shown. In fact, there may be a number of cracks parallel to the one, as shown. The reasons leading to the growth of corrosion on reinforcement are the same as those described under *'Corrosion cracks in column'.*

Spalling of Concrete: The phenomenon of spalling of concrete in the case of a beam is also the same as the one discussed in the case of the column. The basic reason for spalling is the formation of corrosion through the carbonation process, as discussed under 'spalling of concrete' in the column.

The other reasons responsible for spalling are the same as those discussed in the column. The spalling of concrete occurs, as shown in figure 6.4(d). In the figure, the spalling of concrete only on the soffit (that too only in one part) has been schematically shown. However, it may occur in other locations, including the sides of the beam covering an area in excess of that shown in the figure, depending on the extent of corrosion. The corrosion keeps on propagating, and therefore, remedial measures need to be taken immediately to address the appearance of the spalling of concrete in any location of the beam.

6.3.2.1.1.3. Structural Distresses/Damages in Slabs

The structural distresses (mostly cracks) are accountable to factors such as overloading, deficiency in design or construction, settlement of foundation, temperature fluctuation, chemical reactions, etc. Some of the commonly observed structural defects are schematically shown in figure 6.5. These defects are briefly discussed below.

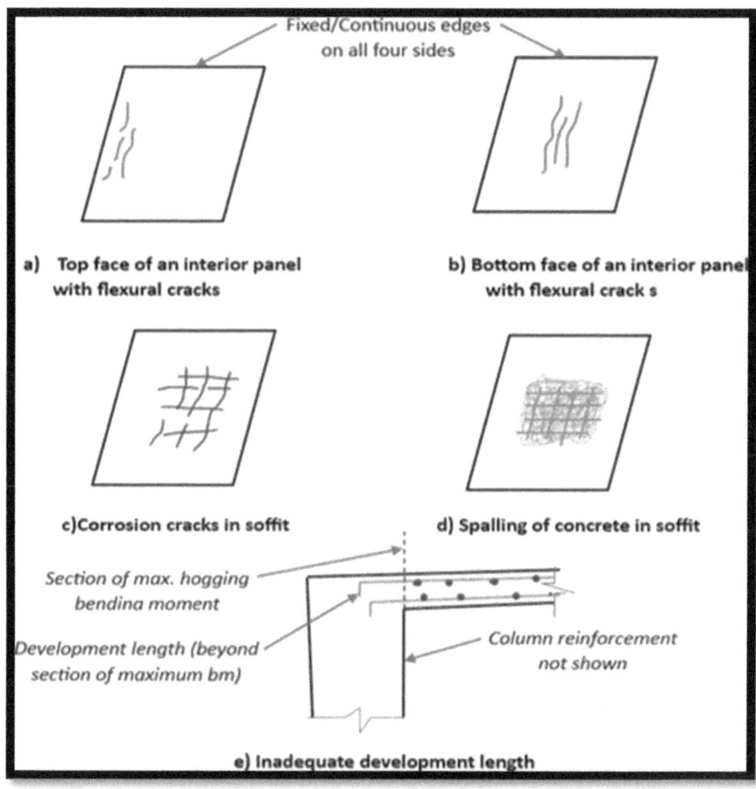

Figure 6.5: Structural Distresses in Floor/Roof Slab of a RCC Building

Flexural Cracks: The flexural cracks caused by the hogging bending moment *(being maximum along the shorter span near the supporting beams)* appear along the longer edge, as shown in figure 6.5(a), obviously on the top face of the slab. On the other hand, the flexural cracks caused by the sagging moment *(being maximum along the shorter span in the mid-span) appear along the longer span, as shown in figure 6.5(b),* obviously on the bottom face of the slab.

The major reasons for the flexural cracks are attributable to deficient design *(with respect to section and/or amount of reinforcement)* and/or faulty construction. The commonly observed fault in construction is the inadequate development length provided beyond the section of maximum hogging bending moment of the slab, particularly in the case of slab-beam connection in the beams beyond which the slab is discontinuous. This situation is illustrated in figure 6.5(e). In many cases, it is observed that the development length to be provided, as shown in the figure, does not exist.

Corrosion Cracks: The phenomenon leading to the development of corrosion cracks in slabs is the same as the one described in the case of columns and beams. These cracks are commonly observed on the bottom face (soffit) of the slab, as shown in figure 6.5(c). The reasons leading to these cracks are also the same as those given in the case of the column.

Spalling of Concrete: The phenomenon, as discussed earlier in cases of columns and beams, applies to the slab as well. It occurs normally on the soffit of the slab, as shown in figure 6.5(d). There have been cases of spread of spalling over larger areas. This is because remedial measures have not been taken immediately on the appearance of the spalling of concrete over a small area. Consequently, the corrosion goes on propagating along rebars thereby causing the spread of spalling area.

6.3.2.1.1.4. Structural Distresses/Damages in Shear Walls

The shear walls are not adopted in all the RCC framed buildings. These walls are basically provided in some selected areas only with the basic objective of increasing the lateral strength and stiffness *(under lateral forces caused by wind, earthquakes, etc.)*. The shear walls, in fact, carry both the gravity loads and lateral loads and structural stresses/damages on these elements depend on their positions and orientations in the building[123]. The possible distresses/damages on shear walls *(under cyclic loading)* may lead to typical failure mechanism[124] such as sliding shear failure, flexural failure, diagonal tension failure, diagonal compression failure and hinge sliding failure. Therefore, any distress indicative of shear crack, crushing of concrete, diagonal tension crack, etc., has to be taken care of immediately upon appearance on the shear walls through the adoption of appropriate remedial measures for averting the possibility of failure.

6.3.2.1.1.5. Structural Distresses/Damages in Infill Walls

As stated earlier, infill walls are invariably adopted in a building for obvious functional reasons, with or without openings. However, in design, its contribution to lateral strength and stiffness was not accounted for in India prior to the publication of the revised seismic code[25]. Even then, the infill walls placed along planes of the building frames (between columns) have been known to act as structural elements when the building is subjected to lateral forces caused by wind, earthquakes, etc. These infill walls carry no gravity loads in contrast to shear walls. Therefore, structural distresses on infill walls are basically caused by lateral forces only. In most of the cases, the infill walls are of unreinforced brick masonry. Some of the commonly observed distresses/damages in infill walls are shown in figure 6.6. The basic structural actions brought into play by the lateral force P acting on the building frame *(as shown in the figure)* are tension, compression and shear. The tension occurs along the diagonal BD, and the compression occurs along the diagonal AC, as long as the direction of lateral force P is shown in the figure. However, on the incidence of P in the direction opposite to that shown, the tension will occur along the diagonal AC, and obviously, compression will then occur along diagonal BD. The shear force induced does act horizontally. The effects of these structural actions are briefly discussed below with reference to the figure.

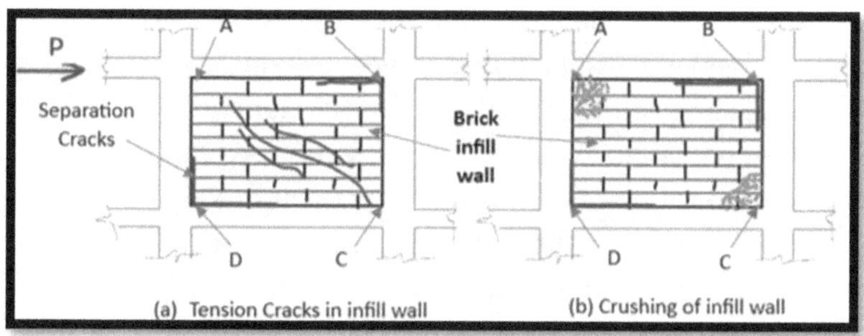

Figure 6.6: Some Distresses in Brick Infill Walls

Tension Cracks: Under the lateral load P, the tension develops in a direction perpendicular to the compressed diagonal AC, and as a result, the tension cracks develop along this diagonal as shown in figure 6.6(a), the tensile strength of brick wall being very small. As a result of the compression along the diagonal AC, the separation cracks too develop along interfaces between the infill wall and the frame at the corners B and D, as shown in figures 6.6(a) & (b). These separation cracks develop because of the poor bond strength in the mortar adopted for the joints along the frame. These types of stresses were observed even in many footages of structural damages caused by past earthquakes in addition to observations made in model-tests conducted by the author himself[125,126] and others.

Crushing of Infill Wall: In many cases, the crushing of the infill wall occurs at the corners of the compression diagonal, as shown in figure 6.6(b) (at corners A & C in the figure). The reason for this type of crushing is attributed to the development of compressive stress in excess of the compressive strength of brick infill. The crushing occurs before the tensile stress produced under the lateral load P in the diction along diagonal BD reaches the tensile strength of the infill.

Horizontal Shear Crack: There exists the possibility of the formation of horizontal shear cracks along the mortar joints (horizontal ones) since horizontal shear develops on the infill under the lateral load P. It normally develops when the mortar used for jointing bricks is of poor quality having poor shear capacity. The distresses appearing on the infill wall need to be taken care of immediately on appearance for a number of reasons. The most important reason is the fact that the infill walls (existing in the building frames) do provide a reserved lateral strength that gives protection against the possibility of serious damages to the building under severe occasional events such as wind, earthquakes, etc, which give rise to lateral forces. However, they (infill walls) do not carry gravity loads except for their self-weight. The appropriate remedial measures depend on the extent of distress on the one hand and, on the other, on the type of structural action that causes the distress. The type of strategy/method to be adopted will be discussed later, based on the flowchart given in figure 6.2.

6.3.2.1.2. Non-structural Distresses and Damages

Non-structural distresses/damages may appear in both the structural and non-structural elements of the building fabric. These distresses do not adversely impact the stability and integrity of the building. However, they do affect its (building's) functionality in terms of inconveniences to the users, aesthetic values, etc., apart from decreasing the lifespan of the building components. Therefore, the adoption of timely remedial measures is an absolute necessity. Many types of non-structural defects are commonly observed in the building fabric. Salient ones appear in the foundation, masonry works, concrete and reinforced concrete works, steel members, timber works, finishing works and plumbing works (in the building). For a systematic discussion of different types of non-structural defects, two broad areas of the building fabric have been considered: the building envelope and the interior. The most commonly observed non-structural defects are discussed below under these two broad areas.

6.3.2.1.2.1. Non-Structural Defects in the Building Envelope

The building envelope basically consists of the roof, external walls, doors/windows/ventilators (on external walls), ground/basement floor slab *(as the case may be)* and architectural elements such as vertical fins, horizontal chajas, etc. The different defects are briefly discussed below with reference to each of these elements/components.

6.3.2.1.2.1.1. Roof

The defects depend on the type of the roof. In India, the common types of roofs are pitched roofs (with roofing sheets such as CGI/Dyna/Asbestos sheets) and flat RCC roof slabs with terrace treatment. In the case of pitched roofs, the common defects are leakage of rainwater through the roofing sheets and the gutters and downpipes. The basic reason for these defects is attributable to poor installation with respect to both the roofing sheets and the ridging sheets. During installation, non-adoption of the adequate lap length (as recommended by the applicable code of practice) in the joints of roofing sheets and those of ridging sheets leads to the leakage of rainwater. In addition, at times, the sagging of the roof on account of the settlement of the supporting structure leads to the development of the source of leakage. The rainwater passing through the sources of leakage falls into the ceiling of the topmost floor and causes decay of the ceiling board and the frame (if the frame is of timber or steel) supporting the ceiling. In the case of the RCC roof slab, the defects in a terrace depend greatly on the types of use on the one hand and, on the other, on the type of treatment adopted for the terrace. The roof is, indeed, the climatic barrier upwards. However, many a time, it (the terrace) is used for a roof garden or a traffic-bearing surface. Nowadays, the terrace is even used as a parking deck[127]. The terrace roof is built basically with two principles. One is the terrace roof without roof membrane with or without thermal insulation, and the second one is the terrace roof with roof membrane with or without thermal insulation[127]. However, in India, the most commonly adopted roof terraces do not use thermal insulation. The commonly adopted treatment of the terrace is indicated in figure 6.7. In most of the buildings, the thermal insulation is not provided particularly in areas having no extreme heat from the sun. The normal practice is to provide a cement concrete topping mixed with adequate waterproofing compound *(against cement concrete, there is a practice of adopting lime concrete also),* as shown in figure 6.7(a). The purpose of providing the topping is primarily to provide a proper slope up to the outlets of roof drains.

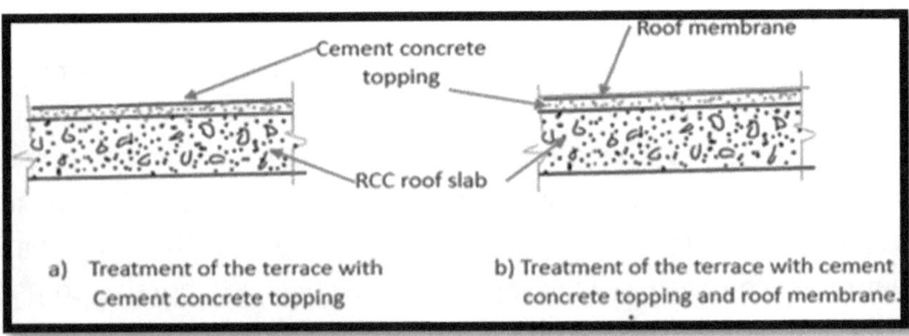

Figure 6.7: Sectional Views of Roof Slab with Roof Treatments without Thermal Insulation

Extreme care needs to be taken when laying the topping by providing expansion joints at appropriate spacings to avoid cracks that are accountable for thermal expansion. In addition, the trowelling finish of the top of the topping is desirable, though it needs more time and skill on the part of the masons. Providing a proper roof membrane on the top of the topping, as shown in figure 6.7(b), is a preferred practice for superior roof protection. The adoption of thermal insulation in a roof terrace is a specialized job. A detailed discussion on this aspect has been avoided in this chapter.

The most commonly observed defect in a flat terrace roof is water leakage, as in the case of a pitched roof. The reasons for the leakage are attributable to many factors, such as reckless traffic in the roof *(leading to a worn-out state)*, the development of fine cracks on the roof membrane or the topping itself (as the case may be) due to its exposure to the sun, seasonal variation in temperature, poor drainage including clogging of outlets, downpipes, etc. Through the cracks, the rainwater comes in contact with the RCC roof slab and slowly seeps in, thereby causing corrosion on the rebars of the slab and eventually, some spots appear as wet areas on the soffit. The appearance of these defects is a clear indication of a poorly maintained roof terrace.

6.3.2.1.2.1.2. External Walls

The commonly observed non-structural distresses/damages in external walls of RCC framed buildings include cracks, rising dampness, peeling paints, fungi and small plant attacks, insect or termite attacks, defective plaster rendering, efflorescence, etc. The reasons for these defects are briefly discussed below so that the appropriate remedial measures may be adopted.

Cracks: In a framed building, the cracks considered are only non-structural since the structural cracks that may develop even in non-load-bearing walls under lateral loads have already been discussed under the subhead of *structural distresses/damages.* The basic reason for the development of non-structural cracks is the process of expansion and contraction of the materials of the wall on account of its exposure to moisture resulting in alternate wetting and drying process. This type of cracks may occur anywhere in the wall depending on its exposure to moisture and also on the properties of thermal expansion and contraction of the materials concerned. In addition, it depends on the quality of workmanship and age. The cracks developing along the interfaces between the wall and beam/column and also along the sides of the frames of doors/windows/ventilators are commonly observed. These cracks do not pose a risk to the stability of the building under gravity loads.

Dampness: The dampness in external walls *(Internal walls being discussed separately)* is a common defect in many of the buildings. It is caused by many factors, such as rainwater, condensation, rising dampness from groundwater and flooding, service leaks, moisture in the air, etc. The rainwater falling in external walls *(which are not well-protected with proper finishing)* gets into the brick and mortar joints through capillaries of materials, and the portion concerned becomes damp. The leakages in downpipes, roof drainage, and service pipes also cause dampness on external walls. The condensation of humid air on the cooler face of a wall is also a factor causing dampness. The most commonly observed reasons for dampness on walls on the ground floor of a building are rising dampness and flooding. The dampness is caused by the groundwater/floodwater that is carried through the plinth wall that is in contact with the soil below the ground floor level. This dampness gets transported through capillary actions to the walls above the plinth level if there is no barrier (in the form of Damp Proof Measure in place, i.e. on the top of the plinth wall). The provision of a proper DPC layer or a proper plinth beam with waterproofing compound is to be duly made for creating this barrier. However, in the case of many of the old buildings, this provision is found to be absent or inadequately made, and as a result, the dampness in the ground floor walls develops. The flooding in excess of the plinth height (even in the presence of the DPC layer) will naturally cause dampness. If due remedial measures *(to be discussed under Phase II(b) Figure 6.2)* are not taken, the dampness on walls will lead to the development of injurious effects on the walls, such as the growth of plants, the peeling of paint, the growth of mold and fungi, the decay and disintegration of brick walls by sulphate, the efflorescence, blistering/flaking/bleaching of paint. Some of the commonly observed defects on external walls are shown in the photos (taken on some buildings of Guwahati City (Assam) given in image 6.1).

The Growth of Plants: The leakage in waste downpipes causes dampness and creates an ideal location for the growth of moss and plants, as shown in image 6.1(a).

The Peeling of Paint: The dampness in walls leads to the peeling of paint, as shown in figure 6.1(b). The peeling normally occurs on building facades (primarily on plastered areas subjected to dampness). The peeling is also caused by improper preparation of the surface before painting. The leakage of waste downpipes additionally causes dampness on the walls, leading to discoloration, as shown in image 6.1(c). This photo shows additionally the growth of a plant just at the source of leakage.

The Growth of Mold and Fungi: The growth of mold and fungi in areas of dampness in walls (both external and internal) is very often observed. A photo showing this growth appears in image 6.1(e). As stated by Bakri[128] *et al: "The terms fungi and mold are often used interchangeably, but mold is actually a type of fungi. Concerning about indoor exposure to mold has increased along with public awareness that exposure to mold can cause a variety of adverse health effects."* They grow in areas with water leakage, high humidity, or dampness.

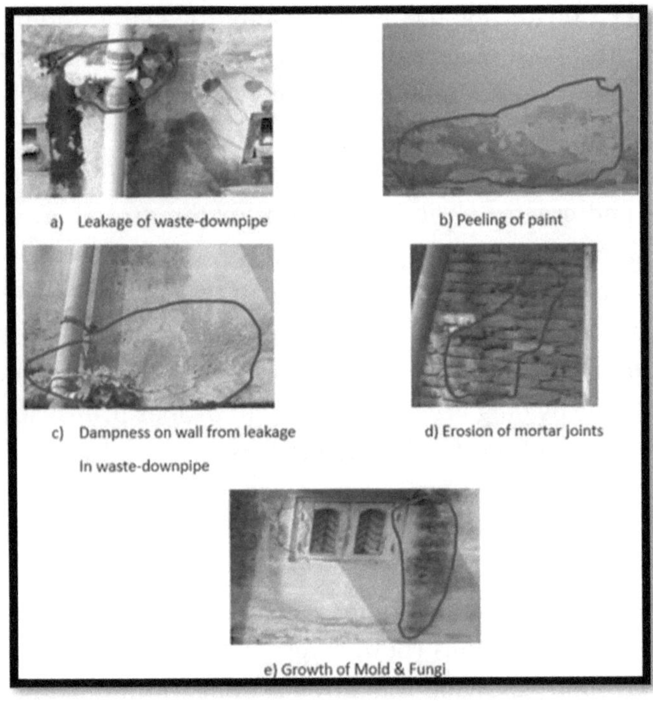

Image 6.1: Photos Showing Some Non-Structural Defects on External Walls
Source: Photo Taken by Author in Some Buildings of Guwahati City

Decay and Disintegration of Brick Walls Caused by Sulphate: As stated by IS Code[129], the sulphate present in brickwork causes decay and disintegration of the bricks and mortar joints: *'Sulphates present in brickwork react in the presence of water with alumina contents of the cement and hydraulic limes in the mortar and rendering, forming other salts with a considerable increase in volume, and consequently, chip and spall the bricks, produce cracks in the joints and renderings, and disintegrate the mortar'.* The photo in image 6.1(d) shows the erosion of mortar joints of an exposed brick wall (not plastered).

Efflorescence: This is a process given rise to by *the Crystallization of Salts*[129]. In many cases, the bricks used in the brickwork contain soluble salts. When water enters the brickwork, the salts present get dissolved out and then get deposited on the face of the brickwork in the form of fine crystals. This phenomenon is commonly observed, particularly in new construction, and the reason is attributed to cleaning the dried wall with water instead of dry brushing. This is because, when cleaned by water, the efflorescence appearing on the dry surface gets dissolved and again gets reabsorbed by the brickwork.

6.3.2.1.2.1.3. External Doors/Windows/Ventilators

In buildings, the commonly adopted types of doors/windows/ventilators are timber, aluminium and steel. However, in most of the older buildings in India, timber doors/windows/ventilators are used. Therefore, the defects in aluminium/steel ones have been kept outside the scope of this discussion. There are many commonly observed defects[130] in timber doors/windows/ventilators. The salient ones are briefly discussed below.

Separation Crack around the Frames: It is a common defect. These cracks occur basically on account of different coefficients of thermal expansion of timber and masonry work. The gap so produced facilitates the attack by pests such as beetles, termites, carpenter ants, etc., because of the accumulation of moisture from different sources, including air. *(The termite attack is treated in greater detail under a separate subhead below).* When attacked by the pests, the frame or shutters become hollow inside (not visible from the outside), producing wooden dust. In frames and shutters, at times, some holes develop because of dead knots existing initially in timber as live knots[130]. In addition, very often, the buckling of the shutter is observed due to the use of unseasoned timber in its manufacture. The use of unseasoned timber is additionally responsible for the development of cracks in the frame and shutter as well. The peeling off of the laminations (if adopted) is also a common occurrence because of the poor quality of pasting coupled with the presence of moisture.

The fittings of doors/windows/ventilators create many defects basically on account of poor manufacturing quality, poor quality in fitting and use of unseasoned timber.

Termite Attack: Termite attack in buildings is a common occurrence. There are basically two types of termites[122]— ground nesting or subterranean type and wood nesting or non-subterranean type. The most commonly observed type is the first one. This type is the most destructive for wood. The termites find ways through cracks and gaps to reach the timber components such as doors/windows/ventilators, ceiling frames of timber, etc. and attack the wood for their food. The second type lives in the dry wood. The termites of the first type construct mud tubes for their movement from their underground colonies to different sources of food, such as timber doors/windows/ventilators, etc. The moist environment is ideal for the survival of the community of termites. Once the element of timber is attacked, it turns into a serious issue of damage and poses a problem for the eradication of termites. There are various means[122,131] for the treatment of buildings invaded by termites.

6.3.2.1.2.1.4. Ground Floor/Basement Floor

While dealing with the ground floor of a building, two situations come to the front. The first one is the ground floor without a basement floor, and the second one is the ground floor with a basement floor. Therefore, the ground floor becomes a part of the building envelope only when there is no basement floor. On the other hand, when the basement floor exists, then obviously the basement floor along with the outside walls (concrete or reinforced concrete or brickwork) comes under the components of the building envelope. The discussion on non-structural defects of the elements of the building envelope is taken up as follows.

6.3.2.1.2.1.5. Ground Floor Having No Basement Floor

As already stated earlier, the ground floor slab constitutes a component of the building envelope. In most of the buildings, the floor slab is of the cross-section, as shown in figure 6.9. The ground floors constructed with the layers, as shown, have been found to have no non-structural damages such as dampness, cracks on floors, seepage of underground water, termite attack, sagging of floor, etc. in many buildings exceeding their 40–50 years of lifecycle, demonstrating thereby the desired qualities both in workmanship and materials used.

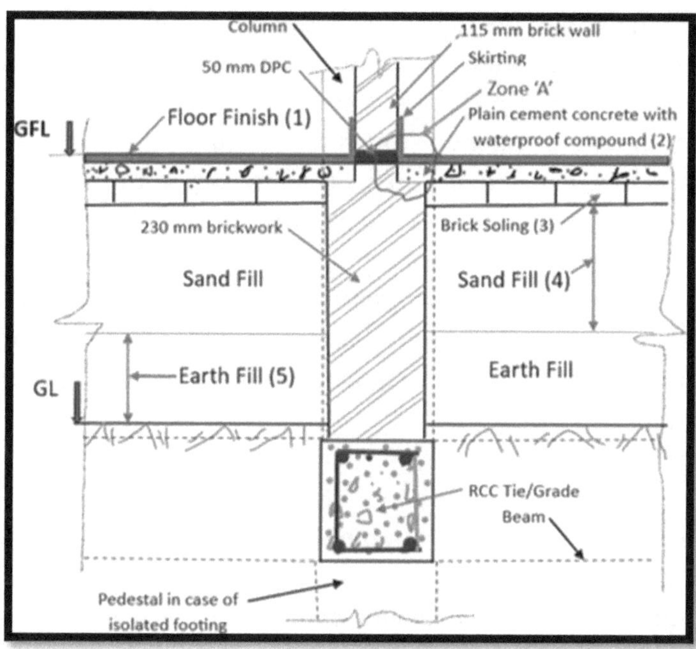

Figure 6.8: Sectional View (Taken On an Interior Panel) Showing Details of a GF Slab

However, there are many cases of buildings, including some new ones, which undergo a number of non-structural damages on the floor basically on account of poor workmanship and poor quality of materials used. The varieties of defects are naturally dependent on the types of construction of floors (on GFL). In this discussion, the defects relate to the commonly adopted type, as shown in figure 6.8. The most commonly observed defect is the water leakage and rising dampness from the portion underneath the GFL (figure 6.8). This defect is caused by the rise of the water table during monsoon and flooding, the reason thereof basically being the lack of water-tightness of the two layers marked 1 and 2 in the figure. In addition, at times, the sagging of the floor takes place due to improper compaction of the layers marked 4 and 5 in the figure. The sagging so occurring results in cracks in both the layers marked 1 and 2, thereby facilitating the rising of dampness beneath the GFL. Very often, the cracks along interfaces between the brick wall and skirting and also along the interfaces between the brickwork and layers 1 and 2 (in the zone marked as 'A' in the figure) facilitate the termite movement from the underground colonies of subterranean type (described earlier). The termites normally cannot make their way through the sand. However, their movement through the sand fill (marked 4 in the figure) becomes possible because of heavy clay-content. Very often, mud tubes are visible on the top of the skirting. These mud tubes indicate the movement of termites towards their destination of food (i.e. timber in doors/windows/ventilators and ceiling frames). There have been many cases of termite attacks even through the gaps found to exist in the base layer of tiles of skirting and floors due to faulty fitting of tiles.

6.3.2.1.2.1.6. Ground Floor Having Basement Floor

The defect in the basement of a building, commonly observed, is the leakage of water from both the side walls and floor. This is accountable to faulty design and construction. There are cases of basements being out of use in the monsoon season because of water accumulation, like in a pond. The sidewalls are subjected to earth pressure and water pressure in places where the water table rises above the basement floor level. The design fails to duly account for these forces. On the other hand, the upward pressure on the base slab (of the basement) increases with an increase in the rise of the water table. Summarily, the basement floor is subjected to structural actions similar to those of an empty tank below ground level. On account of inappropriate design and construction, various non-structural defects such as cracks, leakage of water, dampness, growth of plants, peeling of paints, growth of mold and fungi, etc. (as discussed earlier) are given rise to.

6.3.2.1.2.1.7. Architectural Elements Such As Vertical Fins, Horizontal Chajas, Etc

There are many architectural elements including vertical fins, chajas, parapet walls, etc. The defects in these elements appear primarily for two reasons. The first one is the wrong design, including its connection to the structural elements, while the second one is the wrong construction. A commonly and appropriately designed/constructed chaja is described in figure 6.9 given below. There are many buildings as old as 40-50 years, with the chajas designed and constructed in the ways described through the views in (a) and (b) of this figure. No significant defects have been observed in this type of design and construction, even in old buildings. Against this situation, in many buildings, including new ones, the cracks, such as flexural cracks along the joint of the chaja with the lintel and transverse cracks, as shown in figure 6.9 (a), have been very often observed. The normal thicknesses (excluding the thickness of finish) provided for the reinforced concrete chaja are 65 mm to 75 mm at the joint end and around 40 mm to 50 mm at the cantilever end (i.e. at the edge). The common error found to be responsible for the development of the flexural cracks (as shown in figure 6.9 (a)) is the non-provision of the reinforcement in the tension zone (on the top face). Because of the ignorance of the supervising persons concerned, the main reinforcements are placed along the neutral axis or in the compression zones in contrast to the correct positioning of rebars as shown in figure 6.9 (b). On the other hand, the transverse cracks (as shown in figure 6.9 (a)) appear because of the non-provision of expansion/contraction joints along the length at appropriate spacings.

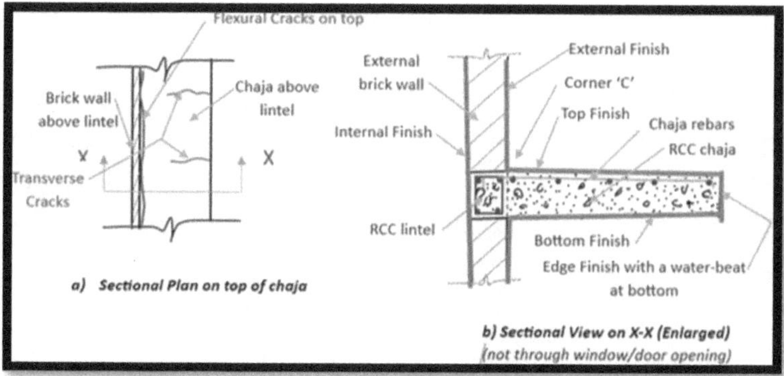

Figure 6.9: Views Describing the Construction of a Normal Chaja

A mild slope on the top face of the chaja needs to be given to avoid the accumulation of rain water in/near the corner on top face marked as 'C' in figure 6.9 (b). The rainwater accumulating on the top of the chaja results in dampness in the external wall, thereby facilitating the growth of mold and fungi, as evident in image 6.2(b). This photo additionally bears evidence of poor maintenance of the chaja as well. On many occasions, the chaja gets overloaded due to the movement of the maintenance persons and the placement of superimposed dead loads such as those of the AC compressor (as shown in image 6.2(a)). Under this type of overloading, there arises the possibility of the development of flexural cracks (Figure 10(a)). It has to be noted that the chaja, being truly a non-structural member, carries loads due to its self-weight in addition to superimposed dead load (as stated above) and occasional live load from the movement of the maintenance persons. There are cases of even partial/total collapse of chaja on account of these factors.

The design and construction of both the horizontal chaja and vertical fin have to be based on the consideration of aesthetic values and functional necessities *(primary ones being the protection of walls/openings/doors/windows/ventilators, etc., against rainwater and sun).* Image 6.2(c) shows the case of a properly designed and constructed system of horizontal chaja and vertical fins in a building that is, by now, about 10 years old with due consideration to the aesthetic values. No non-structural defects have so far been observed. The point to be noted is the transfer of the load from the vertical fins (marked 1 & 2 in image 6.2(c)) through secondary columns (marked as 3 & 4 in the figure) to the structural element (beam), as shown. The designer has to ensure the effective transfer of load from these non-structural elements to the structural elements (beam in this case). In a similar way, the parapet wall, if adopted, will have to be duly connected to the structural member to which its self-weight is transferred.

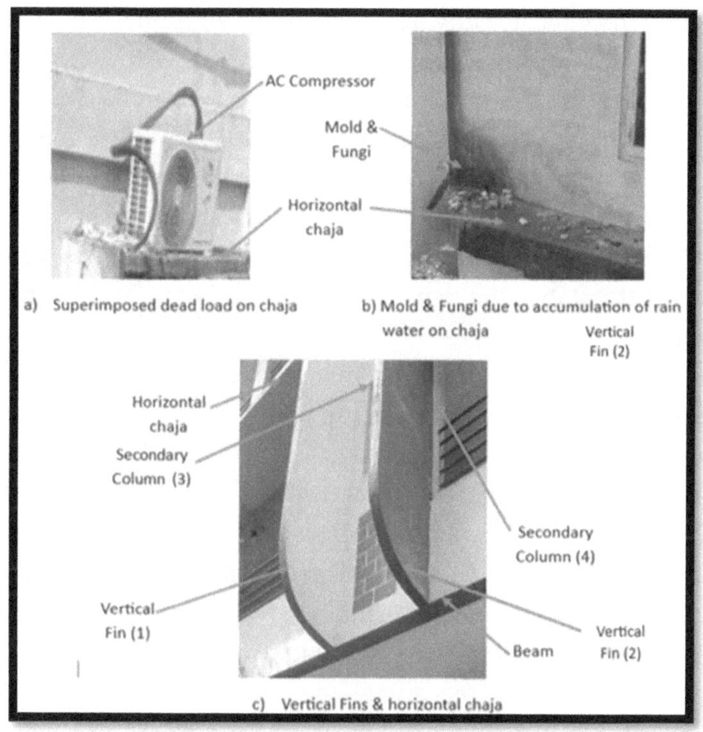

Image 6.2: Photos Showing Issues on Vertical Fin & Horizontal Chaja
Source: Photo Taken by Author in Some buildings of Guwahati City

6.3.2.1.2.2. Non-structural Defects in the Interior

The interior of a building includes salient elements and components such as partition walls, internal doors, floor slabs (excluding roof and ground/basement floor), and finishing items on floors and walls. As defined earlier, the building fabric includes all civil works done in a building, excluding the building services. The plumbing system (though it comes under building services) has been stated above only with respect to a possible source of leakages that will adversely impact different items of civil works in the building.

Internal Walls: Many of the non-structural defects already dealt with in the case of external walls are common to interior walls as well. The defects discussed under external walls, such as cracks, dampness, peeling of paints, growth of mold and fungi, decay and disintegration of brick walls caused by sulphate and efflorescence, are commonly observed even in the case of internal walls. The reasons for this have already been discussed under external walls.

Floor Slabs: The floor slab has two faces — the top and the bottom. In most of the buildings nowadays, the top is finished with tiles of various types (commonly adopted ones are marble and ceramic tiles), while the bottom face (the ceiling for the next lower floor) is finished with plaster and painting. The poor installation of tiles is the major reason for the appearance of the defects on the top face of the floor slabs. The major defects include cracking and bulging. The reasons attributable to these defects are the installation of tiles with insufficiently wide joints, shrinkage of mortar base and air gaps in the base material. The standards of laying tile, as set by the code of practice, are not strictly followed by the builders. The size of the tiles also has an impact on these defects. Apart from the poor installation of tiles, the structural defects developing in the RCC floor slab will naturally cause damage to the floor finishing. Some issues, such as slippery surfaces, loose carpeting, etc., caused by poor cleaning practices can create safety risks to occupants of the building.

The issues, such as shrinkage cracks, peeling of paints, dampness, etc., are commonly observed on the bottom face of the floor slab. The dampness is caused by the leakage of water from plumbing defects, which include minor and major leaks in concealed water pipes, drains and fixtures. The water from the source of the leakage very often finds ways to enter into the floor slabs, thereby creating areas of dampness *(apart from rainwater falling on external walls)* on internal walls and floor slabs. This dampness is responsible for corrosion in the rebars of the slab, spalling of concrete/plaster, peeling of paints, etc., from the bottom face of the floor slab. Therefore, the plumbing defects need to be addressed immediately on observation. Another source of water leakage is the toilet- floors (sunken floors, in particular). The gaps developing on the joints of tiles fitted on the floor and the poor drainage of wastewater from the bath area are responsible for causing dampness in these floor slabs, resulting in the above-noted defects.

Internal Doors/Windows/Ventilators: The defects on timber doors/windows/ventilators, as discussed under the building envelope, are common even to those in the interior of the building.

However, some additional defects commonly observed in the case of timber doors of the toilets are discussed herein. The timber doors in toilets are susceptible to attack by beetles, pests, etc., on account of their exposure to water from inside, particularly to the lower parts of both the frame and shutter. The special measures taken by providing waterproof lamination sheets in the lower parts of both the frame and shutter have been found to be effective in avoiding moisture absorption (by these two elements). Another practice of providing concrete blocks (up to a certain height around 30 cm) on the bottom of the timber frame has also been very effective in many cases. As in the case of timber doors/windows/ventilators on external walls, all timber items, including internal doors/windows/ventilators, are also susceptible to termite attack. In many of the buildings designed and constructed by the author (even at sites having under-ground colonies of termites), the complete sealing by concrete at the level of ground- floor (with the layer of DPC and PCC below floor finish) has been found to be effective for blocking the movement of termite from underground. However, the termites might find their way to attack timber items in the building by making their way through the formation of mud tubes on the outside of plinth walls. These mud tubes are visible, and hence, the source of termite movement is easily identifiable and may then be appropriately taken care of. Maintaining air quality indoors is a common problem. The means of natural ventilation, such as doors/windows/ventilators, need to be appropriately opened and closed for the exchange of indoor air. The mechanical ventilators, if adopted, have also to be operated and maintained properly. There are many indoor sources that release gases or particles adversely impacting the indoor air-quality. Some of these sources include fuel-burning combustion appliances, tobacco products, building materials and furnishings, household cleaning and maintenance products, excess moisture, outdoor sources, etc. Inadequate exchange of indoor polluted air may cause various health issues.

6.3.2.2. Type of Strategy/Method (Phase II(b))

After the distresses/damages under both the categories, i.e. structural and non-structural, have been duly identified, the strategy/option/method for their *(defects')* remedy has to be ascertained/designed based on the appropriate analysis of the respective technical reasons, as involved. A brief discussion on the strategies/options/methods normally adopted as remedial measures is presented below under two broad sub-heads:

- Remedial measures for structural distresses/damages and
- Remedial measures for non-structural distresses/damages.

In each of these cases, the objective of choosing an appropriate type of strategy consists of adopting a suitable method of repair/rehabilitation along with the materials to be adopted (for the chosen method). Today, there are many options/methods and materials to carry out the repair and rehabilitation activities, including retrofitting[121,122,132]. A judicious choice of the method(s) and material(s) does require a knowledge of the available strategies/options/methods and materials for this purpose in the respective location of the building concerned.

6.3.2.2.1. Remedial Measures for Structural Distresses/Damages

As stated earlier, the remedial measures for structural defects with respect to maintenance have a clear contrast with the measures necessary for strengthening a building found to be deficient with respect to the requirements as per the modern codes of practice *(as discussed in Chapter 2 under subhead 2.5).* This contrast consists of the fact that the purpose of maintenance is to maintain a building in its original operational condition without any consideration being given to the aspect of deficiency/vulnerability against the requirements of modern codes. Therefore, in view of this contrast, the remedial measures for taking care of the structural defects have to be decided upon primarily on the basis of the reasons leading to the identified defects as discussed under the subhead of 'identification of distresses/damages' *(presented earlier).* In this chapter, during Phase II(a), the structural elements, namely columns, beams and slabs, are taken into account. The foundation is excluded. Therefore, the remedial measures for the structural defects on these elements need to be decided only by engineers who are well-aware of the structural actions leading to the defects under consideration. The reasons for the commonly observed structural defects in columns, beams and slabs have already been discussed with reference to figures 6.3, 6.4 and 6.5, respectively. Strictly, the measures to be adopted depend on the severity of the distresses. The primary objective of repair/rehabilitation is to ensure stability and structural integrity, as it existed prior to the development of structural defects, and, on the other hand, to protect the elements against further deterioration. Keeping these objectives in mind, the strategies/options/methods for the repair/rehabilitation of the distressed element/component have to be chosen. For a judicious choice, the engineer concerned has to be well-equipped with the required level of knowledge and experience in the domain of available strategies/options/methods in the field of repair of structural defects. This domain is, indeed, a huge one, as reflected by its treatment in different technical literature *(some of which are included under references).*

Depending on the type and severity of structural distresses, the first step in the process of repair/rehabilitation is to decide upon the strategy to be adopted for a particular distress. Many of the available pieces of literature do not discuss, in clear terms, the adoptable strategies. However, the Handbook of CPWD[121] does deal with this aspect in clear terms. As stated in this handbook, the strategy to be adopted for a particular distress may include one or more of the available strategies. The salient ones[121] are: *Reduction of dead/live loads, repair/strengthening of columns, beams and slabs, improving the compressive strength of concrete, attending to cracks and joints, and providing protective cover against the aggressive deteriorating chemicals.* To adopt the appropriate strategy, the engineer concerned has to duly appreciate the reason(s) leading to the structural defect. For example, the strategy of reduction of dead/live loads may be taken. An attempt to reduce the dead/live loads needs to be made only when the basic reason leading to the structural defect (as discussed earlier) is the overloading accountable to change in use or otherwise. Similarly, adopting other strategies also has to be strictly based on reasons leading to the respective defect.

There are different options available for repair/rehabilitation of structural defects. The salient options, as given by the handbook[121], are: *Grouting & crack repair, patch repair, replacement of structurally weak concrete, replacement of spalled, and/or delaminated concrete, replacement of carbonated concrete surrounding steel reinforcement, cleaning and passivating the corroded steel reinforcement, concrete overlays with normal, low or highly fluid concrete, latex modified concrete & corrosion protection such as jacketing, etc., re-alkalization of carbonated concrete, electro-chemical removal of chloride from concrete and waterproofing and/or protective coating.*

Various methods are available to execute the options described above. The salient ones, as stated by the Handbook of CPWD[121] are: *Repairs using mortars, Dry pack and epoxy bonded dry pack, Pre-packed Aggregate Concrete (PAC), Shotcrete, Concrete replacement, Epoxy bonded concrete, Silica fume concrete, Polymer concrete system, strengthening concrete by surface impregnation using vacuum methods, Thin Polymer overlays, Thin Epoxy overlay, Resin/Polymer modified cement slurry injection, Protection seal coats on the entire surface, Ferro-cement, Plate bonding, RCC jacketing, Propping and Supporting, Fiber Wrap Technique, Chemical and Electro-chemical method of repair.*

A detailed discussion of the above-noted strategies, options and methods has been treated as outside the scope of this discussion. However, the same is available in full in the handbook[121] and partly in other literature covered under references. The proper choice of an option/method does need the due consideration of factors such as environmental conditions of the location of the site, the availability of the required materials, the availability of skill and equipment, the time required for execution and above all, the cost of repair/rehabilitation.

6.3.2.2.2. Remedial Measures for Non-Structural Distresses/Damages
The non-structural elements having defects in the building fabric (both the envelope and the interior), as already identified under the

subhead *'Non-structural distresses and damages,'* need to be repaired/rehabilitated by adopting appropriate remedial measures. As in the case of structural defects, there are many strategies/options/methods even for this case. Obviously, the choice of the appropriate technique for repairing any defect has to be based on the correct appreciation of the reason thereof. The major reasons leading to non-structural defects have already been discussed. Remedial measures for some of the defects caused by the rising dampness in walls of the ground floor and floor slabs of the ground/basement floor, the water leakage, temperature effects, termite attack, etc., are briefly discussed below.

6.3.2.2.3. Remedial Measures for Defects Caused by Rising Dampness and Leakage of Water

Many defects (as discussed earlier) are caused by rising dampness and leakage of water. The basic measures for repairing these defects initially consist of permanently blocking the path of rising dampness from the ground and closing the sources of water leakage. The dampness on the walls of the ground floor rises on account of the ineffectiveness or non-provision of the DPC layer at the position marked in figure 6.8. The author tackled this issue in a new building about 40 years back. The building developed a lot of defects due to rising dampness since no DPC layer at the position shown in figure 6.8 was provided during the design/construction. A new layer of DPC (with standard specifications) was introduced in the way described through figure 6.10. On the top of 230 mm brickwork (i.e. the plinth wall), gaps in the portions marked 'A', leaving out initially the portions marked 'B' in the figure (alternately), were created manually. After cleaning the gaps so created (having a thickness varying from 40–60 mm), the concrete *(having the nominal proportion of 1:1.5:3 with the damp-proof compound in specified proportion, the coarse aggregate of broken stones being of 10mm down size)* was injected manually *(since then no concrete-injecting equipment was locally available).* After the layer was placed in the portions marked 'A' and hardened for 7—10 days, the left-out portions marked 'B' in the figure were taken up, and the DPC layer was introduced in a similar way. In all the walls (both exterior and interior), the DPC layers were placed in a similar way.

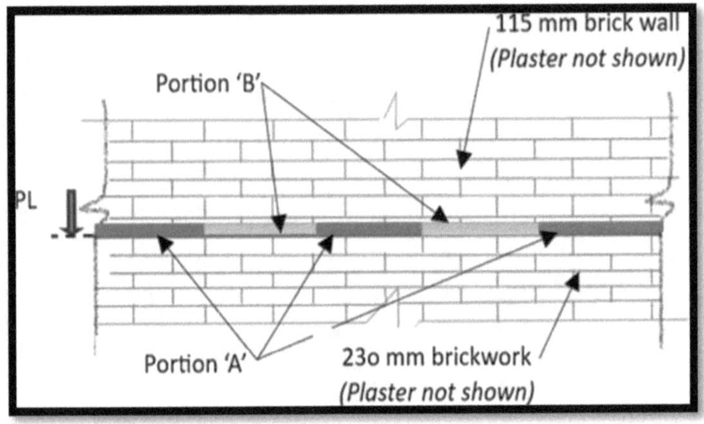

Figure 6.10: Steps Adopted for Introducing a New Layer of DPC

All the walls developing various defects caused by the rising dampness were allowed to dry up, and eventually, the replastering and, subsequently, the repainting was done. Eventually, it was observed that the DPC layer so placed succeeded in stopping the rising dampness. Those days, the procedure of laying a DPC layer *(the way explained above)* was, indeed, labor-extensive and time-consuming. However, in today's context of mechanization and the development of new techniques and materials, it will be easier to introduce a DPC layer in the walls of an old building with the problem of rising dampness.

The problems of rising dampness and seepage of water through the floor-slab of the ground floor/basement floor *(as the case may be, as discussed earlier)* may be resolved in a number of ways, as briefly discussed below with reference to figure 6.8 & figure 6.11.

In many cases of rising dampness in the ground floor (without the basement floor), the method of relaying of layer marked '2' in figure 6.8 *(after compacting the layers below it)* with concrete of good quality, followed by the laying of the Floor Finish layer marked '1' has been found to be effective in addressing this issue. In fact, there are many examples of buildings with no issue of rising dampness, such as buildings 40—50 years old with a ground floor (of the type shown in figure 6.8) built with good workmanship and materials of good quality. Nowadays, there is the practice of providing a water-proofing membrane below layer '2' as well.

An effectively adopted method for addressing the problem of dampness and seepage of water in the basement floor of a building is schematically described in figure 6.11. The elements marked '1', '2' and '3' in figure 6.11 (a) are the existing vertical wall (masonry or concrete), the floor slab and the foundation *(as existing, may be shallow or deep as per design/construction)*, respectively. The sources of dampness and seepage of water are indicated by the green arrows shown in this figure. The hatched portion represents the earth below GL, as shown.

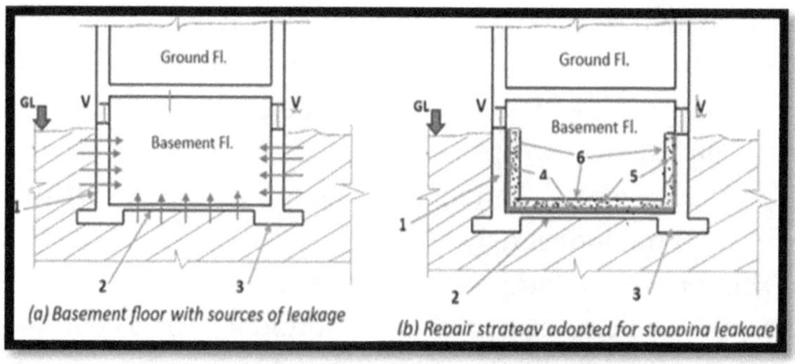

Figure 6.11: Schematic Representation of a Repair-Strategy for Rising Dampness & Seepage of Water in Basement Floor

The 'V' marked in the figure shows the position of the ventilators. The method consists of providing three new elements marked '4', '5' and '6', as shown in figure 6.11 (b). The element '4' is a water-proofing membrane of any approved brand to be laid after proper preparation of the inner surfaces of the old vertical walls '1' and the top of base slab '2'. Then, the duly designed RCC wall and base slab (marked '5' in the figure) is constructed. Thereafter, the inner surfaces will be given the finishing layer (marked '6'). The design/construction of RCC walls and the base slab will be just like those of a water tank (the major part being below GL). Therefore, the design considerations must account for the earth pressure and water pressure based on the expected rise of the water table during monsoon on side walls and the upward water pressure likely to be caused on the base slab if the water table rises above the basement floor level. Depending on the existing condition of the old side wall, a decision to replace it with a new brick wall before placing the elements '4', '5' and '6' may also be taken. Similarly, the existing base slab may also be replaced with a new plain cement concrete layer over brick-soling, over which the new elements '4' and '5' may be laid. A final choice needs to be governed by all the technical considerations, as briefly stated.

The problem of rainwater leakage in buildings is a serious one in the sense that it leads to many other defects, including both structural and non-structural ones *(as discussed earlier in this chapter)*. The common sources of rainwater leakage are obviously flat roof slabs, pitched roofs, shell roofs, junctions of walls and sunshades, cracks on external walls, expansion joints in buildings, etc. These sources of leakage need to be duly sealed before the defects are repaired. The strategies/options/methods and materials, as dealt with in available codes, handbooks and other pieces of literature, need to be adopted judiciously.

The sources of dampness/leakage of water in the bathing area (including the sunken ones) are also commonly observed. The main sources of leakage are joints of pipes (water supply or waste) and sanitary fittings, joints of floor tiles, leakage from floor traps, etc. These defects normally occur due to poor workmanship, use of substandard materials /fittings and incorrect usage by occupants[133]. Remedial measures need to be taken to identify the reasons correctly.

After the sources of dampness and leakage of water have been duly taken care of, as discussed above, the elements having various defects should be left to dry up completely before other defects are repaired. A brief discussion of different methods normally adopted for the repair of some of the non-structural defects is presented below.

Repair of Cracks on Masonry Walls (Non-Structural Elements— Load Bearing Walls Are Outside the Scope of This Discussion): The repair of surface cracks is a simple one. The plaster is removed along the cracks, and if the crack is observed on the masonry wall, a V-cut is made and then filled with cement mortar not leaner than 1:4. After that, the wall is replastered. Apart from cement mortar used to seal the cracks, it is common nowadays to adopt chemicals[122] to seal the cracks. If the cracks are appreciably wide, more than 1.5 mm, the technique of 'Stitching' may also be adopted by using thin mortar blocks or large concrete blocks. The cracks along the joint between structural elements (beams and columns) and brick walls are very common. Since these cracks are caused by temperature effects (accountable to different thermal coefficients for reinforced concrete and brickwork), the repairing of these cracks needs a separate treatment. The normal practice[122] is to grout these cracks with a water-proof chemical and then to paint that strip with a special paint.

Repairing the spots of efflorescence is an important aspect. The normal procedure is to remove the plaster and then scrub the area with a hard brush to remove the salts formed. Then, the area has to be cleaned by using a chemical solution. A mild solution with hydrochloric acid (one part of hydrochloric acid + five parts of clean water)[122] may be used. After that, it has to be replastered and dried before repainting the area.

The erosion of mortar joints (reasons dealt with earlier) has to be repaired by racking out the old mortar (to a certain depth depending on the extent of erosion) and then by injecting new mortar of the appropriate proportion (normally 1:4). The joints have to be wetted adequately before injection of new mortar for avoiding the absorption of water of the new mortar by the bricks.

Termite attacks in existing buildings are a major issue, as discussed. There are different ways for the treatment of this termite attack. The broad guidelines for anti-termite treatment in an existing building are given in the IS code of Practice[131]. The fundamental approach to the treatment of this attack consists of accurate identification of the source(s) of the entry of the family of termites into the building on the one hand and, on the other, of locations of their hideouts in the building, such as ceilings, timber doors/windows/ventilators, switchboard, gaps behind tiles, etc. Once these two aspects have been duly identified, the measures for their treatments need to be judiciously taken as per the guidelines given in the IS code of practice. The objectives of the preventive measures against termite attack are primarily:

> To provide a barrier for the movement of termites from soil below ground level (outside the building),
> To provide a barrier for the movement of termites from soil below ground floor level and
> To kill all the termites already in different hideouts in the infected building. Even after the anti-termite treatment has been done as per the code, frequent checking of the building needs to be conducted to find if any sign of re-entry of termites into the building is observed. If any sign is observed, remedial measures will be immediately taken.

Repairing of Chaja: As discussed under the head of identification of defects, the chaja develops flexural cracks, transverse cracks (Figure 6.9 (a)) and other non-structural defects. If the cracks are not extensive, repair may be carried out with polymer-modified cement mortar after cleaning the top surface (where the flexural cracks have appeared) and applying a bond coat. The transverse cracks shown in figure 6.9 (a) normally appear when the length of the chaja is very long. These cracks are normally found to extend for the full depth of the chaja and may be repaired by injecting cementing mortar only after providing expansion joints at suitable spacings. These repairing measures become effective only when the reinforcements are in the proper position (as discussed earlier with reference to figure 6.10 (b). Other non-structural defects on chaja may then be taken care of as discussed earlier. However, when mistakes are found to exist with respect to design and construction, the damaged chaja needs to be dismantled and recast with proper design and construction (indicated in figure 6.9 (b). Alternatively, the damaged RCC chaja may be completely dismantled, and chajas with other materials, such as precast ferrocement slabs[122] fitted on light frames, may be opted for.

6.3.3. Execution of the Strategy/Strategies

The last phase of maintenance management is the execution of the strategy/strategies (Phase III of figure 6.2), which is eventually finalized upon completing the due technical analysis of the observed distresses in the building fabric. The salient aspects involved are indicated in the flowchart given in figure 6.12 below.

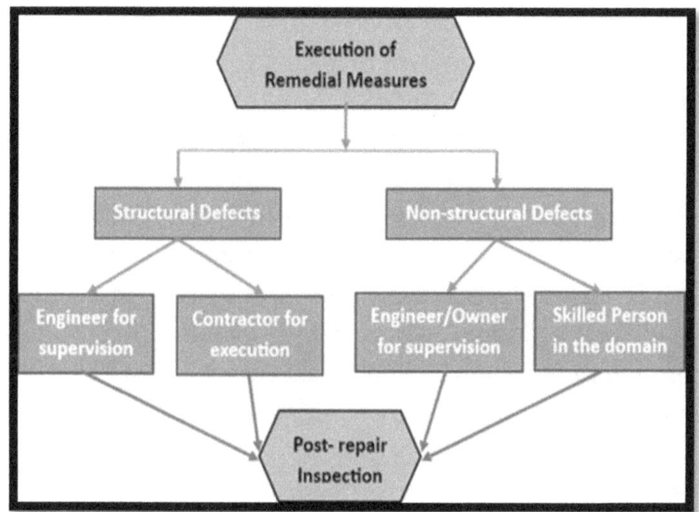

Figure 6.12: Flowchart Summarizing the Salient Aspects of Repair Strategies

6.3.3.1. Structural Defects

The task of executing the method(s) finalized as discussed under the subhead of *Remedial measures for structural distresses/damages* is the most important stage of the whole process of maintenance management for the building fabric. This is because the structural elements/components relate to structural stability and integrity. Therefore, all work to be executed for repair/rehabilitation of the structural elements/components undergoing structural distresses/damages needs to be carried out by an experienced contractor under the strict supervision of a competent engineer (as indicated in the Flowchart of figure 6.12). The engineer needs to be a person from the consulting engineer/firm/company who finalizes the strategies/options/methods (including detailed specifications for each item of work involved). On the other hand, the contractor to be engaged must be adequately experienced and equipped to execute the respective item(s) of work in conformity with the terms and conditions, as duly approved by the owner concerned. The repairing of structural defects is, indeed, a highly specialized job in view of the importance of ensuring structural stability and integrity on the one hand and, on the other, in view of the availability of modern materials and techniques for repair/rehabilitation works (*as reflected by the discussion presented under the subhead of type of strategies/methods*).

6.3.3.2. Non-Structural Defects

There are many types of remedial measures for non-structural defects, as reflected in the discussion presented under the subhead of *Remedial measures for non-structural distresses/damages.* These measures include various domains, techniques, and materials. Obviously, for the effective execution of the chosen method for a particular defect, a skilled person in the related domain is required. The supervision of the works under this category may be done by an engineer or the owner themselves, depending on the nature of the defects.

6.3.3.3. Post-repair Inspection

After completing all works of repair/rehabilitation of all defects (both structural and non-structural), the engineer, contractor, skilled worker and owner involved in the whole process need to develop a mechanism for periodical inspection (as necessary) of the works executed. The primary objective of this periodical inspection is to monitor if the works executed have duly ensured the durability and performance requirements of the strategies/options/methods so adopted. If any discrepancy is observed, it needs to be duly attended to. If the volume of the works of repair/rehabilitation is of an appreciable extent, the necessary terms and conditions for periodical inspection and follow-up actions for deficiencies (if observed) may also be formulated, and an appropriate agreement to this effect may be duly signed between/among the parties involved.

6.4. Concluding Remarks

In dealing with the maintenance of the building and its management, the general principles involved for all the elements of the hard services (defined earlier) have been briefly discussed. On the other hand, only the building fabric has been treated in greater detail. The other elements of hard services, such as (a) Plumbing and Drainage Systems, (b) Electrical Installations, (c) Heating, Ventilation and Air Conditioning (HVAC) systems, etc., have not been taken up for a detailed discussion in this chapter.

The full potential of many of the buildings in our country, particularly in the public sector, does not appear to be utilized because of a number of reasons. The salient ones are:

- There are many non-engineered buildings,
- Even in the case of many engineered buildings, deficiencies in design and construction aspects are apparent and
- There exists the lack of awareness for a fully integrated approach to the maintenance management of building among many of the owners.

The integrated approach to maintenance management of the building fabric, as briefly presented in this chapter, clearly reflects the growing importance attached to the maintenance sector by the national government[91,115,116,117,121] and many others covered in the literature referred to. Today, there is a wealth of information about the availability of technology and materials for carrying out any task relating to design, construction and maintenance of buildings. The issue is obviously the appropriate utilization of the available technology and materials on the ground.

The appropriate adoption of the available stock of information with respect to both technology and materials relating to repair/rehabilitation of building distresses/damages warrants a greater awareness among all three salient stakeholders: the consulting engineers/architects responsible for the identification of defects and formulation of repair/rehabilitation methods thereof, the contractors/skilled persons responsible for the execution of the measures and the owners responsible for following an integrated approach for maintenance. The creation of this awareness does require measures such as training, culture of knowledge through workshops, seminars, studies, etc. for all the stakeholders. The recent trend of introducing specialized courses on repair, rehabilitation and retrofitting structures in some of the technical institutes at the levels of both undergraduate and postgraduate courses has been encouraging. The most important aspect involved in the execution of the measures of repair/rehabilitation activities is the selection of appropriate techniques and materials for any particular defect. For a judicious choice of the same, the basic requirement on the part of the engineer/contractor/skilled person concerned is a clear knowledge of the relevant technique and materials. Against this requirement, it is often seen that repair strategies are executed blindly based on ignorance about the proper reason or the proper technique/materials.

The design and construction of a new building have a great bearing on the issues of its maintenance, which develop as it (the building) starts growing in the age of its useful life.

Therefore, the required considerations for reducing the possible maintenance issues need to be duly accounted for during the phases of planning, design and construction. It is in this context that the planner, designer, and contractor are expected to be aware of the different reasons that lead to the growth of different types of stresses/damages during the lifecycle of a building's fabric.

Chapter 7 |
Articles on Miscellaneous Topics

7.1. Introduction

A number of articles have been written on different topics. These articles have been included in the last chapter of this book since an individual chapter for each topic has not been considered to be appropriate in view of the short contents (for each topic). The topics cover some aspects considered to be of interest to young readers, including both budding and fresh engineers. These articles are arranged with the names of individual topics, as given below.

7.2. Lessons Learnt from the Demolition of the Twin Towers of Noida (India)

The demolition of the Twin Towers of Noida has been possibly the greatest demolition of structures in India. The two towers: Tower 16 (Ceyane) and Tower 17 (Apex) were the two blocks of the Emerald Court Project, constructed by Supertech Limited. The total number of flats contained in these two towers is 915, out of which 633 were booked. Three numbers of revisions of the original plan of the Emerald Court project were made on the basis of increased FAR and the acquirement of additional land in the same plot. As per the revised sanctioned plans, the heights of these two towers were raised from (G+ 24) to (G+ 40) in each case. As a result, the height of these two towers increased to 121 metres. In the original sanctioned plan, a green area was shown in front of tower T1. Eventually, T16 and T17 were constructed in this green area.

The demolition of these two towers within 10-12 seconds clearly demonstrated the modern technique of destruction of structures without any appreciable damage to the environment of the surrounding area. Against this situation, an analysis of the reasons leading to the SC verdict for demolition reflects the extent of degradation of moral values in society in general and on the parts of those involved in the execution of this project. Obviously, the Residents' Welfare Association (RWA) of Emerald Court Group Housing Society has to be credited for instituting the writ petition in the Allahabad High Court. The verdict of the High Court given in favour of the demolition of the two towers was challenged in the Supreme Court by Supertech Limited (Appellant). Eventually, the Supreme Court upheld the high court verdict with a lot of strong observations which need to be looked into seriously by all those involved in urban development.

The whole episode, starting from the violation of the rules and regulations set by the authorities controlling the construction of building infrastructure and eventually culminating in the demolition of the two towers, truly presents a series of lessons to be learnt by planners, engineers, contractors, the different authorities involved in the process of controlling construction activities in the country. In addition, this demolition clearly demonstrates the extent of conflict of interest in India in the arena of different developmental activities of the country. It is in this context that the author has made an attempt herein to look into the salient technical aspects, the undermining of which led to this type of demolition, possibly the greatest in India so far.

The RWA filed the writ petition in the Allahabad High Court with a view to getting relief on some major aspects (stated below under subhead 7.2.2.1). The aspects of relief prayed for by RWA indicate the extent of awareness available with it (RWA) with respect to empowerment imposed on the Apartment Societies by the Apartment Acts of different states of the country. It is in this context that the different housing societies may have a relook at their present positions with respect to legalities and the areas of empowerment, as granted by the Apartment Acts of the relevant states.

7.2.1. Technical Grounds Forming the Basis of the Court's Verdict for Demolition

7.2.1.1. The Main Reliefs Sought by RWA before the High Court, Allahabad

The main reliefs[134] sought by RWA before the high court included:

- *Quashing the revised plan for the construction of T-16 (Ceyane) and T-17 (Apex) and the demolition of structures constructed pursuant to the plan* and

- *Quashing the permission granted to link T-1 with T-16/ T-17.*

In addition, there were, in fact, some more reliefs sought; they are not specifically discussed herein. The judgement of the High Court of Allahabad was given in favour of the demolition of the two towers (T-16 & T-17) primarily on the grounds of violations of a number of rules and regulations of the authorities concerned. The areas of violations have been made abundantly clear in the verdict of the Supreme Court, as briefly discussed in the next subhead.

7.2.1.2. Technical Areas Violated by the Appellant (Supertech Limited — the Developer of the Real Estate)

The approval of the 3rd revised plan and the construction of T-16 & T-17 were challenged primarily on the grounds of violation of a number of codes, Acts, etc., namely, NBR 2006, NBR 2010, NBC 2005, UP 1975 Act, UP Apartments Act and Fire safety norms. Before coming to the verdict, the honorable Supreme Court (SC) made a critical analysis and interpretation of all factors bearing on the relief sought by RWA (as mentioned in the preceding para) and the subsequent judgement of the Allahabad High Court in light of relevant Acts and documentary evidence. The critical analysis[134], made by the SC reflects a number of technical areas, which should draw the attention of all the stakeholders of construction industry in general and those involved in the development of real estates in our cities/towns.

The SC critically analyzed the documentary evidence placed before it by both the appellant and the respondent and eventually drew a number of conclusions. The salient points relate to the following violations:

Minimum Distance Requirements between Blocks: The sanction given by NOIDA for the construction of T-16 and T-17 is violative of minimum distance requirements (between towers) under NBR 2006, NBR 2010 and NBC 2005. For example, the distance between Blocks T1 and T-17 may be taken. Against the requirement of 20.45m, the one envisaged in the third revised plan was only 9m. The attempt made by the appellant to treat T-1 along with T-16 and T-17 as one cluster of buildings under one block by providing a space frame between T-1 and T-17 was rejected. It was directly contrary to the appellant's own position, as stated to the HC through affidavit and also through the representation to the flat buyers.

Violation of Fire Safety Norms: The spaces around the blocks need to conform to the minimum values, as specified by the NBC. The NOC issued by the concerned CFO was conditional. It (the NOC) clearly stated that the NBC 2005 must be complied with regarding the fire safety norms. However, as observed by the SC, the norms were not complied with. According to this code, the minimum rear and side spaces for a building having a height over 55m should be 16m. Against this requirement, the distance between T-1 and T-17 was only 9m.

Elimination of Common Garden Area in Front of T-1: As per the first revised plan of 2006, there was a provision for a common garden area in front of T-1. In fact, it was promised to the buyers of the first 15 blocks. In the subsequent revised plans (2nd & 3rd), this garden area was eliminated for the construction of T-16 & T-17. This action violated the provision of UP Apartments Act 2010, since the consent of the flat owners of the first 15 blocks was not duly taken.

7.2.2. Act of Collusion between officers of NOIDA and Supertech Limited

The violations, to the extent as evidenced by the brief analysis given under subhead 7.2.1, were possible only on account of the 'Conflict of Interest' leading to collusion among the office bearers of both NOIDA and Supertech Limited. This collusion has been abundantly clear in the interpretation of documents and evidence placed before both the courts (HC and SC). The honorable Supreme Court, while giving this verdict, made a strong observation, which goes as: *The rampant increase in unauthorized constructions across urban areas, particularly in metropolitan cities where soaring values of land place a premium on dubious dealings, has been noticed in several decisions of this Court. This state of affairs has often come to pass in no small measure because of the collusion between developers and planning authorities.* In addition, the honorable SC gave a few excerpts of its verdict with respect to some similar cases in other states. These cases also conclusively referred to collusion between regulatory bodies and builders. The honorable Supreme Court further observed: *From commencement to completion, the process of construction by developers is regulated within the framework of law. The regulatory framework encompasses all stages of construction, including allocation of land, sanctioning the plan for construction, regulation of structural integrity of structures under construction, obtaining clearances from different departments (fire, garden, sewerage, etc.) and the issuance of occupation and completion certificates.*

7.2.3. Final Verdict of the Honorable SC

The final verdict of the Honorable Supreme Court is *'The order passed by the High Court for the demolition of Apex and Ceyane (T-16 and T-17) does not warrant interference and the direction for demolition issued by the High Court is affirmed'.* The complete verdict, including the conditions of demolition, appears in Appendix VIIA.

7.2.4. Execution of the Demolition

The party engaged in the task of demolishing the Twin Towers was Edifice Engineering (a Mumbai-based unit), along with a South African firm called Jet Demolitions as its partner.

Image 7.1: Twin Towers (before Demolition) with Other Buildings of Emerald Court and Its Village Societies[160]
Source: https://www.india.com/explainer/noida-supertech-twin-towers-blast-why-is-the-building-higher-than-qutub-minar-being-demolished-twin-towers-blast-complete-guide-here-5595799/ (Ref. No. 160).

It was demolished using Implosion Technic. Around 3,700 kg of explosives were infused in the two towers. A lot of preparations were made before the demolition was done on 28 August, 2022. Salient preparations included the vacating of the flats by around 5000 residents of the societies, removal of around 2500 vehicles, parking fire tenders and ambulances at suitable locations, arrangement of around 50 beds in hospitals, covering the buildings near the twin towers with suitable coverings, etc.

The actual process of demolition took around only 9 seconds. At the end of this short period, the Twin Towers *(taller than even the Qutub Minar of Delhi)* turned into dust and rubble. The total quantity of debris yielded by the demolition was estimated to be around 80,000 tonnes. A major part of this quantity was reportedly utilized to fill the basement of the two towers. About 30,000 tonnes of debris and 4,000 tonnes of iron and steel were to be removed from the site.

<u>7.2.5. Post-demolition Effects on the Surroundings:</u>
The post-demolition effects need to be analyzed primarily with respect to: (a) Structural stability and integrity of structures (mostly buildings) existing in the vicinity of the demolition site and (b) Impact on the surrounding environment.

Some studies on these two areas have been conducted during the post-demolition period. A brief discussion on these two aspects is presented below:

Structural stability and integrity of buildings in the adjoining areas: There existed a number of challenges confronting the demolition of the Twin Towers with respect to the stability and integrity of buildings surrounding the site of demolition. The paper[135] by Anil Joseph et al. dealt with different challenges. Apart from the preparatory measures, as mentioned under subhead 7.2.5, a number of structural safety measures were also taken prior to the start of the actual demolition process. As stated in the paper[135], the major issues of structural stability existed with respect to Aster 2, an apartment in Emerald Court, which was only 9 metres away from the site of demolition. In addition, the challenge consisted of ensuring the safety of the buildings in both ATS Village and Emerald Court. The GAIL gas pipeline supplying CNG for Noida and East Delhi, which existed underground (only 4m below the ground level) at a distance of 23m from the Twin Towers, posed another challenge.

Various precautionary measures were taken, particularly in Aster 2. The structural analysis of Aster 2 was conducted to check the displacements and storey drift with the earthquake and blast loads as per the applicable loads and to see if these parameters were within the permissible limits. For all other buildings within the safety zone of 50m, a rapid visual assessment[135] was also conducted to record if any structural defect existed in any of these buildings. No. of instrumentation systems such as Geophones and accelerometers for the record of ground vibrations were placed at many critical locations. In addition, crack meters were placed at the locations of existing cracks in the buildings within safe zones.

After the demolition was done, the data collected through different instrumentation systems so placed were analysed[135] and no major impact on the stability and integrity of the buildings around the site of demolition was found.

Impact on Surrounding Environment: The impact of the demolition of buildings on the environment is truly a complex issue since the possible impacts are multi-dimensional and some effects to come to light are time-dependent. Some of the different aspects of complexity have been dealt with by S.S. Sahu[136] *(a student of TERI School of Advanced Studies, Delhi).*

The method of 'waterfall implosion', as adopted for demolishing the Twin Towers, is internationally recognized as an environment-friendly technique. Even then, there have been many challenging areas, including air pollution, noise pollution, adverse impacts on the biodiversity of the region, etc., which are likely to be caused by a demolition of this magnitude. Whether any detailed test has been conducted or not *(after demolition)* is not known at this stage. However, as understood from different sources, the CPCB has plans to monitor the impacts on the environment. Detailed information on the execution of these plans is not yet available.

7.2.6. Lessons Learnt from the Demolition

The demolition of any structure prior to the end of its utility period is not desirable since it (the demolition) leads to a huge national loss in different forms. The reasons leading to this demolition have been basically the violations of the building rules, which are well set by the respective authorities responsible for the control of the construction in urban areas through different Acts, Codes of practice, byelaws, etc. (as reflected in the discussion, presented in this article). Therefore, the social menace of violating the well-set rules and regulations for vested interest is the root cause of this type of demolition. This menace is deeply rooted in India at the moment. How to eradicate this social nuisance is the major question faced in our country. The verdicts of our honourable courts for demolition of structures—that too after a long period of 9 years will not possibly improve the situation. More effective measures are necessary to infuse ethical values into the minds of all those involved in the country's developmental activities.

7.3. Flood Problem of Assam with Specific Reference to River Embankment

The flood problem in the state of Assam is a perennial one. The rivers Brahmaputra and Barak, along with their tributaries and sub-tributaries, traverse the state. Rastriya Barh Aayog (RBA) identified[138] in 1980 that 40% of total land area is prone to flood in Assam against only 10.2% of land area being prone to flood in the whole country. This data indicates the depth of the flood problem in Assam. The drainage area of the sub-basins[139] of rivers Brahmaputra and Barak in India are shown in table 7.1. The huge drainage area of the sub-basins is responsible for the flood in Assam.

Drainage Area of Brahmaputra Sub-basin		Drainage Area of Barak Sub-basin	
State	Drainage Area(sq.km)	State	Drainage Area (sq.km)
Arunachal Pradesh	81,424	Meghalaya	10,650
Assam	70,634	Manipur	9,567
West Bengal	12,585	Mizoram	8.866
Meghalaya	11,667	Assam	7,224
Naga Land	10,803	Naga Land	728
Sikkim	7.300	Tripura	4,688
Total	194,413	Total	41,723

Table 7.1: Drainage Area of Sub-Basins of Rivers, Brahmaputra and Barak in India (Based on data of Assam Water Resources[139])

The fact that it has been getting aggravated each year indicates several gaps in the efforts made so far in taking the appropriate measures for mitigation or control of flood in an effective manner, keeping in mind the huge catchment area of rainfall that includes many areas of the countries and states *(Table 7.1, countries not covered))* surrounding this state. The measures to be taken for mitigation or control of floods are well- understood. These measures[137] broadly include:

- Structural measures,
- A combination of structural and bioengineering (vegetative) measures and
- Watershed protection

In fact, the whole approach to flood management consists of taking measures covered broadly under three categories: immediate measures, short-term measures and long-term measures. These three categories of measures constitute the policy statement[138], announced by the Government of India on floods and remedies after the unprecedented floods in the country in 1954.

The responsibility for flood control basically lies with the state government since this problem is not included in the legislative lists[138] of the Constitution of India. Therefore, the problem of flooding in Assam, as in the case of other flood-prone states, is not treated as a national issue. However, the Brahmaputra Board, a central autonomous body, was created in 1980 for all the states of NER, including Sikkim and North Bengal. The main functions of this body have been to survey, investigate, and prepare master plans to control floods in the region and construct and maintain dams. In addition, it is mandated to recommend and monitor the projects of centrally sponsored Flood Management Programmes.

Various structural and non-structural measures for the control of floods in various flood-prone basins were suggested by the National Water Policy (NWP), 2002. For the structural measures, the preparation of master plans basin-wise is a basic necessity. The non-structural measures, such as flood plain zoning, flood forecasting and warning, etc., were also stressed by NWP.

The Water Resource Department of the Government of Assam has been primarily taking only immediate and short-term measures to control floods in Assam. An account of these measures, as given in the CAG's report138, appears in table 7.2 from 2007 to 2017.

Item *(Col.1)*	Position as on March 2007 *(Col.2)*	Addition during 2007--2017 *(Col.3)*	% of addition during 2007 --2017 *(Col.4)*	Position as on March 2017 *(Col.5)*
Construction of Embankment (in Km)	4,465.85 (Since 1954)	8.57	0.192	4,474.42
Anti-erosion works (in Km)	746	212	28.42	958
Removal of drainage congestion under Drainage development scheme (in KM)	854.19	27.776	3.25	881.966
Major sluice (in number)	86	12	13.95	98
Minor sluice (in number	539	6	1.11	545
Raising and strengthening of embankment (in Km)	4465.85	807.894	18.09	***

***No new addition

Table 7.2: Position of Short-Term Measures Taken by WRD of Govt. of Assam, As of 2017 (Prepared on the Basis of Data of Cag Report[138])

The different short-term measures, taken by the WRD of Govt. of Assam, appear in column 1 in table 7.2. The total length of embankments existing as of 2017 is 4474.42 Km (Column 5 of the table). The major portion of this total length (4465.85 Km, Column 2) was constructed in the period from 1954 to 2007. Since then, the addition of new embankments till 2017 (a period of 10 years) has been minimal (only 0.192%), as evidenced by column 5 of the table. During this period, the major thrust was laid on raising and strengthening 18.09% of the existing embankments (last row— column 4). A substantial amount of anti-erosion work (28.42%, column 4) was executed during the same period. However, the drainage development works done were nominal (only 3.25%). Some major and minor sluices were also provided during the period under discussion.

As stated in the CAG Report[138], the WRD of Assam had taken no long-term measures, such as the construction of the reservoir, treatment of catchment area, etc, for a permanent solution to the problem of flood in Assam. The aspects of long-term measures were dealt with by many in the past. The WRD of Assam, in response to this point, as raised by CAG, stated[138] that it (WRD) could not take up any long-term measure on account of the non-establishment of a basin-level organization involving all stakeholders, since the rivers, the Brahmaputra and Barak, including their tributaries, originate from neighbouring states/countries. To what extent this stand taken by WRD is tenable is a debatable point since there exists (as stated above) the Brahmaputra Board, a central autonomous body with the mandate of preparing master plans for the control of flood in the states of NER, including North Bengal. In fact, the BB has suggested, by now, a number of long-term measures such as catchment area treatment, afforestation, flood plain zoning, construction of reservoirs, and short-term measures such as the construction of embankments, anti-erosion works, construction of raised platforms, etc. and immediate measures such as repairing and maintenance of embankment, regulating sluice gates, etc., through a number of master plans. As stated in the CAG Report[138], from 1986 to 2010, the BB formulated 57 Master Plans, out of which 49 were approved by the Govt. of India. As observed in the CAG Report, no further action of detailed investigation and study of schemes contained in the BB's master plans were taken up by WRD for implementation till 2017.

In view of the major thrust being laid on the embankments by the WRD of Assam, an attempt has been made in this article to deal with the embankments from the perspective of planning and design.

7.3.1. River Embankments in Assam

Extensive damages leading to loss of life and property, apart from the tremendous sufferings of the affected ones, are caused during every monsoon by the breaches of embankments in the state of Assam. It is truly in this context that the stakeholders responsible for planning, designing, constructing, and maintaining the embankments are expected to look for the technical reasons for the frequent breaches and then formulate the remedial measures as soon as possible.

As appropriately observed in IS Code[141], *the construction of embankments to control floods is an age-old practice and is still being used due to its proven suitability.* Obviously, the suitability is dependent on a number of parameters relating to technical considerations. These considerations broadly cover the aspects of planning, design, construction and maintenance of river embankments. The Bureau of Indian Standards has extensively dealt with all these aspects and set guidelines through the codes[140,141]. A brief discussion of these technical aspects has been attempted herein.

The planning of an embankment plays the most significant role in ensuring its effectiveness. The broad aspects to be duly taken care of are:
- The area to be protected from inundation by flood water,
- The degree of protection to be provided and
- The alignment and spacing of embankments.

These aspects are duly dealt with in IS code[140].

With respect to design, the aspect of adopting a suitable cross-section is of paramount importance. The two types of embankments recommended in this IS code of practice are:
- Homogeneous Embankment and
- Zoned Embankment.

The salient parameters of the typical sections of these two types of embankments to be adopted in design are given through two figures: Figure 1 and Figure 2 of the code[140]. A detailed discussion on other technical aspects, such as design HFL, hydraulic gradient, free board, side slopes, top width, stability, etc, is outside the scope of this article. However, the aspect of the side slope of the embankment needs special mention since some of the existing embankments appear to be deficient with respect to what is recommended by the code.

The other major areas demanding appropriate technical expertise include constructing and maintaining embankments. The code of practice[141] covers the guidelines for these two aspects. This code duly deals with the salient factors such as borrow pits, laboratory tests, preparation of foundation, earthwork (including embankment profile, embankment involving mechanical compaction, embankment involving manual compaction, remodelling of embankment, incomplete embankment), compaction, slope protection, etc.

The maintenance of the embankments is another aspect that requires proper attention. The code of practice[141] states: *Proper maintenance of embankments is extremely important, as breaches in them can be disastrous and may cause even greater damage than the inundation by the floods where no embankments are provided.* The different measures to be adopted for pre-monsoon maintenance and monsoon maintenance are recommended in the code. The broad objective of proper maintenance is to maintain the original design section of the embankments by repairing or reconditioning. The most important design parameter to be checked during the pre-monsoon period every year appears to be the HFL in view of the rise in the bed level of the rivers caused by heavy siltation.

The discussion presented above clearly reveals the fact that all the salient technical aspects of river embankments have been duly codified by the BIS with respect to planning, design, construction and maintenance. Despite this situation of codified technical knowledge, there have been so many breaches of river embankments in our state. This situation of breaches raises the question of whether the existing embankments conform to the guidelines and recommendations of the relevant codes of practice. It is indeed the time when all the stakeholders of river embankments should sit together and review the situation of embankments. A huge amount of the state budget is spent every year on repairing and strengthening embankments. Obviously, the proper utilization of this fund may be done only when the technical knowledge made available to us is duly honoured.

In conclusion, it may be stated that a critical review of all the existing river embankments needs to be taken up by a competent team of experts in the related areas. The concept of third-party quality assurance, as followed nowadays nationally and internationally in many projects, may necessarily be taken recourse to.

(Note — A part of this article was published in the Assam Tribune on 28.08.2022)

7.4. The Draft Professional Engineers' Bill, 2019 Yet To Become an Act

Now, it has been more than 50 years since the necessity of an Engineers Bill in India was first conceived. A series of efforts were made at different times by different bodies/organizations/individuals to get the bill enacted. A group of more than 4000 engineers took the initiative of putting individual petitions to our Prime Minister in November 2014 for taking the necessary initiative to get the Draft Engineers Bill passed in the parliament. The first para of the individual petition[142] goes as: *"We, the undersigned, request the present Government at the Centre to take cognizance of the importance of engineers and initiate speedily the process of passing 'Engineers Bill', which has already been prepared by the Union Human Resource Development Ministry"*. However, till date, the Engineers Bill has not become an act.

A perusal of the situation leading to this delay (almost 54 years since its initiation by the Planning Commission in 1970) in getting this bill placed in the parliament reflects a number of reasons, as briefly mentioned below:

As outwardly seen, the enactment of the Engineers Bill should have been already in place long back, particularly in view of the fact that in our country, there exist a number of Acts for other professions such as Architects, Doctors, Chartered Accountants, Cost Accountants,

Lawyers, etc. The apparent complexity leading to the delay to this extent may be attributed basically to the involvement of a huge number of engineers covering many disciplines of engineering and technology. These engineers are covered by many professional bodies. Some of these bodies are: Institution of Engineers (India), Association of Consulting Engineers (India), Institution of Surveyors, Institution of Valuers, Institution of Chemical Engineers, Association of Consulting Civil Engineers (India), Institution of Mechanical Engineers, Institution of Electrical Engineers, Institution of Marine Engineers, Institution of Electronics and Telecommunication Engineers, Aeronautical Society of India, Engineering Council of India, etc. In addition to these professional bodies, there are many other organizations involved in the engineering profession, including: AICTE, NBA, Indian Railways, Indian Army, CPWD, etc. To bring all these bodies/organizations to a consensus on the draft of an Engineers Bill was apparently the basic reason for the delay up to 2007. A perusal of different kinds of literature available elsewhere on this issue indicates the fact that all the professional bodies/organizations readily agreed on the necessity of the enactment of the Engineers Bill. The delay was apparently caused by the major issue of *'modalities and authority to effect the regulation'.*

7.4.1. Present Status of Engineers Bill

Mr. Raj and Mr. Mull[143] summarize the sequence of developments taking place with respect to the efforts made so far for the Legislation for Engineers in India. While giving the present status of the Engineers Bill, they observed: *Engineers are available in our country, but we need a mechanism to ensure that those of high caliber can be identified and given the responsibility to make decisions to execute the required tasks. They also need to be tasked with mentoring the next generation of Engineers so that the country is never in want of them. Legislation is required in the country to regulate the profession of engineering and create a cadre of engineers of high caliber in all disciplines in a sustained manner.*

The First Draft of Engineers Bill was prepared[143] by the Association of Consulting Engineers (India) in around 1985.

However, the Ministry of Human Resource Development (MHRD) was identified in 1990 as the nodal ministry for this bill, and eventually, the Hon'ble Minister of HRD directed his ministry to process the bill. However, the draft bill was not taken for enactment. Thereafter, a PIL was filed[143] by 'Association of Consulting Engineers (India)' and 'National Association of Consulting Engineers India' against the Government of India (MHRD) for the enactment of the Engineers Bill. As stated by Raj[143] et al, a positive affidavit was submitted by MHRD. Eventually, the judgement on the PIL *directed the Engineers to form a consensus and go back to the Government with the draft bill'.* Apparently, this judgement came in around 2000.

Subsequently, a confederation called the Engineering Council of India, with all the engineering associations and societies, was formed in 2002. Thereafter, the ECI prepared the Second Draft of Engineers Bill in 2004 and presented the same to MHRD for onward processing for enactment. However, in lieu of processing the Second Draft for enactment, the MHRD decided to give the responsibility[143] to AICTE for regulation of the engineering profession. This decision of MHRD was again fought by Engineering Consultants in the court, which eventually decreed: *'AICTE had no mandate to regulate the Profession of Engineering and a separate body had to be created for that purpose'.* Subsequently, MHRD set up a committee with representatives from ECI, CEAI, IE(I) and AICTE. This committee prepared the Third Draft of Engineers Bill in 2005. Again, in 2007, MHRD set up another committee headed by a member of the Union Public Service Commission and with members from ECI, CEAI, IE(I), etc. Eventually, the Fourth Draft of Engineers Bill was prepared by this committee and finalized in 2008. Thereafter, it was presented to MHRD. The Fourth Draft was then circulated to all ministries, and the comments thereto were obtained. Based on the comments so received, the Fourth Draft was finalized in 2008 and then put on the process of placement in the Parliament for enactment. Surprisingly enough, in the process of its placement in Parliament, at a certain stage, a view was placed by the HRD Ministry (in the Parliament) in response to a question to the effect that the Royal Charter given to IE(I) is adequate, and therefore, the Engineers Bill is not necessary. After a lot of clarifications given on the issue and persuasion, MHRD revived the issue of Engineers Bill and, in 2018, appointed another committee under the aegis of AICTE with Prof. A. S. Ananth of IIT Madras as its Chairman for the preparation of the Draft of Legislation for the profession of Engineers. It is understood[143] that it (the Committee) submitted the Draft Engineers Bill to MHRD in 2019, and it is now under processing. This bill is now known as *Draft Professional Engineers Bill 2019*, which is now awaiting its placement in the 18th Lok Sabha.

7.4.2. An Analysis of the Situation of Delay in Legislation of Engineering Profession

An analysis of the dragging-on of the process of legislation of the engineering profession over a period of about 50 years since its initiation by the Planning Commission in 1970 raises a lot of questions. The salient ones creeping into the author's mind are:

- *Why has the Draft Engineers Bill (DEB) not been enacted yet?*

- *What are the factors responsible for delaying it so long against the consensus arrived at by so many engineering associations and societies representing lakhs of professional engineers in the country?*

- *Can this delay be linked in some ways to the extent of impunity of corruption in our systems?*

The possible answers to these questions might lead to a number of debatable points. The last question has come to the author's mind in view of the comparison of the Corruption Perceptions Index Rank of India[144] with those of a few top-ranking and bottom-ranking countries out of 180 countries considered for rankings for 2023, as brought out by figure 7.1. As reflected in the figure, India secured a CPI score of only 39 (out of 100) and has been placed in the 93rd position in the ranking list. A comparison of India's score with that of top-ranking countries like Denmark (holding the 1st rank with a score of 90) and Finland (holding the 2nd position with a score of 87) indicates the extent of corruption perceptions in India. Bhutan, a neighbouring country of India, has a better ranking

(26th position), though other neighbouring countries, namely Pakistan and Bangladesh, hold ranks lower than India's.

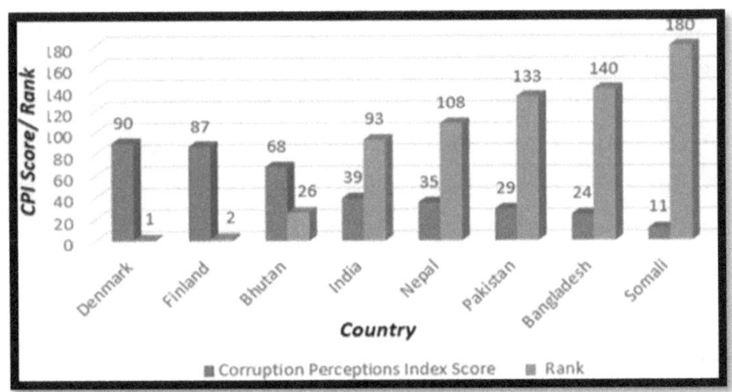

Figure 7.1: Chart Showing Corruption Perceptions Index (CPI) Score with Rank for A Few Countries among 180 Countries[144]

The basic objective set in the Draft Professional Engineers' Bill consists of ensuring the performance of all engineering activities by qualified persons so that sustainable development is ensured with the safety and welfare of the people. In addition, it aims to develop a mechanism that will set the norms of professional conduct and accountability for professional engineers. A detailed account of the proposed bill is avoided at this stage for the possibility of incorporating some changes before it finally becomes an Act.

A Statutory Council, to be known as the Indian Council of Engineers, will be constituted. However, it is not clear at this stage whether the Engineering Council of Engineers (ECI), established in 2002, will be the Statutory Body, as referred to, since the Draft Bill is yet to become an Act. The Council so constituted will "operationalize registration through professional institutions functioning under delegated authority of the Council as per regulations made by the Council." All persons holding a recognized degree-level qualification in engineering are eligible for initial registration for a period of five years. For this initial registration, no experience will be necessary. Once registered, they will be a "Registered Engineer," with a registration number, and will be authorized to use the title "Engineer (Er)." However, for the second level of registration for ten years at a time, one shall have to apply with proof of continued engagement in engineering activities and "Continuous Professional Development (CPD)" as per the regulations of the Council. Once an engineer is a "Registered Engineer", they will be deemed to have been registered by any central or state government, municipal or local bodies or any other public bodies which require registration of engineers under other laws or rules.

Year	Accidents*	Deaths*	Average death per accident
Col.1	Col.2	Col.3	Col.4
2012	2764	2682	0.97
2013	3074	2832	0.92
2014	1833	1821	0.99
2015	1830	1885	1.03
2016	1896	1984	1.05
2017	1997	1997	1
2018	1953	2018	1.03
2019	1866	1929	1.03
2020	1481	1536	1.04
2021	1576	1630	1.03
*Includes residential buildings, commercial buildings, bridges, dams and others[145]			

Table 7.3: Accidents & Deaths Due To Collapse of Structures during the Period from 2012 to 2021 (Prepared by author on the basis of data of Factly[145])

The absence of an Act for regulation and development of the engineering profession so far has been responsible for creating a lot of problems in the developmental activities of the country. The salient issues include: failures of many development projects, delays in the completion of many projects leading to excessive cost-over run, inferior qualities of many projects resulting in failures to serve the society with respect to their purposes, collapse of many structures including bridges and buildings, environmental pollution, growth of many structures vulnerable to natural calamities including earthquakes, etc. There have been reports of heavy losses with respect to both human lives and properties. For the period of 10 years (from 2012 to 2021), the data[145] relating to accidents and deaths (of persons) due to the collapse of structures are indicated in table 7.3. In addition, confusion and conflict among planners and engineers are also seen very often in the construction industry. A perusal of one Madhya Pradesh High Court Verdict[146] (given in

Appendix VIIB) indicates the extent of confusion very often given rise to by the non-legislation of the engineering profession. Even a verdict of this type has been found to be disputed by many on different grounds (which are beyond the scope of this book). The basic cause of disputes, confusion, etc., is obviously the non-coverage of the engineering profession by an Act of the country. It is truly in this context that the efforts of the fraternity of engineers have to go on till the enactment of the Draft Professional Engineers Bill 2019.

7.5. A Few Incidents of 'Conflict of Interest' in Author's Professional Life
The main objective of writing on a few incidents concerning 'Conflict of Interest' has been to share with the younger generation of engineers a few incidents of the author's professional life, which truly created a heavy impact on his journey through the construction industry. The incidents are briefly discussed below with a disclaimer to the effect that he (the author) has no intention of casting any aspersion on any individual/organization/institution in any form.

7.5.1. Incident A

In the capacity of the Managing Director (MD) of RGT Consulting Engineers Pvt. Ltd. (*that was registered in 1988 after he put in his services in teaching for about 13 years and 10 years in the construction industry*), the author designed a prestigious project for a reputed organization. Based on the approved Schedule of Rates (SoRs) of the organization concerned, a detailed estimate *(based on the item rates of the said SoRs)* was prepared for the project. The design submitted was fully approved with respect to concept design and structural design. However, the engineers of the organization concerned with the project implementation came to the author's office and wanted him to inflate the estimate submitted by about 10 Percent. In response to his query on the reasons thereof, it was stated that the execution would need some extra money for solving social problems, basically accountable to issues bearing on insurgency and other issues (not clearly stated but implied). The MD (the author) declined to inflate the estimate, as wanted by them. Eventually, it was known that the project was executed at a cost higher than the estimated cost.

The net impact of the decline to inflate the estimated cost was that no further project was achieved by his company from that organization. This was indeed a great setback to the company at the infant stage of its life, particularly in view of the then-existing pipeline of many valuable projects with that organization. This setback has always been a glaring example of a *'Conflict of Interest'* in the author's professional life.

7.5.2. Incident B

A big building project was in the offing in another reputed organization. The head of the organization came to the author at a stage when the project was about to be awarded to a firm of an architect on a turnkey basis at a floor-area rate per sqm sometime in the early 90s. He (the author) reacted by saying that the rate was very high, and in those days, the reasonable rate would have been around 20 to 30% less than what he stated. He was surprised to hear the comment on the cost since the reduction to accrue on the basis of the reduced rate *(as stated)* would be of the order of around Rs. 40 lacs—indeed a huge amount by the standard of money-value during those days. The author was then advised by the Head of the organization to submit a proposal without making commitment of award of the project. However, it was assured that the proposal with the concept design would be placed before his council of management for a revision of the first decision of awarding the assignment to the architect's firm. Eventually, the assignment was awarded to the author's company at the projected cost. The project was then converted into the delivery model of 'Design—Bid—Construct' *(a model that was defined in the article on project construction management).* The company (the author being the MD) played the role of project consultant, taking full responsibility for the design and supervision of the whole project. Finally, the project was completed successfully on time, and within the stipulated cost. The objective of briefly stating the background of this project is honestly to share with readers of the younger generation the *'agony, insult and adverse criticism'* the author had to digest during the stage of implementation of this project, as briefly discussed below.

The first query came from important quarters about the credential as a designer for doing the 'concept design' of the project since I am a structural engineer—not an architect, though, by then, I was a member/fellow of the Association of Consulting Civil Engineers, India (ACCE(I)). I successfully defended my position by taking support from a Bombay(then) High Court's verdict to the effect that a civil engineer is appropriately qualified to sign the 'concept design' of a building. *(A similar verdict from a High Court appeared in Appendix VIIB).* Then, there was a series of queries, which kept on coming during the period of execution from the Auditor's Team. Even at times, some of the members of Auditor's Team used to come to the construction site and used to raise a lot of irrelevant queries. One day, a senior officer of the Auditor's Team came to the site and asked the author why the CGI roofing was adopted *(this was a double-storey building)*. On being irritated by a technical question of that type, he (the author) replied, *'You know, I have a paper published long back in the Indian Concrete Journal, which contains the answer to your question. By the way, may I know if you are a Civil Engineer?'* He got angry and left the site since he was truly an accounts person. Finally, an audit report on this project came to the organization's head, who took the initiative to get this company engaged. The report contained objections of a serious nature that adversely reflected on the author (as MD of the company). Simultaneously, the objections getting into the hand of a reporter through some sources got published with a lot of colouring in a daily newspaper, creating thereby a strong aspersion on the author's personal integrity, in particular, and on the credentials of the company, in general. The author refrained from giving any response to the newspaper report. However, he gave his official response to the Head of the organization systematically on each of the objections raised through the auditor's report. Eventually, everything settled down since the response to the auditor's report nullified all points contained therein to the satisfaction of all members of the council of management of the organization. The due 'commissioning and handing over' of the completed project to the organization closed the chapter of that assignment. However, the extent of obstacles, agonies, and criticism the author (as the MD of the company) had to manoeuvre during the stage of its execution left a deep dent in his professional life in the construction industry. This dent, if critically analyzed even today, leads to a vital question as to how to get rid of issues created by the' *Conflict of Interests'*, so deeply rooted not only in the construction industry but also in other domains of activities in the society, particularly in countries like ours. In addition, the dent so created compelled the author to relook at his decision to enter into this scenario of the construction industry with a strong conviction of maintaining *'honesty and integrity'*, leaving behind his first decision of starting his professional journey in the teaching profession (in which he put in 13 years). Since then, the question that started striking his mind from time to time was whether he (the author) should return to the teaching profession. However, the final and immediate impact of that dent on him was that he declined to take up the second project, which was offered thereafter by the organization under discussion. Now, it has been about 30 years since this project was completed. The building has been proudly serving its users in a dignified manner. This is what gives the author immense pleasure and pride as a consultant against all odds, briefly described herein.

7.5.3. Incident C

The company of the author got an assignment of a Project consultant for a construction project of an industry. The scope of works for the assignment was limited only to the stage of project construction, which included phases of construction planning and physical construction, including quality control, cost control, time management, etc. *(as dealt with in Chapter 5 of this book of construction project management).* The stages of design and bidding were completed before the assignment was awarded to our company. The author accepted the assignment with a specific condition to the effect that all the structural drawings submitted by the designer of the project would be subject to our critical review before execution. This condition and other terms and conditions, including our fees and terms of the payment, were duly incorporated into the agreement signed between the company and the client concerned. A Technical

Advisory Committee (TAC) duly constituted by the Client for this project was, by then, already in place. The Organizational Set Up (OSU) after this assignment primarily included the Head of the industry, the TAC, Project Consultant (the author himself being the MD of the company) and Contractors concerned. Before the Project Consultant (the author's company) was appointed, four contractors – one for each of the four industrial buildings (to be constructed) were already selected. Incidentally, the period of days then was the one during which the insurgency activities were at their peak in Assam. It was, indeed, a challenging task to gather the courage to take up a project of that type during that period full of social problems due to the obvious compulsion of surviving as a company with a limited number of employees. Anyway, the works had started at the site, and simultaneously, problems, too, started cropping up basically on account of again *'Conflict of Interests'* among different parties, thereby bringing in new challenges to the task of completing projects with control of quality, cost and time. The author would like to share with the readers only a few of these challenges to lay emphasis on adverse impact of this factor *(conflict of interest)* in construction industry.

Field tests conducted on a certain quantity of aggregates brought by a contractor to the site indicated poor quality with respect to gradings, and the contractor concerned was advised to remove the same from the site. The next day, a group of unknown young persons (presumably representing the supplier of the rejected materials) came to the site and strongly pressurized the Project Consultant (represented by the author himself) to accept it and utilize the same. He refused to do so and replied,' *I have been engaged by the client for maintaining the quality of work. If you pressurize me like this, the only option left to me will be to withdraw myself from the project'*. They left then, apparently being offended. The next day, again, a message came through one of my contractors to the effect that some persons from the insurgency group would meet me soon and demand money from me. Eventually, nobody came, and the author was convinced that those were only the pressure tactics adopted by self-styled agents of insurgency groups.

Another incident connected with this project has been considered to be worth discussion in relation to the basic theme *'Conflict of Interest'*. One young Assistant Engineer (with a B. E. degree) and one experienced supervisor (with no formal technical qualifications) were placed at the site for constant supervision of work in addition to the author's own frequent visits to the site. This incident took place on a day of casting of concrete of a big floor slab of one of the four buildings. The task of concreting started a bit early and by the time the author reached the site, the work already proceeded for two to three hours supposed to be in the presence of Project Consultant's Assistant Engineer and the supervisor. The Assistant Engineer (of the PC) and the contractor concerned were not available at the site. However, the PC's supervisor and the supervisors and sub-contractor for concreting of the contractor were available. Concreting work was done with about 100 people, including both skilled and unskilled workers. Initially, the author went to the persons working with concrete mixers. On asking the concerned persons, it was known that the proportion of ingredients adopted for each batch of mixing was invariably lower than the one as specified. This was found to be so on his (author's) physical checking of the mixed concrete dumped for placing in position. Then, the immediate action of stopping the casting of concrete for the remaining portion was taken and the decision so taken was reported to the Client. The matter was discussed in the TAC, and a decision was made to dismantle the portion of the slab that was cast and to advise the contractor to recast the slab. On this decision, the contractor concerned was naturally upset and came to the author's office and stated, *'Sir, I honour your decision, but please advise how I will recover the money which I had to pay to some parties (?) for getting the contract'*. He (the author) politely responded by saying, *'I am helpless. However, if you desire, I am ready to withdraw myself from the project, provided this action helps you in getting that recovery'*. It did not go to that extent, and the work was completed by the contractor concerned. However, this incident of *'conflict of interest'* again created a sharp *'conflict of the author's mind'* as to *'whether he should compromise on his conviction to maintain honesty and integrity or to go back to his teaching profession'*. This conflict of mind continued for a long time till 2010, the year in which the author joined his second span of teaching profession. There are, in fact, many more incidents of the types stated herein. It may be reiterated that the issues accountable to *'Conflict of Interest'* in the construction industry constitute a great challenge to all the stakeholders in general and to the engineers of the construction industry in particular.

7.6. Lack of Clear Understanding of Code-Provisions

The lack of proper understanding/interpretation of provisions of codes at times leads to confusion and disputes at construction sites. An incident briefly described below relates to a technical point over which a dispute came up at a construction site for which the author, as the MD of his company (RGT Consulting Engineers Pvt. Ltd.), was in charge of structural design and supervision of a government-financed Project of Sports Stadium in Assam. Since it was a project financed by the Assam Government, a construction committee was constituted by the state government to provide overall guidance and supervision. The committee was chaired by a Cabinet Minister with a few members, including an Architect. The Committee used to visit the construction site from time to time. During one of its visits to the site of construction, the Architect raised an objection to the bend length provided at the end of a beam rebar in its connection with an end column, as shown in figure 7.2. The bend-length under question is marked as "x" in the figure. He stated that the bend-length provided was wrong. His statement to this effect clearly demonstrated his lack of understanding of the related code-provisions.

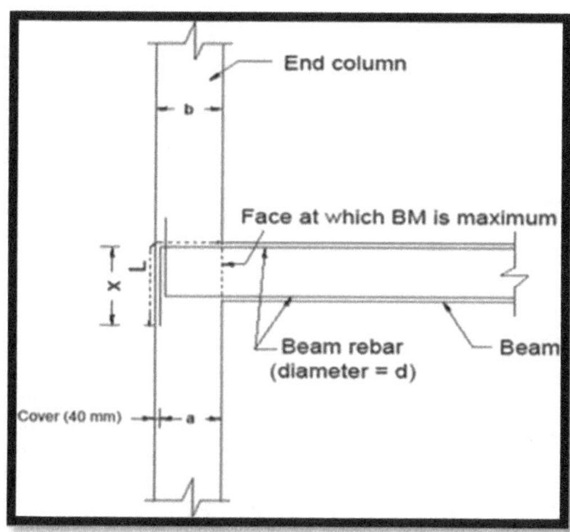

Figure 7.2: Development Length (L) at Joint between a Beam with an End Column

The bend-length 'x' (shown in the figure) depends on the total anchorage length 'L' (as shown in figure 7.2). This 'L' is given by the code29 as:

L = l + 10d, where 'd' is the diameter of the rebar concerned and 'l' is the development length of the bar in tension.

x = L – y, where 'y' is given by: y = a + c, 'c' being the anchorage value of the bend (in this case, the bend is 90 degrees, and hence the anchorage value is 2x 4d = 8d) and 'a' is (b- cover), 'b' being the width of column in the direction of stress in the bar.

The calculation of the development length, 'l', is given in the Appendix.

For a particular diameter and permissible stress in the rebar, the appropriate bend-length 'x' can be appropriately obtained depending on the width of the column along the direction of rebar, as shown in the figure. The most important point to be noted is the face from which 'L' has to be considered (it is shown in the figure). The lesson learnt from this incident has been: "Once we are confident about our work, we should politely defend our work, without getting annoyed and with a due explanation of the issue concerned". An approach of this type contributes towards maintaining an ideal atmosphere of work at the site.

The author very often observed mistakes in many of the

constructions supervised by him with respect to anchorage/development lengths particularly in the case of joints between beams and end columns and joints between slabs and edge beams (over which the slab is discontinuous). These mistakes resulted from a lack of understanding of the principles of code provisions, an example of which has been dealt with herein.

7.7. Concluding Remarks

This chapter has covered a number of topics relating to different aspects of construction industry. The demolition of the Twin Towers of Noida reflects the consequences of violation of standards and norms well set by the authorities controlling the construction activities of the country. Similarly, the second topic on floods in Assam has also dealt with the areas requiring the attention of all stakeholders involved in the planning, design, execution, and maintenance of different measures of flood control. The third topic of legislation of engineering profession in India ought to be a major issue of concern for all the engineers in view of its impact on the overall scenario of developmental activities of the country, as briefly discussed.

It was strongly felt by the author during his long professional life that the 'Conflict of Interest' is an issue that is predominantly existing in different developmental activities of the country. A few of the incidents of the author's own professional life have been described in this chapter with the aim of drawing the attention of all the stakeholders of developmental activities in general and the young generation of engineers in particular.

The last topic of this chapter on 'the lack of understanding of code-provisions' on the part of some supervising engineers has also been an issue strongly felt by the author during his professional life. The culture of knowledge among the young generation of engineers of the construction industry, on the one hand, and the laying of more stress in the process of teaching in the technical institutes, on the other, are apparently necessary on this issue of understanding code-provisions.

Appendices

Appendix IIA: List of Salient Non-Destructive Tests (Based on the list given by the Constructor[47])

Sl. No.	Name of Tests	Objective of Test
1	Rebound Hammer Test or Schmidt NDT	Conducted for finding the surface hardness of concrete(which is indicative of strengt5h of concrete
2	Carbonation Measurement	Conducted to assess the depth of concrete affected by atmospheric carbondioxide and moisture (thereby increasing the possibility of corrosion in rebars)
3	Permeability Test	Conducted to measure the extent of flow of water through the concrete
4	Penetration Resistance or Windsor Probe Test	Conducted to measure the hardness of surface and near-surface layers of concrete
5	Half-cell Electrical Potential Method	Conducted to assess the corrosion potential of rebars
6	Covermeter Test	Conducted to assess the cover to rebars
7	Radiographic Test	Conducted to detect voids in concrete and to identify position of stressing duct
8	Ultrasonic Pulse Velocity Test	Conducted to find compressive strength of concrete
9	Sonic Integrity Test Method	This method uses an instrumented Hammer which provides both sonic echo and transmission methods for testing the quality of concrete structures.
10	Tomographic Modelling	This adopts the data from ultrasonic transmissions tests in two or more directions to detect voids in concrete.
11	Impad Echo Test	Conducted to detect location and extent of defects such as cracks, voids, delamination, honeycombing in concrete structures
12	Ground Penetratin Radar (or Impulse Radar	It is used to detect position of rebars or stressing ducts
13	Infrared Thermography	It is used to detect defects such as cracks, voids, delamination and other anomalies in concrete. This method is also adopted to locate water entry points in buildings.

Appendix IIIA: Definitions of Types of Urban System as Per Census 2011 *(Taken from the Report[51] of NITI Aayog)*

Statutory Towns: Settlements that are notified under law by the concerned State/UT government and with local bodies such as municipal corporations, municipalities, municipal committees, etc., irrespective of demographic characteristics.

Census Towns: Settlements that are classified as urban in the census after they have met the following criteria: a minimum population of 5000, at least 75% of the male 'main workers' engaged in non-agricultural pursuits, and a density of population of at least 400 persons per sq. km. These are governed as villages and do not necessarily have urban local bodies.

Outgrowths: These are viable units, such as a village, clearly identifiable in terms of their boundaries and locations. Outgrowths possess urban features in terms of infrastructure and amenities, such as pucca roads, electricity, etc., and are physically contiguous with the core town of the agglomeration.

Appendix IIIB: Projects Planned for Smart City of Guwahati (Assam) *(Based on data given in smart City Mission of Mohula[58])*

Name of Projects	*Cost in Rs. Cr.*
Borosola Beel (Lake) Project: *(1.Construction of Treatment Plant, 2. Cleaning & Re-section of Beel (Lake) and 3. Development of Parks)*	80.00
Mora Bharalu River Project: *(4 Treatment Plant at every one Kilometre,5. Cleaning & Re-section of drain and 6. Construction of Embankment & Compaction)*	421.00
Area Based Development (ABD): *(7. Solar, 8. Walkway and Cycling Track, 9. Shops etc. and 10. Restaurants over bridges etc.)*	Cost not shown
Bharalu River Project: *(11. Treatment Plant at every one Kilometre, 12. Cleaning & Re-section of Drain, 13.Construction of Embankment and Compaction, 14. Solar, 15. Walkway and Cycling Track, 16. Shops etc., 17. Restaurants over bridge etc.*	296.00
Brahmaputra River Front Project: *(18. Embankment (Filling and Cutting), 19. Construction of concrete sloping wall with rock filling, 20. Construction of infrastructure work*	532.00
Deepar Beel Project: *(21. Base Work –Development for half area, 22. Construction of infrastructure---solar, walkways, shops etc.*	290.00*
Pan City---ICT Project on Public Transport System: *(23. Development of ICT application, 24. Development of Hydraulic Information System, 25.Installation of GPS, Wifi network, computer and other electrical equipment*	150.00
Bus-stop wholly developed by private organizer (100%) on BOT Model: *(26. Construction of Bus Bay and Bus Stop with all facilities on all two-lane roads, 27. Marking of Bus Bay on three-lane road)*	423.00
Improvement of Road/Foot Path/Traffic Junction on PPP Mode Cost: *(28. Construction of Foot Path, 29, Construction of Road Crossing)*	40.00
*TOTAL***	*Rs. 2235.00 Cr.*

*It includes Rs. 40 cr. considered as adjustments for computation, **The total cost does not include the cost of DPR preparation, PMC, O & M etc.*

Appendix IIIC: Statutory Towns Covered for GIS-Based Master Plans under Amrut 2.0 for the States of NER *(Prepared by the author on the basis of data of the PIB Release[65])*

States of NER	Name of Statutory Towns* under AMRUT 2.0
Arunachal Pradesh	Seppa, Roing, Tezu, Changlang and Khonsa. ***Total--5***
Assam	Bongaigaon, Dhubri-Gauripur, Tezpur, Goalpara, Sibsagar, Tinsukia, Jorhat, Diphu, North Lakhimpur, Karimganj, Borpeta, Golaghat, Bilasipara, Kokrajhar, Rangia, Mangaldoi, Dergaon, Nazira-Simaluguri, Namrup, Naharkatia, Biswanath Chariali, Haflong, Lanka, Hojai, Borpeta Road, Hailakandi, Lumding, Morigaon, Nalbari, Margherita, Kajolgaon, Silapathar, Digboi, Dumdooma, Dhekiajuli, Mariani and Chapor. ***Total--37***
Manipur	Thoubal, Kakching, Lilong (Thoubal), Mayong Imphal and Nambol. ***Total--5***
Meghalaya	Tura, Jowai, Nongstoin, Williamnagar, Resubelpara and Nongpoh, ***Total--6***
Mizoram	Lunglei and Serchhip. ***Total--2***
Nagaland	Zunheboto, Mokokchung, Tuensang, Mon and Wokha. ***Total--5***
Sikkim	Namchi. ***Total--1***
/Tripura	Udaipur, Dharmanagar, Kailasahar, Khowai, Bishalgarh, Teliamura, Ranirbazar, Melaghar, Belonia, Kumarghat, Sonamura, Panisagar, Santibazar, Kamalpur, Mohanpur and Jirania. ***Total--16***

**AMRUT cities are not included*

Appendix IIID: Institutional Mechanism for the Implementation of Amrut 2.0 Mission (Prepared by the author based on the mechanism given in the Guideline[64])

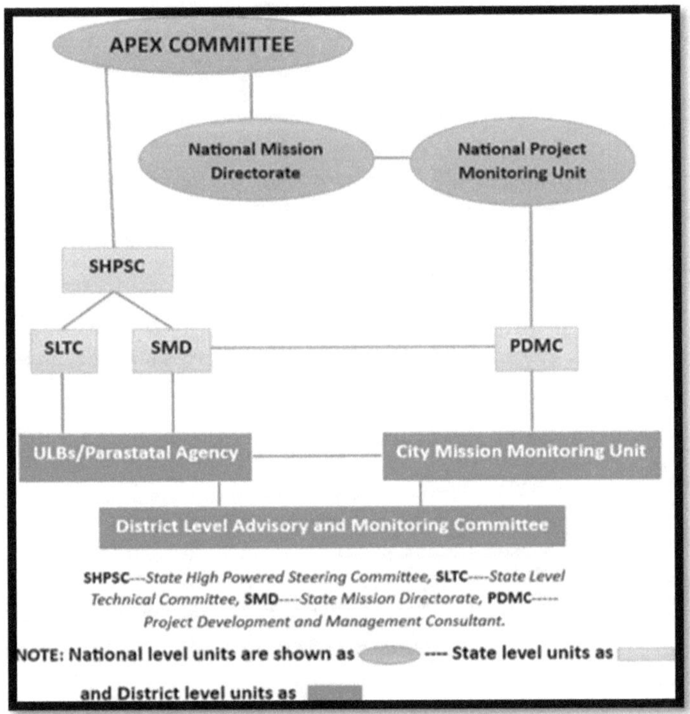

Appendix VIIA: Verdict of Honorable Supreme Court on Demolition of Twin Towers of Noida[134]

The order passed by the High Court for the demolition of Apex and Ceyane (T-16 and T-17) does not warrant interference, and the direction for demolition issued by the High Court is affirmed;

The work of demolition shall be carried out within a period of three months from the date of this judgement;

The work of demolition shall be carried out by the appellant at its own cost under the supervision of the officials of Noida. To ensure that the work of demolition is carried out in a safe manner without affecting the existing pleadings, Noida shall consult its own experts and experts from Central Building Research Institute, Roorkee-38. The work of demolition shall be carried out under the overall supervision of CBRI. In the event that CBRI expresses its inability to do so, another expert agency shall be nominated by NOIDA. The cost of demolition and all incidental expenses, including the fees payable to the experts, shall be borne by the appellant. The appellant shall, within a period of two months, refund all existing flat purchasers in Apex and Ceyane (T-16 and T-17), other than those to whom refunds have already been made, all the amounts invested for the allotted flats, together with interest at the rate of twelve Percent per annum, are payable with effect from the date of the respective deposits until the date of refund in terms of Part H of this judgement and the appellant shall pay to the RWA costs quantified as Rs. 2 crores, to be paid in one month from the receipt of this judgement.

Appendix VIIB: An HC Verdict on Conflict between Architects & Engineers[146]

Appendix VIIC: Calculation of the value of "k" used for the development length of deformed reinforcement bar in tension

This calculation is given for the benefit of fresh and budding engineers. A question was set for the Gate examination as given below:

Question: The development length of a deformed reinforcement bar is expressed as: $l^\wedge = (d\,f)/(kp)$

Where:

d = nominal diameter of the bar,

f = stress in the bar at the section considered at design load,

p = design bond stress

*From IS Code[147], the value of k can be calculated as... ... ... *... ...*
... ...

(* the value of k has to be put in this place as the answer)

(*Note: Notations are different from those given in the question or code for the convenience of writing in the author's computer, though the definitions of respective notations have been appropriately maintained).*

The value of 'k' given in the code[147] is 4, which is deduced for plain bars. However, in the question, 'k' relates to the deformed bar. The design bond stress in limit state method for a plain bar in tension is given in the code[147]. Since, in the question, 'k' required corresponds to deformed reinforcements, the value of 'p' (design bond stress) has to be increased by 60 percent as per the code for a deformed bar in tension. Hence, we get: k = 1.60 x 4 = 6.4

Therefore, the answer* to the question is 6.4.

References

1. Forbes India. (2024). *World GDP ranking (2024).* Retrieved from https://forbesindia.com

2. International Monetary Fund. (2024, April). *World economic outlook (April 2024) – Population.* Retrieved from https://www.imf.org

3. Knight Frank. (2023). *Skilled employment in the construction sector in India.* Retrieved from https://www.knightfrank.com

4. Adda247. (2023). *Union budget 2023–24: Highlights and complete budget analysis.* Retrieved from https://currentaffairs.adda247.com

5. Housing.com. (n.d.). *Bharat-mala project (Bharat Pari-yojana).* Retrieved from https://housing.com

6. Ministry of Road Transport and Highways. (2017, October). *Bharat-mala Pari-yojana.* Retrieved from https://morth.nic.in

7. Invest India. (n.d.). *Construction industry in India.* Retrieved from https://www.investindia.gov.in

8. The Times of India. (2023, April 16). *[Article title, if available].* Retrieved from https://m.timesofindia.com

9. Oxford Economics. (n.d.). *Future of construction.* Retrieved from https://resources.oxfordeconomics.com

10. Forbes India. (2023). *Engineers Day 2023: A shout out to modern civil engineering marvels.* Retrieved from https://www.forbesindia.com

11. United Nations. (2022). *The sustainable development goals report 2022.* Retrieved from https://sdgs.un.org

12. All India Council for Technical Education. (n.d.). *Engineering education in India – Short and medium-term perspectives.* Retrieved from https://www.aicte-india.org

13. All India Council for Technical Education. (2023). *Dashboard.* Retrieved from https://facilities.aicte-india.org

14. American Society of Civil Engineers. (2025). *The vision for civil engineering in 2025.* Retrieved from https://ascelibrary.org

15. Ekxam. (n.d.). *[Relevant title, if available].* Retrieved from

https://www.gate2016.info

16. Tilak, B. G., et al. (n.d.). *Employment and employability of engineering graduates in India. Journal of Contemporary Educational Research, 5*(3).

17. Tener, R. K. (n.d.). *Industry-university partnership for construction engineering education. ASCE Library.* Retrieved from https://ascelibrary.org

18. SYSTRA. (n.d.). *[Relevant title, if available].* Retrieved from https://www.systra.com

19. Building Materials & Technology Promotion Council. (n.d.). *Vulnerability atlas of India (First revision).* Government of India.

20. BBC. (n.d.). *[Relevant title, if available].* Retrieved from https://www.bbc.com

21. The Conversation. (n.d.). *[Relevant title, if available].* Retrieved from https://www.theconversation.com

22. Tsunami Warning. (n.d.). *[Relevant title, if available].* Retrieved from https://www.tsunami-warning.com

23. Owlcation. (n.d.). *[Relevant title, if available].* Retrieved from https://www.owlcation.com

24. Quigley, M. (n.d.). *[Relevant article title]. The Hindu.* Retrieved from https://www.thehindu.com

25. Bureau of Indian Standards. (2016). *IS 1893: Part I: Criteria for earthquake-resistant design of structures—Part I: General provisions and buildings.* In Y. Guyon, *Prestressed concrete* (Vol. I).

26. Supreme Court of India. (2021). *In the Supreme Court of India Civil Appellate Jurisdiction, Civil Appeal No. 5041 of 2021.* Retrieved from https://main.sci.gov.in

27. Bureau of Indian Standards. (2013). *IS 15988: 2013 – Seismic evaluation of existing reinforced concrete buildings – Guidelines.* BIS.

28. Bureau of Indian Standards. (2016). *IS 13920: 2016 – Ductile design and detailing of reinforced concrete structures subjected to seismic forces.* BIS.

29. Bureau of Indian Standards. (1986). *IS 1904: 1986 (Reaffirmed*

in 2006): Code of practice for design and construction of foundations in soils: General requirements. BIS.

30. Srivastava, A., et al. (n.d.). *Review of causes of foundation failures and their possible preventive and remedial measures.* Retrieved from https://researchgate.net

31. Bureau of Indian Standards. (2021). *IS 1892: 2021 – Subsurface investigation for foundations – Code of practice (2nd revision).* BIS.

32. Yuan, X., et al. (2004). *Simplified method for evaluating earthquake-induced differential settlements of buildings on cohesive subsoils.* In *Proceedings of the 13th World Conference on Earthquake Engineering.*

33. United Nations Office for Disaster Risk Reduction. (2015). *Sendai Framework for Disaster Risk Reduction 2015–2030.* Retrieved from https://www.undrr.org

34. U.S. Geological Survey. (n.d.). *Can you predict earthquakes?* Retrieved from https://www.usgs.gov

35. Esri. (n.d.). *Understanding earthquake early warning systems.* Retrieved from https://esri.com

36. Cremen, G., et al. (2021). *Earthquake early warning: Recent advances and perspective. Earth Science Reviews, 205.* Retrieved from https://www.sciencedirect.com

37. Kumar, A., et al. (n.d.). *Earthquake early warning system: Its relevance for India.* Retrieved from https://link.springer.com

38. Drishti IAS. (n.d.). *India's first earthquake early warning mobile app.* Retrieved from https://www.drishtias.com

39. National Disaster Management Authority. (2014). *National disaster management guidelines – Seismic retrofitting of deficient buildings and structures.* Government of India. ISBN: 978-93-84792-00-8

40. National Disaster Management Authority. (2019). *Earthquake disaster risk index report (50 towns & 1 district in seismic zones III, IV, and V).* Ministry of Home Affairs, Government of India.

41. Bureau of Indian Standards. (2009). *IS 13935: 2009 – Seismic evaluation, repair, and strengthening of masonry buildings – Guidelines.* BIS.

42. Indian Institute of Technology Roorkee. (n.d.). *Seismic retrofitting strategies of reinforced concrete buildings.* Retrieved from https://www.iitr.ac.in

43. Indian Institute of Technology Kanpur & Gujarat State Disaster Management Authority. (2005). *IITK-GSDMA guidelines for seismic evaluation and strengthening of buildings (provisions with commentary and explanatory examples).* NICEE. Retrieved from https://www.iitk.ac.in

44. Barua, H. K., & Mallick, S. K. (1977, January). *Behavior of one-story reinforced concrete frame infilled with brickwork under lateral loads.* In *Proceedings of the Sixth World Conference on Earthquake Engineering.*

45. Barua, H. K., & Mallick, S. K. (1977). *Behavior of mortar infilled steel frames under lateral loads. Building and Environment, 12,* 263–277.

46. The Constructor. (n.d.). *Non-destructive tests on RC structures: Basic methods and purposes.* Retrieved from https://theconstructor.org

47. Chen, Y. T., et al. (2008). *Seismic design of structures with supplemental Maxwell model-based brace damper systems.* In *Proceedings of the 14th World Conference on Earthquake Engineering, China.* Retrieved from https://www.iitk.ac.in

48. Singhai, K., et al. (2021). *Seismic strengthening of existing RCC structures by FRP jacketing. International Journal of Innovative Technology and Exploring Engineering, 10.* Retrieved from https://www.ijtiee.org

49. United Nations, Department of Economic and Social Affairs. (2024). *Population of India (2024 and historical).* Retrieved from https://worldometers.info/world-population/India-Population

50. NITI Aayog. (2021). *Reforms in urban planning capacity in India (Final report, September 2021).* Government of India.

51. Government Reports & Publications: Ministry of Housing and Urban Affairs, Government of India. (2021). *Annual report 2021.* https://mohua.gov.in

52. Ministry of Housing and Urban Affairs, Government of India.

(2019). *Handbook of urban statistics*. https://mohua.gov.in

53. NITI Aayog. (2022-2023). *Annual report 2022-2023.* https://www.niti.gov.in

54. Ministry of Housing and Urban Affairs, Government of India. (2015, June). *Smart Cities Mission and guidelines.* https://smartcities.gov.in

55. Ministry of Housing and Urban Affairs, Government of India. (2021, October). *Operational guidelines, AMRUT 2.0.* https://mohua.gov.in

56. Ministry of Housing and Urban Affairs, Government of India. (2021, October). *Operational guidelines for Swachh Bharat Mission—Urban 2.0.* https://mohua.gov.in

57. Ministry of Housing and Urban Affairs, Government of India. (2017, October 5). *Guidelines for Swachh Bharat Mission—Urban (Revised).* https://mohua.gov.in

58. Ministry of Housing and Urban Affairs, Government of India. (2022, December 8). *Status of AMRUT* [Press release]. PIB Delhi. https://pib.gov.in

59. Ministry of Housing and Urban Affairs, Government of India. (2024, July 25). *Projects under AMRUT 2.0* [Press release]. PIB Delhi. https://pib.gov.in

60. Parliament of India. (2023, March 20). *Report of Standing Committee on Housing and Urban Affairs (2022–2023), presented in 17th Lok Sabha* [Digital library]. https://eparlib.nic.in

61. Press Information Bureau (PIB), Delhi. (2024, July 3). *Smart Cities Mission extended till March 2025* [Press release]. https://pib.gov.in

62. Press Information Bureau (PIB), Delhi. (2024, August 1). *Projects for infrastructure facilities to small and medium cities* [Press release]. https://pib.gov.in

63. Press Information Bureau (PIB), Delhi. (2023, February 6). *Progress details of Swachh Bharat Mission* [Press release]. https://pib.gov.in

64. Lok Sabha Secretariat. (2023, December 21). *Swachh Bharat Mission, Urban (Lok Sabha Unstarred Question No. 3141).*

https://www.indiaenvironmentportal.org.in

65. Reports from International Organizations: United Nations. (2023). *The Sustainable Development Goals Report 2023: Special edition.* https://sdgs.un.org

66. Oxford Economics. (n.d.). *Global cities index.* https://www.oxfordeconomics.com

67. National Institute of Urban Affairs (NIUA). (2020). *Ease of living index 2020.* Ministry of Housing and Urban Affairs. https://smartnet.niua.org

68. World Bank. (n.d.). *Urban development overview.* https://www.worldbank.org

69. World Bank. (n.d.). *World Bank open data—Urban population (percentage of total population).* https://data.worldbank.org

70. Web Sources & Articles: IndiaSpend. (2023, July 3). *8 years on, are India's smart cities ready?* https://indiaspend.com

71. Mathur, O. P., et al. (n.d.). *State of the cities, India.* WRI India. https://wri-india.org

72. Smart Cities Mission. (n.d.). *Smart Cities Mission.* https://www.india.gov.in

73. Smart Cities Mission. (n.d.). *List of projects under Smart Cities Mission.* https://164.100.161.224/content/innerpage/list-of-projects.php

74. Ministry of Housing and Urban Affairs, Government of India. (n.d.). *List of smart cities.* https://164.100.10

75. Internet Geography. (n.d.). *What causes urbanization?* https://www.internetgeography.net

76. SDG Transformation Centre. (2023). *SDR—2023.* Retrieved from https://dashboards.sdgindex.org

77. Press Information Bureau. (2021, June 3). *NITI Aayog releases SDG India index and dashboard, 2020—21.* Retrieved from https://www.pib.gov.in

78. Narayan, J. L. (n.d.). *The sustainable development in India: A brief presentation on how engineers can lead economic growth.* Retrieved from https://www.ecindia.org

79. Sachs, J. D. (2023). *The sustainable development report 2023.*

Retrieved from https://sdgtransformationcenter.org

80. Sachs, J. D., et al. (2023). *The sustainable development report 2023*. Retrieved from https://sdgtransformationcenter.org

81. NITI Aayog. (2021–22). *North Eastern Region District SDG Index & Dashboard—Baseline Report*. Retrieved from https://sdgindiaindex.niti.gov.in

82. Press Information Bureau. (2021–22). *NITI Aayog releases North Eastern District SDG Index and Dashboard*. Retrieved from https://www.pib.gov.in

83. NITI Aayog. (n.d.). *SDG Urban Index and Dashboard*. Retrieved from https://sdgindiaindex.niti.gov.in/urban

84. Ministry of Urban Development, Government of India. (2018, September). *A guide to decision-making: Technology options for urban sanitation in India.*

85. Ministry of Housing and Urban Affairs (MoHUA). (n.d.). *Data maturity assessment framework*. Retrieved from https://smartnet.niua.org

86. Ministry of Statistics and Programme Implementation, Government of India. (2022, March). *Guidance on monitoring framework for SDGs at sub-national level.*

87. Ershadi, M., et al. (n.d.). *Core capabilities for achieving sustainable construction project management*. Retrieved from https://researchgate.net

88. Constructing Excellence in Built Environment. (2015). *Plain English guide to sustainable construction*. Retrieved from https://constructingexcellence.org.uk

89. Consult Leopard. (n.d.). *Sustainable practices in construction project management*. Retrieved from https://consultleopard.com

90. Ministry of Environment, Forest and Climate Change (MoEFCC). (2022). *Draft building construction environment management regulations*. Retrieved from https://environmentclearance.nic.in

91. Bureau of Indian Standards (BIS). (2016). *National building code of India* (Vols. 1 & 2).

92. Bureau of Indian Standards (BIS). (2016). *Guide for using*

National Building Code of India 2016.

93. Ministry of Environment, Forest and Climate Change (MoEFCC). (2017). *Guidelines on environment management of construction & demolition (C & D) wastes.*

94. Kumar, A. (n.d.). *The construction project management—The ultimate guide.* Retrieved from https://sprintzeal.com/blog

95. Sears, S. K., et al. (2021). *Construction project management: A practical guide to field construction management* (5th ed.). John Wiley & Sons.

96. ASANA. (n.d.). *Project initiation: The first step to project management.* Retrieved from https://asana.com

97. ASANA. (n.d.). *How to write an executive summary with examples.* Retrieved from https://asana.com/resources/executive-summary

98. Bureau of Energy Efficiency, Government of India. (n.d.). *Design guidelines for energy-efficient multi-storey residential buildings.* Retrieved from https://beeindia.gov.in

99. Bachmann, H. (n.d.). *Seismic conceptual design—Basic principles for engineers, architects, building owners and authorities.* Retrieved from https://preventionweb.net

100. Duggal, S. K. (n.d.). *Earthquake resistant design of structures.* Oxford University Press.

101. Bureau of Indian Standards (BIS). (1982). *SP 22 (S&T): Explanatory handbook on codes for earthquake engineering (IS: 1893—1975 and IS: 4376—1976).*

102. The World Bank. (2023, April). *Evaluating bids and proposals (including use of rated criteria for procurement of goods, works, and non-consulting services).*

103. Blackridge Research. (n.d.). *Evaluating bid proposals for construction projects.* Retrieved from https://blackridgeresearch.com

104. Comptroller and Auditor General (CAG) of India. (2016). *Evaluation of bids and selection of contractors—Chapter 7: Performance audit report on contract management in road works for the year ended 31 March 2016.* Retrieved from https://cag.gov.in

105. The World Bank (IBRD – IDA). (2018, February). *Procurement guidance – Negotiations and best and final offer (BAFO)*. Retrieved from https://pubdocs.worldbank.org

106. Alhady, A., et al. (n.d.). *Analyzing resource allocation and leveling in construction projects. American Journal of Engineering Research, 2*(104), 108–117. Retrieved from https://www.ajer.org

107. Galagali, A. A. (2017, August). *Time-cost-quality trade-off in construction project management. SSRG International Journal of Civil Engineering, 4*. Retrieved from https://www.internationaljournalssrg.org

108. Scribed. (n.d.). *Scope management plan*. Retrieved from https://www.scribd.com

109. Vets2PM. (n.d.). *Scope management plan: Housing construction project*. Retrieved from https://vets2pm.com

110. Bureau of Indian Standards (BIS). (n.d.). *IS 15883 (Part 6): Guidelines for construction project management—Scope management*.

111. Bureau of Indian Standards (BIS). (n.d.). *IS 15883 (Part 3): Guidelines for construction project management—Cost management*.

112. Ministry of Housing and Urban Affairs (MoHUA), Central Public Works Department (CPWD). (2022). *Quality assurance manual for building works*.

113. Bureau of Indian Standards (BIS). (2015). *IS 15883 (Part 4): Guidelines for construction project management—Quality management*.

114. Bureau of Indian Standards (BIS). (n.d.). *IS 15883 (Part 8): Guidelines for construction project management—Risk management*.

115. Bureau of Indian Standards (BIS). (2002). *IS 15183: Guidelines for maintenance management of buildings—Part 1: General*.

116. Bureau of Indian Standards (BIS). (2002). *IS 15183: Guidelines for maintenance management of buildings—Part 2: Finance*.

117. Bureau of Indian Standards (BIS). (2002). *IS 15183: Guidelines for maintenance management of buildings—Part 3: Labor.*

118. Ghambari, M., et al. (2021). *Proposing a building maintenance management framework to increase the useful life of buildings. International Journal of Industrial Engineering & Management Service, 8*(1), 52–61. Retrieved from https://www.ijiems.com

119. Building Repair. (n.d.). *Types of building maintenance activities.* Retrieved from https://buildingrepair.my

120. Structural India. (n.d.). *What is the difference between repair, rehabilitation, and retrofitting?* Retrieved from https://medium.com/@structural

121. Central Public Works Department (CPWD), Government of India. (n.d.). *Handbook on repair and rehabilitation of buildings.*

122. Verghese, P. C. (n.d.). *Maintenance, repair & rehabilitation and minor works of buildings.* PHI Learning Pvt. Ltd.

123. Desale, D. S., et al. (2022, February). *Effect of positions and orientations of shear walls in structures. International Journal of Advanced Research in Science, Communication, and Technology, 2*(2). Retrieved from https://ijarsct.co.in

124. Tang, T. O., et al. (2014). *Shear and flexural stiffness of reinforced concrete shear walls subjected to cyclic loading. The Open Construction and Building Technology Journal, 8*, 104–121. Retrieved from https://www.researchgate.net

125. Barua, H. K., & Mallick, S. K. (1977, January 10–14). *Behavior of one-storey reinforced concrete frame infilled with brickwork under lateral loads. Proceedings of the Sixth World Conference on Earthquake Engineering.*

126. Barua, H. K., & Mallick, S. K. (1977). Behavior of mortar infilled steel frames under lateral loads. *Building and Environment, 12*, 263–272.

127. Simonsson, C. (2021). *Terrace roof construction.* Royal Institute of Technology, Stockholm. Retrieved from https://www.diva-portal.org

128. Bakri, N. N. O., et al. (2014). General building defects: Causes, symptoms, and remedial work. *European Journal of Technology and Design, 3*(1).

129. Bureau of Indian Standards. (2005). *IS 2212: 1991 (Reaffirmed 2005) – Brick works code of practice.*

130. Bureau of Indian Standards. (2022). *IS 6313: Part 3: 2022 – Code of practice for anti-termite measures in buildings: Treatment for existing buildings.*

131. Bhattacharjee, J. (n.d.). *Concrete structures – Repair, rehabilitation and retrofitting.* CBS Publishers & Distributors Pvt. Ltd.

132. Bureau of Indian Standards. (2000). *IS 13182: 1991 (Reaffirmed 2000) – Waterproofing and damp-proofing of wet areas in buildings: Recommendations.*

133. Supreme Court of India. (2021). *In the Supreme Court of India civil appellate jurisdiction, Civil Appeal No. 5041 of 2021.* Retrieved from https://main.sci.gov.in

134. Joseph, A., & Boominathan, A. (n.d.). Engineering challenges behind the demolition of a high-rise structure by delayed detonation techniques at Delhi, India. Retrieved from https://www.researchgate.net

135. Sahu, S. S. (2023). Impact of infrastructure demolition on environment: A study of the Noida twin towers case. *International Environmental Legal Research Journal, 1*(1), 44. Retrieved from https://iledu.in

136. Jha, H., Jha, S., & Karmacharya, B. (2000). *Flood control measures – Best practices report: An approach to community-based flood control measures in the Terai rivers.* GTZ German Technical Cooperation.

137. Comptroller and Auditor General of India (CAG). (n.d.). *Performance audit of flood control in Assam.* Retrieved from https://cag.gov.in

138. Assam Water Resources. (n.d.). *River system of Assam.* Retrieved from https://waterresources.assam.gov.in

139. Bureau of Indian Standards. (2000). *IS 12094: 2000 – Indian Standard Guidelines for planning and design of river*

embankments.

140. Bureau of Indian Standards. (2001). *IS 11532: 1995 (Reaffirmed 2001) – Construction and maintenance of river embankments (levees): Guidelines.*

141. Change.org. (n.d.). *Give statutory recognition to the engineering profession, pass "Engineers Bill" through an act of Parliament.* Retrieved from https://www.change.org

142. Raj, M., & Mull, A. P. (n.d.). *Legislation for engineers.* Retrieved from https://www.ceai.org.in

143. Transparency International. (2023). *Corruption perceptions index 2023.* Retrieved from https://www.transparency.org/cpi

144. Prakash, S. (2016, May). The Engineers' Bill: Evolution and current status. Retrieved from https://www.svpcpl.com/media/May2016-1

145. Architecture Live. (n.d.). *Engineers will have same powers as architects: HC.* Retrieved from https://architecture.live/engineers-will-have-same-powers-as-architects-high-court/

146. Bureau of Indian Standards. (2000). *IS 456: 2000 – Plain and reinforced concrete – Code of practice.*

147. Bureau of Indian Standards. (2000). *IS 456: Plain and reinforced concrete—Code of practice.* https://www.standardsbis.in

148. Breaking News. (2020, October 30). *19 killed as strong earthquake hits Turkish coast.* BreakingNews.ie. https://www.breakingnews.ie/world/19-killed-as-strong-earthquake-hits-turkish-coast-1027504.html

149. British Geological Survey. (n.d.). *Earthquakes.* https://www.bgs.ac.uk/discovering-geology/earth-hazards/earthquakes/

150. Zee News. (2023, February 10). *Turkey-Syria earthquake: Deadliest quakes in two decades claim over 24,000 lives.* https://zeenews.india.com/world/turkey-syria-earthquake-deadliest-quakes-in-two-decades-claim-over-24000-lives-2572031.html

151. Live Hindustan. (2023, February 7). *Turkey earthquake: Rescue workers and residents in multiple cities searched for survivors.* https://www.livehindustan.com/photos/international/turkey-earthquake-rescue-workers-and-residents-in-multiple-cities-searched-for-survivors-1-7733019

152. Firstpost. (2023, January 4). *Manipur earthquake: Death toll rises to eight, govt announces compensation.* https://www.firstpost.com/india/manipur-earthquake-death-toll-rises-to-eight-govt-announces-compensation-2571184.html

153. Getty Images. (n.d.). *Turkish earthquake photos.* https://www.gettyimages.co.uk/photos/turkish-earthquake

154. Research Publish. (n.d.). *A comparative study on earthquake effects.* Issuu. https://issuu.com/researchpublish/docs/a_comparative_study_on_effect-7480

155. Punjab Kesari. (2023, March 1). *North India trembled due to earth shaking: Know why earthquakes occur and all related questions.* https://www.punjabkesari.com/explainer/north-india-trembled-due-to-earth-shaking-know-why-earthquake-occurs-and-all-the-questions-related-to-it

156. Kihikila. (n.d.). *The Great Earthquake of 1950.* https://kihikila.in/ki-hikiba/history-stories/the-great-earthquake-of-1950/#google_vignette

157. Facebook. (n.d.). *[Post about an earthquake].* https://www.facebook.com/permalink.php/?story_fbid=860976847363818&id=230031747125001

158. Firstpost. (2023, January 4). *Manipur earthquake: Death toll rises to eight, govt announces compensation.* https://www.firstpost.com/india/manipur-earthquake-death-toll-rises-to-eight-govt-announces-compensation-2571184.html

159. Private photo. (n.d.). *Similar images available in Google Search.* https://www.google.com/search?vsrid=CLKRga2B3Jz6OBAC

GAEiJDc1ZDUzMzA0LTljNWUtNGVmMi05NjA3LTVhNmIwM
DZhZWIyYw&gsessionid=56JVeGGvmM0ttFpJfxwrbJFHMHC
0dMeDzGr081JiTxs556Kq

160. India.com. (2023, August 28). *Noida Supertech Twin Towers blast: Why is the building higher than Qutub Minar being demolished?*
https://www.india.com/explainer/noida-supertech-twin-towers-blast-why-is-the-building-higher-than-qutub-minar-being-demolished-twin-towers-blast-complete-guide-here-5595799/